The Hospital

The Hospital

How I survived the secret child
experiments at Aston Hall

BARBARA O'HARE

with Veronica Clark

BLINK
bringing you closer

Published by Blink Publishing
3.25, The Plaza,
535 Kings Road,
Chelsea Harbour,
London, SW10 0SZ

www.blinkpublishing.co.uk

facebook.com/blinkpublishing
twitter.com/blinkpublishing

Paperback – 978-1-911274-63-6
Ebook – 978-1-911274-64-3

Typeset by seagulls.net
Printed and bound by Clays Ltd, Elcograf S.p.A

15

Blink Publishing is an imprint of Bonnier Books UK
www.bonnierbooks.co.uk

While the events described in this account are true to the best of the author's knowledge, belief and memory, some names have been changed to protect the integrity of the on-going police inquiry into allegations surrounding the scandal of treatment at Aston Hall.

Contents

Prologue

Monday, 9 January 1995

The rush-hour traffic snakes back as we inch forward, nose to tail, and make our way along the road.

Stop, start, stop, start.

I turn the heating up, the condensation drips from the front and side windows. There are smudge marks against the glass where I've tried to rub it clear. The car heater suddenly kicks into life, stealing our breath away, as I chat to my friend in the passenger seat.

Reckless teenagers run across the road, darting in between the cars as I pull on the handbrake for the umpteenth time. Car fumes build up outside as exhaust pipes pump grey chemical clouds out and up into the air.

"Oh, turn it up, I love this one," my friend says, as 'Whatever' by Oasis blares from the radio.

I tap my fingers against the steering wheel in time to the music.

The schools have just turned out. Young children, dressed in uniforms, clutch at their mothers' hands and line up, waiting to cross the busy road. The traffic lights change to red. I stop

again and watch as they pass, some walking, some skipping –
all carefree and happy that their day is done. My eyes and mind
wander as I glance out of the car window. And that's when I see
it – the nondescript red-brick building. The fire station – solid,
workman-like, practical. I take in the huge chimney and the
bricks – small and symmetrical. There are large, white wooden-
framed windows… exactly like the ones at Aston Hall. My
heart pounds and my mouth feels bone dry. In an instant, I'm
back there, at the hospital. He's the doctor and I'm his human
guinea pig. I'm his experiment.

I feel his hot breath against my neck as I try to twist my
face away from his. The stench of ether fills my nostrils. I'm
paralysed and helpless. I see his hand and feel the sharpness of
the wire mask as he presses it hard against my face.

Drip, drip, drip…

The weight of his body pins me down, crushing me; I gasp
for breath and uncurl my fist. In desperation, I clutch at the
cold rubber cover of the mattress. The room is dark. His soul
is dark.

I'm trapped, drugged and imprisoned – a 12-year-old girl
begging to die…

Chapter 1

The Tinker's Daughter

Standing inside a strange, dark house, I turned and looked through a window that faced out onto a backyard. There was a sad strip of dying grass in a cluster, surrounded by grey cobbled stones, but very little else. Underneath the window sat a big Silver Cross pram, its chrome reflecting the sunlight like a mirror.

"Come on, Barbara. Climb in," a slim lady with blonde hair urged as she waved her hand to try and hurry me up.

I stretched out, grabbed at the side and heaved myself in. The lady held onto the big handle to keep it still as I curled up and tried to squeeze into the space where the baby was supposed to lie. It was no good; I was four years old and far too big to sleep in a pram. I sat up and looked around.

"Get in," the woman said.

I couldn't see Dad's face, but the lady turned to him.

"She'll be alright. We'll just stick her in here."

I smile and say nothing because I don't dare complain. The cramped pram is my bed for the night. With my eyes closed, I pretend to sleep. I hear voices and the sound of a door closing. The adults have disappeared and suddenly I am all alone. There's the faint sound of footsteps as the lady's heels click-clack down the hallway and the banging of the door to a downstairs bedroom. Muffled laughter floats from underneath the door as I hear sounds of the blonde lady and my father together. I can't see them, but I know something is happening and I'm not wanted.

I closed my eyes and tried to remember my mother, but it was like trying to catch a cloud in my hands. Without a photograph, the image I had of her in my head thinned and evaporated until I was left with nothing. Dad had told me my mother abandoned me when I was a baby. He said she was an Irish gypsy with bright red hair and that being a gypsy's daughter made me a tinker. I imagined her riding wild and free on horseback, her long, flaming red hair trailing behind – a Celtic beauty. I prayed that she'd come back for me, but as the days and months passed, I realised I'd probably never see her again. Dad told me she'd left when I was 11 months old and still in nappies. He said she'd remembered to pack her prize possessions – her fine trinkets and best porcelain, but had left me behind like a pile of old rags. I watched the door, hoping she'd return for me.

Meanwhile, our house was never short of women. To the outside world, Dad was a real charmer with an eye for the ladies. Tall with dark, quaffed hair, everyone said he was a dead ringer for Elvis Presley, but he was my dad and I'd seen the other side of him. He used his good looks to snare any pretty ladies who crossed his path. But this blonde lady was unusual because she'd stayed longer than the rest. Her name was Marion. Although our house had no carpet and a small gas fire in the front room, Dad always seemed to find enough money to take Marion out. By now, I was five years old, but I was always left alone when they went for a night down the pub.

Our council house was pretty basic. We lived in a three-bedroom mid-terrace, with a brown leather couch that doubled as a spare bed downstairs. My bedroom was at the back of the house and it contained a single bed and a large walnut wardrobe that had been pushed up against the wall. I was expected to stay up in my bedroom all day, especially when Marion called around. One afternoon, I heard the front door slam and the sound of her high heels on the bare wooden floorboards. The smell of her perfume wafted along the hallway, filling the house, and then Dad's bedroom door closed. There was laughter and the sound of glasses being chinked downstairs in the kitchen, and I smelled Marion's perfume as she climbed the stairs and opened up my bedroom door. She was holding something in her hand, and it took me a moment to register what it was because it seemed so out of place – it was an egg box. She took a step forward and gave it to me.

"If you need to go to the toilet, use this, that way you won't go traipsing around the place, making a commotion flushing all the time," she insisted, pushing the small grey carton into my hands.

"And don't go near the window. Or the curtains!"

I watched as Dad carried the old stepladder and perched it underneath the attic hatch. Reaching up, he lifted off the attic door, leaving a black hole in the ceiling.

"Barbara, come over here," Marion beckoned me forward.

I wandered towards her, all the time keeping my eye on the hole above her head.

"See that?" she said, pointing up at it. "That's where the monster lives. If you come out of the room when me and your dad are out, then he'll jump down and eat you up."

I gasped and stepped back into the safety of my bedroom. I glanced up at the open space, my eyes searching for the monster.

"Don't worry," her voice softened a little. "As long as you stay inside your room and be a good girl, he won't hear you or gobble you up. Do you understand?"

I nodded, but inside my chest my heart was beating furiously. I was terrified.

"Good girl," she said, ruffling her hand through my blonde hair. "Now, I've made you something to eat."

She was holding a milk bottle full of water.

"No, it's inside the egg box. Go on, open it up."

I lifted the cardboard lid to find two hardboiled eggs. The shells had cracked where they'd been boiled for too long.

"Two eggs. That should fill yer. Now, you be a good girl and eat them up, eh? Oh, and I nearly forgot."

She turned and handed me the milk bottle.

"There's something to drink."

Leaving me with my milk bottle, egg box and two hardboiled eggs, Marion closed the door and went back downstairs. Moments later, I heard the sound of the front door closing, and that's when it hit me – I was alone with a monster in the attic. Terrified, I ran and hid underneath the dark green eiderdown on my bed. I was too frightened to move or use the egg box. Instead, I wet myself and the bed but at least the warmth brought me comfort as I waited for Dad to return. By late evening, both my clothes and the bed stank of piss. I heard Marion's voice and the sound of giggling as glasses chinked and music blared up through the floorboards.

After that day, I was permanently frightened – too scared to cross the landing even if the attic cover was on. Soon, it had almost become a daily routine with me being left alone with the monster, an egg box and two hard-boiled eggs. At weekends, they'd leave at lunchtime and wouldn't return until last orders. My loneliness and fear seemed relentless – just me and the monster.

I trembled beneath my eiderdown because I was certain I'd heard a creak and I convinced myself it had come from the attic.

The monster was on his way to get me!

I pictured him as a wolf with long, sharp teeth. There was another creak. I gulped, closed my eyes and wrapped the eiderdown tight around my body. I was so quiet that all I could hear was the sound of my own breath as my heart pounded inside my chest.

One day, as Marion handed me my egg box she looked at my face, exhausted through lack of sleep.

"What's wrong?"

"It's the monster," I wept. "I'm so scared. He's there, up in the attic."

A wicked grin spread across her face.

"But he doesn't just live in the attic, Barbara," she said, resting a concerned hand against my shoulder. "He lives in the wardrobe, too."

I gasped. My eyes darted from her to the wardrobe and back again.

"But I thought he lived in the attic?"

I felt anxious and the palms of my hands were clammy with sweat.

"No, he's everywhere," she said dramatically. "He's always watching to make sure you're behaving yourself."

I buried my face in my hands and began to whimper, but Marion lifted my chin towards hers.

"Barbara, do you know how to tell if the monster is inside the wardrobe?"

I shook my head.

"See the black marks in the wood of the wardrobe?" she said, tracing a finger along the dark wooden grains.

"That's when you know the monster is inside, because he leaves black marks on the outside of the wood where his long nails have been."

Marion had sensed my terror. She walked out of the room, leaving me with the black marks and the monster. Terrified, I ran and hid beneath the eiderdown. I lived this way for another nine months. I couldn't even turn on my bedroom light for comfort when it got dark outside because Dad wouldn't put a light bulb in my bedroom. Instead, I'd tremble beneath the covers, praying for Dad and Marion's return. As soon as I heard the front door open and the sound of Elvis Presley from the record player, I knew I was safe because Dad was home. The sound of Elvis filled the house as Dad and Marion jived downstairs. Elvis made me feel safe, so did the sound of dancing and the smell of alcohol and tobacco, because Dad was happy. The long days and nights continued, until one day Marion returned home with a bundle in her arms. She'd given birth to a beautiful baby boy – my half-brother, Stephen. I adored Stephen from the moment he arrived. He was so small and precious that I wanted to protect him. I had never had a sister or brother before, but now I finally had someone to love. However, Marion insisted I wasn't allowed to go near him or any of his things.

It became so bad that I was terrified to look at Stephen in case I got into trouble. One day, I was downstairs when I spotted a beautiful blue heart that had a picture of a rabbit on the front. There was a small white cord hanging from it, which, when you pulled it, played the lullaby 'Sleep little baby don't you cry'. Stephen was resting inside his cot, but I wanted to show him the heart. I looked over my shoulder to check the coast was clear, picked it up and went over to him.

"Look what I've got," I whispered.

Stephen's eye caught mine and he grinned back at me – a big, wide, gummy smile that only a baby can make. I desperately wanted to play the lullaby but was worried I'd be caught. Stephen was smiling and holding out his hand like a little starfish, trying to take it from me.

"Is this what you want?" I asked.

Without warning, Dad burst into the room and saw me holding the toy above Stephen's head.

"Give me that!" He snatched it from my hand. He was shouting so loudly that Stephen burst into tears. "Now look what you've done!"

My eyes began to fill with tears.

"I'm… I'm sorry," I stammered.

But he wasn't listening.

"I've told you. You're not allowed to go near the baby. Keep away from him!"

"Sorry…" Huge, fat tears streamed down my face.

"What are you?" he asked looming over me.

I cast my eyes towards the floor because I didn't want to make him angry – it was the last thing I wanted.

"I said, what are you?"

"I'm a tinker," I whispered.

"Yes, you are. And what are they? They're fucking useless, that's what they are. So, what does that make you?"

"Useless," I replied, not daring to look up.

"Yes, you're useless. Now, get up those stairs, Tinker, and stay away from Stephen."

I'd already left the room before he could finish his sentence – my legs climbing two steps at a time.

Although I wasn't allowed near him, Stephen's arrival had changed things for the better. Now she was a loving mother, Marion started to show an interest in me. Before I'd been largely ignored, but now she insisted on washing my long blonde hair.

"If I let it dry naturally, it falls into ringlets. There," she said, taking a step back to admire her handiwork, "you don't look half bad, even if I do say so myself."

My chest swelled with pride. I was grateful that someone — even Marion — was showing an interest in me.

Eventually, Dad secured a job working on the oil rigs. It was good money, but it meant he'd no longer be around, so Marion moved in with her sister Lorraine, who lived a few doors away. Dad had suddenly found himself cash rich and would send us parcels every week. Often they contained pretty dresses for me, not that I was allowed to wear them because they were always kept for best. One day, a box arrived at Lorraine's house.

"Oh, would you look at that," Marion sighed, beckoning her sister over.

She pulled out a beautiful pale-blue dress and held it aloft as both women admired it. It was trimmed with lace and had a huge petticoat sewn underneath to make the skirt stick out. It was the loveliest thing I'd ever seen. I realised that Dad had sent it for me, but they refused to let me wear it or even try it on. One day, Marion took Stephen and me to Lorraine's house so that she could look after us. Lorraine had five children of her own, so her house was always fit to burst. It was warm outside, but no one would play with me so I hung around bored stiff. Lorraine opened a cupboard and wheeled out an old sewing machine to repair a dress. I was mesmerised as the silver needle darted up and down, dipping and nipping the blue frayed fabric. She looked up and caught me watching her from a corner of the room.

"What you doing hanging around? Go and see your brother. He's in the living room," she snapped, waving me away with her bony little hand.

I didn't need telling twice. I loved spending time with Stephen and now that Dad was working away, Marion seemed happy to have someone else to entertain the baby, even it was me.

"And don't sit on the furniture!" Lorraine called. "I don't want a dirty tinker sitting on my couch. You can sit on the floor where you belong."

I did as I was told and flopped myself down onto the floor. The carpet was thick, red and plush, and it felt like I was sinking my fingers into velvet. I anchored myself into a sitting position with my hands behind me and both palms flat against the floor. I watched as Stephen played with his toys. I so wanted to pick them up and show him how they worked, but I was too scared in case I was caught. I glanced around the living room, trying to take it all in. It was nothing like my house. Although she had a brood of children, Lorraine's front room was immaculate. Delicate ornaments of bone china were dotted along the mahogany mantelpiece and gold-framed pictures hung from the walls. There was a big black-and-white television that stood in the middle of the room. It was the 1960s and hardly anyone owned a TV, so it was Lorraine's pride and joy. Suddenly, the living room door scraped against the carpet as it opened. It was Peter, one of Lorraine's twin boys. He was tall, and although he was still a teenager, he had the build of a man. Peter observed me from the doorway and stepped inside the room, closing the door behind him. I was nervous because I knew he didn't like me and, whatever he wanted, I knew it'd get me into trouble.

"I've not touched anything." I began gesturing over towards Stephen and his toy.

But he wasn't listening; he walked over, his brown heavy boots crushing the carpet. I turned away, afraid of what he might say or do. Suddenly, I felt a pain shoot up my arm as he ground his boot against my fingers. The heavy sole cut into my skin as I began to scream and pleaded with him to stop, but he didn't.

"You dirty tinker."

The pain was so intense that I begged him to stop.

"What the..." a voice suddenly said, cutting through my cries. It was Lorraine. She'd heard the commotion and had come tearing into the room, followed close behind by Marion. She ran across the room, scooped Stephen up in her arms and started to check him over.

"Oh my God, for a moment I thought you'd hurt him," Marion gasped, glaring at me.

I was in so much pain that I didn't register what she'd said. And then it dawned on me. They thought I'd hurt the baby.

Peter lifted his foot from my hand as soon as he'd spotted his mother. I was certain that Lorraine had seen, and she was furious, but not with him, with me. My hand continued to throb. Every finger felt as though it'd been snapped in two.

"What's wrong with you?" Lorraine bellowed.

She shot Peter an icy stare, but he just shrugged his shoulders.

"Don't look at me; I've only just come in..."

I could barely hear any of them because the pain was still searing white hot inside my brain. I knew I had to stop crying, but I couldn't help it. It felt as though my hand had been crushed beneath the wheels of a car.

"Shut up!" Lorraine snapped, grabbing my shoulder angrily. "Do you hear me? I said, shut up!"

I tried to tell her. I tried to tell them all, but I couldn't get my words out. No one was listening anyway.

"That's it," Lorraine decided, standing up straight. "You're too much trouble. Go on, get up, because you're going back to your own house."

My hand began to turn blue-black, as Marion led me back to Dad's house. It was only a few doors away, but I knew I'd be locked in there with the pain and the monster. She opened the living-room door and gestured for me to go inside.

"Now stay in there and be quiet, and whatever you do, don't go near the windows or touch the curtains. We don't want the neighbours knowing our business," she said, slamming the door behind her.

The front door closed and she was gone. I was alone again, only this time I knew Dad wouldn't be back. There was no smell of beer or tobacco and the sound of Elvis Presley had long faded away. This time I was on my own, apart from the monster upstairs. I was terrified my cries would wake him, so I made myself as still and small as possible, sobbing silently into the shoulder of my T-shirt. The hours dragged by, but as I had no toys to play with, I sat and made shapes out of the patterns in the wallpaper. The house was stifling hot, but I wasn't allowed to open a window to let the cool breeze in. Instead, I sat there as the temperature rose around me. I was desperately thirsty and needed to find water. I opened the door to check for the monster before bolting into the kitchen to gulp down water from the tap. As soon as I'd quenched my thirst, I fled to the safety of the front room and closed the door. My heart was beating fast as I leaned against it. I remained there for the rest of the day, until day became night and then day again. Eventually, Marion opened the door.

"Come on. I'm taking you back to Lorraine's house."

My right hand had swollen to twice its normal size and I couldn't put any weight on it, so I had trouble getting up from the floor. I'd hoped against hope that I'd been forgiven. But I was wrong.

"Come 'ere, you fucking Gypo," Lorraine cackled as soon as I walked in through the back door.

I spotted a large cardboard box on the table and wondered what she'd taken delivery of. She saw me looking at it.

"This?" she said, tapping the top of it with the palm of her hand. "Ahh, we've got plans for this."

A few hours later, the other children were told to sit down to a plate of chips at the dinner table. Meanwhile, I was given half a sugar sandwich, or a 'piece' as Lorraine called it, and told to sit on the back step. The bread had no butter and was dry and hard to swallow. It hurt my throat as I tried to digest my first bite, but I didn't complain because I didn't want to be sent home again. As I nibbled at the corners of the bread, I glanced down at my swollen belly. My arms and legs were rake thin but my stomach was hard and it stuck out – *I didn't even look like the other children*. I'd been fed on such a scarce diet that it was a miracle I had any energy to function. The reality was that I was barely surviving. After lunch, I was standing outside in the backyard when Marion called me into the kitchen. She had a surprise for me. I felt nervous as I stepped in through the door, but then I saw the beautiful blue dress – the same one Marion had unpacked earlier – laid out across the back of a kitchen chair.

"Here, take a seat," Marion said, tapping one. My eyes darted towards her hand to see what she was holding, but it was grips and hair curlers.

She sensed my apprehension because she added, "We're going to make you look all pretty, aren't we Lorraine?"

I watched as she gave her sister a sly glance and Lorraine smirked back. It made me feel uneasy.

"Come on, you heard what she just said. Sit down!" Lorraine shouted.

The sound of her voice jolted me into action and I hurriedly sat down on the chair.

Marion explained that she was going to wash my hair and put me in the dress my father had bought. I was absolutely dumbstruck.

"You'd like that, wouldn't you?" She smiled.

I nodded and grinned. I wasn't used to kindness, but I was grateful all the same.

She dragged one of the chairs over towards the kitchen sink, told me to stand on it, stripped me of all my dirty clothes and washed me clean. As the soap, cloth and lukewarm water cleansed my skin I began to feel brand new again.

"There, that's better isn't it?"

I glanced over at Lorraine. She was busy, sat at the kitchen table, cutting something out of the cardboard box with a pair of scissors.

Marion washed my hair and set it in curlers. Once it was dry, she picked up a stream of pale-blue ribbon and tied it in my hair. She held up the new dress and fastened me into it. I looked down at myself and gasped. I'd never felt as special in all my life. Marion turned to Lorraine.

"Well, what do you think?" she asked, taking a step back.

"Lovely," Lorraine said. "Just like an angel."

The two women burst out laughing although I had no idea why. I was just so delighted that I could barely believe this was happening to me.

Maybe they'd realised it had been Peter that had stood on my hand? Maybe they felt sorry for me? Maybe they'd start to look after me properly now, like the other children?

Lorraine had begun rummaging through a set of kitchen drawers.

"Now, where did I put them?" she muttered.

"Put what?" Marion asked as she pulled some lace socks onto my feet.

"The nappy pins."

I wondered why Lorraine needed nappy pins.

I wasn't a baby anymore. Maybe she needed them for Stephen. Yes, I thought. That was it. She needed the nappy pins for Stephen.

But the nappy pins weren't for my baby brother – they were for me.

"Now, stand still," she said aggressively as she tugged at the back of my new dress. I felt a sharp point as the nappy pin slid into the fabric and caught against my back.

"Ouch!" I whimpered.

"Well, I won't stab you if you hold still, now, will I?"

My lovely dress was pulled as she fastened something against it. Once she'd finished she stood back and laughed as I twisted my body to try and see what it was she'd pinned to me. When I realised what they were, I was confused. It was a pair of homemade cardboard wings that she'd crudely cut out of the cardboard box.

"You look like an angel, so I've pinned those to yer back," she sniggered.

Marion covered her mouth and began to laugh too, until soon the pair of them were in hysterics. I wasn't sure why they were laughing but I joined in. But if anything my laughter seemed to set them off even more. Finally, once she'd managed to compose herself, Lorraine lifted me off the chair and planted me down on the kitchen floor.

"There," she said. "Now, I want you to walk up and down the street in your pretty dress, wearing your brand-new wings."

I twisted once again. There was something written on them, but I was still young and I couldn't read. I felt wonderful dressed in my new outfit, so I was happy to show it off to the other children. I started to walk up and down the street, just as I'd been told, but as I passed, adults turned to look at me in horror. Most of the other kids playing out were young like me, so they couldn't read either. I giggled and skipped along because, for the first time in my life, I felt special. But the more people I passed, the more I realised something was wrong. It was the way the adults' faces changed as they turned to read what had been written. I didn't find out until much later, but the two women had used a thick black felt tip and had scrawled across my angel wings.

She may look like an angel, but she is the devil – don't play with her.

From that moment on, I'd been marked out in the neighbourhood. I was, and always would be, the tinker's daughter. I'd never be good enough, no matter how hard I tried.

Chapter 2

The Party

Although they'd tried their best to humiliate me with the angel wings, Marion and Lorraine had failed to succeed. I was so used to being told I was useless that I'd almost become immune. Lorraine would look after me during the day because Dad paid her. The two women would stand by the door, waiting for the postman to arrive with yet another envelope stuffed full of cash from my father. Of course, it was meant to pay for me, Stephen and our upkeep. Not that I saw very much of it. They'd stand there rubbing their hands together, waiting to see how much he'd sent through. They'd be disappointed if it wasn't enough, but elated if it was more than expected. There'd be a shopping spree with presents for the women and children, but never anything for me.

One evening, just as I was leaving to return home to spend the night at Dad's house, Lorraine placed a bony hand on my shoulder and stopped me.

"We've got visitors staying," she said.

I looked at her blankly.

Did she want me to stay at the house all day, too?

"There's not enough room here," she continued. "So the twins are going to have to stay with you."

Just then, Marion walked through to the kitchen.

"Have you told her?"

Lorraine nodded.

"Good. I'll come back with you and make up a bed."

My mattress stank of piss, so Marion decided it'd be best if she pulled out the big leather sofa which doubled as a make-shift bed.

"There you go," she said, taking the cushions off and pulling it out flat. "Plenty of room."

She told me to go straight to bed because the boys would be joining me later, but I didn't realise they'd be coming straight from the pub. I could smell the beer on their breath before I saw them pulling off their shoes. Thankfully, they slept in their clothes. Peter and Paul were 18 years old, so I found it intimidating sharing a bed with them, even if it only was for a few weeks. Peter climbed in first on my left, pushing me over to the middle, whilst Paul slipped in on the right-hand side. I pretended to be asleep because I didn't know what to say. I was still frightened of Peter since he'd ground my hand into the carpet, so the thought of sharing a bed with him filled me with dread. Within minutes, Paul was snoring away with his face opposite mine. I didn't dare face Peter, but then I felt a knee pressing hard against the small of my back.

"Tinker," he hissed. "Tinker, wake up. I want you to scratch my feet."

21

I pretended to be asleep, but Peter continued to kick me until I turned around. When I did, I discovered his feet, not his face. He lifted his head up off the bottom of the bed and looked up at me.

"I said, scratch my feet."

I was puzzled.

Why on earth did he want me to scratch his feet?

I was too frightened to say no, so I lifted a hand and began to scratch.

"No, not there!" he scolded. "I want the soles of my feet scratched."

I did as he said, but as this was the same foot that had almost broken every bone in my hand, I wanted to claw his skin off. I continued to scratch his feet for what had seemed like hours. At one point, I even drifted off to sleep. The constant motion of my nails dragging against his skin felt hypnotic. I was woken by a sharp kick against my chest.

"You stop when I say so."

Eventually, I heard heavy breathing followed by a long deep snore. Peter was asleep, so I was able to stop. I found it strange because when he was awake Peter was the ultimate bully. Of course, Stephen and Marion had stayed at Lorraine's house even though it was full of visitors. I continued to share my bed with the twins until one morning when I was awoken with a start. They'd already left for work, and I was all alone in bed when someone pulled the curtains open. Sunshine flooded in through the window almost blinding me. I saw the silhouette of a woman – Marion. She cut a shadowy figure as she moved around the room quickly, picking up clothes and blankets from the floor.

"Come on, get up," her voice was loud and urgent.

I blinked back the sleep.

"Come on. We need to get the house nice and tidy. You can get up and help me."

With that, she dragged the blanket off my bed.

I yawned and clambered to my feet, but I was baffled. Marion had never thought to clean the house before, so I wondered what and who was so important to make her do it now. I watched as she continued to move around, tidying things away, and wiping and dusting with a cloth as she went.

"Here," she said handing me a bottle of cleaning fluid. "You can do the bathroom, and make sure it's spotless, otherwise you'll be in trouble."

I scrubbed and scrubbed, trying my best to reach all the bits the eye could see, knowing it'd be judged. The toilet was horrible, but at least I could reach it. The bottom of the metal bath was another matter. I was only five, and my arms weren't long enough to clean properly. I heard Marion tut in annoyance as she stood and watched from the doorway.

"Give me that," she said, pulling the rag out of my hand. "If you want anything doing round 'ere, you have to do it yerself," she huffed.

I wanted to ask why we were cleaning the house, but I was too scared in case it made her angry. In the end, my answer came the following day when he turned up at Lorraine's front door. It was Dad – he was home. I ran into his arms and he hugged me. But no matter how happy he was to see me, his face lit up when he held Stephen. It was clear he was his blue-eyed boy. Dressed in khaki trousers and shirt and wearing sandy shoes (pumps), Dad looked just like Elvis Presley in the film *GI Blues*. Of course, Marion threw her arms around his neck, but it was clear that she was more interested in how much money was in his pocket. Suddenly, our house came alive as we settled down into some sort of family life. Dad had brought a caramel toffee bar home for Stephen, which he'd left on top of the mantelpiece. But it was a blisteringly hot summer's day and I was worried it'd melt. I wasn't supposed to touch it, but I knew it needed moving. I walked over, picked it up and studied it. It felt much heavier than it looked. I held the wrapper against my nostrils and took a deep breath, savouring the sweet, delicious smell. I was so entranced that I didn't hear Dad's footsteps behind me.

"I wasn't going to take it, honestly..." I said. But it was no good. In Dad's eyes I was a filthy tinker and that alone made me a thief.

"I told you, don't touch any of the baby's things. How many times..."

"But I wasn't... I... I... was just..."

He proceeded to drag me, like a rag doll, through the living room. I was half-lying and half-standing as I trailed behind him caught in his iron grasp. As he turned through the doorway, I was thrown sideways and accidently cracked the side of my face against the doorframe.

"Oww," I cried.

But Dad wasn't listening; instead, he continued to drag me until we were at the foot of the stairs.

"Get up those stairs, you dirty tinker," his voice boomed.

I clutched my throbbing face, ran to the bedroom, and slammed the door to try and keep him out. I was so terrified that I didn't come down until the following morning. Although my face was painful and swollen, nothing more was said, but I noticed Marion exchange a worried glance with Dad across the kitchen table. He was oblivious, because once I'd been punished, the incident had been forgotten. It didn't matter that my face was black and blue. Marion explained that I'd be starting school in two days' time, and I could barely contain my excitement. I'd looked forward to it all summer long because I couldn't wait to meet and play with other children. I hoped I'd fit in and be treated just like a normal child. But it wasn't to be. Two days later, Stephen and I sat having breakfast. He giggled as he pushed a spoon into some baby mush and flicked it up against his mouth. I gasped as it splattered hard against the floor and glanced over at Marion. I waited for her to fuss and complain, but she didn't even flinch because she was deep in conversation with Dad.

"But what are we going to do about school?" I heard her say. Her eyes darted nervously over towards me. I looked down because I didn't want her to think I was listening.

Dad sighed, took a sip of tea and shrugged his shoulders. "Oh, I don't know."

Marion grabbed the kettle and filled it up again. She clicked a switch and the flame on the gas hob fired up as she rested the kettle down on it.

"We could say she walked into the corner of a table?"

"Yes," Dad nodded. "Let's say that."

I was young, so I wasn't sure what they were talking about, but I had a feeling it was something to do with me and the huge bruise on my face. After breakfast, Marion washed and dressed me in some clean clothes. She'd even brought out a pair of white frilly socks for me to wear. I'd been so excited about starting at school, and now she'd cleaned me I felt ready for it too. Marion put Stephen in his pram and we began to walk towards school. The butterflies rose inside my stomach, and I couldn't help but skip because I was so excited. As she walked, pushing the Silver Cross along the street, Marion looked up. Lorraine had come running out of her house towards us but as soon as she saw me her face paled. She stopped Marion dead in her tracks.

"Where are you going?"

"To the school. It's Barbara's first day today."

Lorraine looked at her and then down at me. Grabbing her arm, she pulled her sister to one side and whispered in her ear.

"You can't take her to school looking like that."

"It's alright. I'll say she walked into the corner of the table."

But Lorraine wasn't listening; she was taking me in and every bit of the blue-black bruise that had spread across my face.

"No!" she replied, her voice sounding panicked. "Turn around now and take that child home. If you take her into school looking like that then someone will call social services."

Marion's face fell into a frown.

"You think they would?"

Lorraine nodded. "I know they would. Listen, turn around now before anyone sees her."

So, despite my protests, that's what Marion did.

"But I thought I was going to school today," I sobbed.

"No, you go to your room and you stay there until I say so."

I was heartbroken as I heard the front door slam and I was alone again. I continued to weep because I didn't understand what I'd done wrong. An hour or so later, I heard a key in the door and Marion's voice calling me downstairs.

"Here, you can help me put the shopping away."

Afterwards, I'd wandered off, but she called me back into the kitchen. There was a pile of dirty terry towelling nappies piled up on the side. Marion dragged a chair over towards the big white sink and tapped her hand against it.

"You can climb up here and scrub these," she told me.

Stephen's nappies were disgusting and the smell made me gag, but I didn't dare refuse. Instead, I scrubbed them until they were clean again. It was a revolting job, but at last it was done. I tried my best to squeeze the water out of them but they were heavy and I didn't have enough strength in my arms to hold them up and wring them out. Marion popped her head into the kitchen to inspect my work but she was furious when she spotted the pile of soaking wet nappies dripping on the worktop.

"You're bloody useless! Now, get back up to your room."

A week or so later, I was fast asleep in bed when the door flew open, banging off the wall as it did so. I sat bolt upright in bed, thinking it was the monster. It was Dad. The light illuminated the landing behind him, casting his figure as one long shadow.

"Get downstairs now, Tinker."

I sensed I was in trouble but I didn't know why.

He was furious. I jumped out of bed and ran down the stairs with Dad close behind.

"Living room, now."

The light in the front room was blinding. I'd been asleep one minute, but now I was standing there under the big light, trembling and wondering what on earth I'd done wrong.

"Your mother's gone."

I was confused. I knew my mum had gone. She'd left when I'd been a baby. But he wasn't talking about her, he was talking about Marion.

"She's taken Stephen with her, and it's all your fault. Everyone leaves you. Now, tell me what you are?"

I was too terrified to look up at him in case it made him worse.

"I'm a dirty tinker," I whispered.

"She's taken him. She's taken my boy, and it's your fault. I'll show you, you dirty tinker!"

Dad lunged forward but I was too quick for him. The fact he'd missed only seemed to anger him more as he chased me around the room.

"Get in that bathroom now!"

I cowered in the corner of the bathroom as he pushed the plug in the bath and turned the tap on full.

"Now get in that bath and scrub the dirty tinker out of you."

I did as he said. I picked up a big scrubbing brush with a long wooden handle and began to scour my skin.

"That's right. Now scrub yourself and scrub hard."

I was too frightened to disobey so I scrubbed as hard as I could. I scrubbed so hard that I began to bleed.

Blood was good because blood meant the tinker was coming out of me.

It pricked to the surface and began to steam down my arms, turning the clear bathwater red. Dad came back into the bathroom.

"Look, Dad," I said, showing him my bleeding arm. "The tinker's coming out of me."

He took one look, pulled me out of the bath and threw me into bed. When I awoke the following morning, he'd already left. I heard footsteps on the stairs and I wondered if he'd come back. A hand reached out towards me and then pulled away in horror. It belonged to Paul, Lorraine's son. I heard him bolt downstairs and then the sound of the front door closing. Moments later, Marion was standing over me, her face a picture of pure horror.

"Oh my God," she gasped as she lifted me up and carried me into the bathroom and gently washed my arms.

"You poor, poor child," she whispered.

Marion dressed me and took me to Lorraine's house.

"That's it," she announced as soon as we'd come in the door. "I'm leaving him – this time for good. I don't want any more to do with him."

Marion's disgust made me feel better because I knew it wasn't my fault. As hard-hearted as she was, even Lorraine was horrified. After that day, and to her credit, Lorraine insisted on keeping me at her house even though Marion disappeared shortly afterwards, taking Stephen with her. I'd felt protected, but my new-found security didn't last long. Lorraine told me I'd have to share a bed with two other children, a nine-year-old girl and an eight-year-old boy. They were her children, so when one of them wet the bed and blamed me I was the one she threw out, back to Dad's house.

"Look what I do for you and this is how you repay me."

Dad had left to work on the oil rigs again, so I was all alone. I hated sleeping on my own in the big, empty house. One of the boys would collect me and take me to Lorraine's house where she'd feed me a sugar sandwich. But I always had to go back to that dark house.

One day, I was sitting in the living room when I heard someone banging furiously on the front door. I didn't recognise the voice so I hid behind one of the chairs so they couldn't see me through the window.

"I know you're in there," the voice called.

I didn't dare answer the door because I'd been warned not to.

Dad continued to send cheques to Lorraine to pay for my keep, and she continued to feed me the bare minimum. This carried on for what seemed like months. I'd still not started school and I didn't have a clue when that would be.

One morning, I was sitting in the front room, staring at the wallpaper and making pretty patterns in my head when I heard the front door open and close. I held my breath as I heard voices coming from inside the hallway. I was frightened but desperately lonely, so I opened the door and peered through.

"There's someone in there," one of the voices said.

A hand pushed against the door and it swung open to reveal me. I looked up and saw a tall, blonde lady with her hair fashioned in a beehive, a younger, dark-haired woman and an older man. They were strangers inside Dad's house. The older woman stepped forward and spoke.

"Who are you?" she asked as she took me in from my filthy feet to my knotted hair.

I was about to speak when the younger woman knelt down and held my hand.

"Are you in the house by yourself?" she asked, guessing correctly.

I nodded shyly and watched as her face crumpled with concern. She glanced back at the older couple and then at me.

31

"What's your name?" she asked.

"Barbara."

"Right," the older woman said, rolling up her sleeves. "What that poor child needs is a good wash."

I watched as she unbuttoned her jacket and held out her hand for me to go with her. I did, even though I had no idea who they were. The man, who was called Liam, ran a sink full of water and the older woman, Edna, gave me a bed bath using an old dishcloth.

"I've never seen a child so dirty," she declared, holding a horrified hand against her bosom.

Edna and Liam were married, they explained, and the younger, kind lady was their daughter, Susan. As Edna cleaned me, Liam nipped upstairs to search for some clean clothes I could wear. But Susan was dismayed when she spotted them in his hands.

"I'm taking her into town to get some new things," she declared.

Half an hour later, I was sitting on a bus with Susan. She explained how my father had offered them his house.

"But he didn't tell us you were living there," she smiled.

I smiled back, although I felt too nervous to trust her because I knew from bitter experience that people always let you down. Someone on the bus started smoking and before long someone else had lit up. I'd never been on a bus before. The sensation of the wheels turning combined with cigarette smoke soon made me feel nauseous. Thankfully, the journey was short and before long we were walking down the main street heading towards the marketplace. Susan held my hand as we walked up to a stall that sold socks and underwear.

"I'd like seven pairs of pants and seven pairs of socks," she said as the woman counted them out.

Apart from the pale-blue dress I'd been forced to wear with the angel wings, I'd never had anything new bought for me before, so I was thrilled.

"These are all for you." Susan opened the bag to show me.

I was dumbstruck because I'd never known such kindness. Susan smiled, crumpled the brown bag in her hand and led me over to another stall. The lady was a dressmaker and she measured me up for two new dresses.

"So when can I pick them up? When will they be ready?" Susan asked.

"They'll be ready within the week."

Then we visited a toy shop. I'd only ever watched other children play with toys because I was never allowed any of my own, so, when Susan placed a beautiful little doll in my hands, I wasn't sure what to say or do.

"That's yours, Barbara. It's all yours to keep."

I should have felt happy, but I was traumatised. The little doll, the dresses and the underwear were too much too soon. I'd gone from having nothing to having everything in just one day.

"Here," she said, sensing my discomfort. "Why don't I put the doll back in the bag for you? Would that be alright?"

I gave her a grateful smile. We headed back to the bus stop and caught the next one home. As we sat on the bus I started scratching at my head.

"Have you got an itch?" Susan asked.

I nodded. My head had felt itchy for weeks. On the way home, we stopped off at the chemist so that she could buy something else. As soon as we'd arrived back at the house, she took off her jacket and looked through my hair. Whatever she saw made her jump back in horror.

"Oh my goodness," she gasped. "Your head is alive!"

She pulled a comb and a bottle of lotion from a paper bag and laid some newspaper down on the coffee table. Then she placed an upturned bowl on top of my head and began to cut around it. With my head bowed, I watched as my blonde hair fell onto the paper below. She picked up the comb and began to pull it through what hair I had left before rubbing a strange lotion over my scalp. It stung my eyes and the smell was so acrid that it caught at the back of my throat, making me cough and splutter. But I didn't complain because I'd felt clean for the first time in months. By the time she'd rinsed out the lotion, the itching had stopped.

Liam and Edna walked into the room. They were carrying paintbrushes.

"That looks better," Liam grinned as soon as he spotted me. "Now let's tackle these walls and get them to look as good as you do."

I was so happy that I thought my heart would burst. Happy I was no longer alone, happy that these strangers were kind and wanted to look after me. I didn't realise it then, but Edna had seen me as a way to make a decent living. Dad was on good money, and she knew she could ask him for funds and also receive a wage from Social Services for fostering me.

Shortly afterwards, Edna came looking for me.

"Here," she said calling me over. "I've got something to show you."

I followed her towards the back of the house and out into the garden.

"Look," she pointed towards a mound of rubbish piled up into a bonfire at the bottom of the garden. On the top was my old mattress and eiderdown that she'd cleared from my bedroom.

"Look what I've done for you," she said, nodding towards the old bed.

I was speechless.

"I'm getting rid of it. Now what do you say?"

I wasn't sure, so I said the only thing I knew that kept adults happy.

"I'm a dirty tinker."

Edna looked horrified.

"I'm nothing but a dirty tinker," I repeated.

Her expression had frightened me, but she wasn't angry, she was upset. She grabbed hold of my hand, led me back inside the kitchen and sat down on a chair.

"Barbara, how old are you?"

I shrugged my shoulders – I didn't have a clue.

"Alright. How many birthdays have you had?"

I shrugged again. I'd never had a birthday in my life.

She leaned back in her chair, clearly exasperated.

"Well, if you are a tinker then I suppose you wouldn't know when your birthday is."

She called Susan into the room.

"How old do you think Barbara is?"

Susan studied me.

"About eight?"

I was tall for my age. Even though I didn't know when my birthday was I knew for certain I wasn't as old as eight.

"Have you started school yet?" Susan asked.

"No, I was going to, but I couldn't."

"The letters," Edna suddenly remembered. "There were loads of letters on the floor by the front door. Liam's put them on the side."

They began tearing open a pile of brown envelopes until they found one from the education authority.

"She's five or six," Susan said, jabbing the letter with her finger. "Says here she should've started school."

"Right," Edna said taking my hand. "We're having a party for you, do you understand?"

I understood, but I didn't understand why they were throwing one for me.

They began chatting to the neighbours, and, through Lorraine, discovered that my birthday was in August.

"That's it then you're definitely having a party because your birthday is next week!"

Party preparations got underway and invitations were sent out to all the children in the neighbourhood, even though they'd been warned not to play with me before. The attention made me feel awkward because I wasn't used to it. With the week at an end Susan took me back to the dressmaker so we could pick up my new dresses. One was a beautiful blue dress with the top skirt looped up around the bottom to show off the pretty petticoat underneath. It was perfect. On the day of my party, Edna called me into her bedroom and handed me a big, white box. Inside was a heavy porcelain doll with dark-brown moulded hair.

"Look after that doll," Edna told me. "It cost a lot of money."

I was thrilled, but not as thrilled as she was when she saw me in my beautiful blue dress.

"You look just like Shirley Temple," she sighed.

I was sent outside to play so they could set the table with party food. There was already a girl and boy waiting for it to start so I went over to join them. There was a gorgeous black-berry bush out the back, so I decided to pick some for Susan and Edna, thinking it would make them happy. I wanted to show them how grateful I was. I reached up and plucked the biggest and ripest berries I could find. Soon my hair had come undone and my dress was tucked in my waistband, so I could carry the blackberries back to the house. When I did, all hell broke loose.

"Oh my God, look at that little tinker!" A voice cried in horror. It was Susan.

Having witnessed all her hard work destroyed, Susan saw red and grabbed me by the scruff of my neck. She took a wire coat hanger off the side and whipped the back of my bare legs. As punishment, my party was cancelled and the children sent home. I should've felt sad, angry even, but I didn't because I didn't know what I was missing out on.

Chapter 3

The Doll

I finally started school. Susan walked me there on my first day because Edna had started drinking heavily. The drink made her a darker person.

Around this time I started having problems with my vision. One of my eyes was lazy. Back in the early 1960s there was a myth that all children with lazy eyes were a bit slow, even though it was complete nonsense. One day, Edna was busy downstairs when I spotted the doll she'd given me for my birthday. It was tall and had the face and clothes of a real baby. It was the only big toy I owned, so one day I decided to take it into class to show it off. I was walking near the school when an older boy spotted me.

"'Ere, what's that in your hands?" he asked, spying the doll.

I wrapped my arms protectively around her.

"It's a doll."

"A doll? That looks like a bit of a posh doll to me. 'ere lemme have a look," he said, tugging it out of my arms.

"No! Give it back."

It was no good; he was much taller than me.

"Can your doll fly?" he asked.

39

I shook my head.

"Yes, she can."

With that, he pulled an arm back and threw her hard. I watched as she sailed high through the air and landed with a hard thud on top of the school roof.

"Told you," he crowed as he walked away laughing.

Edna would kill me. She'd told me to look after the doll but I'd sneaked it out and now it was on top of the roof. A day or so later, she was tidying my bedroom when she noticed it was missing.

"Where is it?" she asked, grabbing me roughly.

Through pitiful sobs I told her all about the boy throwing the doll on the school roof.

"I told you to look after it."

Edna's son, Trevor, was visiting, so she sent him to school with a ladder to retrieve it. But as soon as he placed her in my arms, my face fell. Her porcelain head had caved in on impact, leaving a huge, gaping gash. As soon as Edna saw it she beat me. The more she slapped me, the more I begged her not to.

"You're fucking backward," she said, pointing at my eye. "I don't know why I bothered getting you something nice because you don't deserve it. Now, get up them stairs and out of my sight."

The hatred in her eyes had frightened me. I'd initially trusted her because she'd shown me kindness, but in her drink-fuelled rage, I was simply terrified.

Liam was a builder by trade, but had managed to secure some work on a new motorway that was being built. Although they had money, a television and a car, Edna had always wanted the best of everything, so whatever wages Liam brought home, it was never enough. Instead, she'd fund her extravagant tastes with money from finance companies to have the best house in the street.

Not long afterwards, it was a really hot day. I decided to go outside even though all the doors and windows were open. I was sitting on the front step, playing five stones – I had to bounce the ball and try to pick up as many stones as I could with one hand. I was so engrossed in my game that at first I didn't notice the tall, slim man carrying a little boy on the other side of the street. But something made me look up, and that's when I spotted them. It was Dad, and he was carrying Stephen on his shoulders. I felt a pang of envy as I watched them double over in laughter. I hadn't even realised he was home, yet there he was playing the perfect father as though he only had one child. He glanced over, but quickly turned away and began to sing:

"Walk tall, walk straight, and look the world right in the eye."

I was more determined than ever to find my real mother.

One day, I was playing outside when an elderly lady started chatting to me. She was pushing a trolley full of newspapers, and she told me her name was Mrs Watson. I'd seen her many times before, and she was well known in the area for being a little bit odd.

"What's your name?" she asked.

"Barbara," I replied, but I couldn't take my eyes off the enormous pile of newspapers. "What are they for?"

"These?" she said, tapping a hand against them. "They tell me everything I need to know, so that I don't forget anything. They're full of stories and photographs, so they help me to remember."

I wished I had a trolley full of newspapers like Mrs Watson, so that I could picture and remember my mother, and then I'd never forget her.

Soon afterwards, Edna and Liam decided to move house. They'd managed to secure the lease on a local chip shop that had living quarters above it. It was only a two-bedroom flat, so I'd have to share a bedroom with Susan, but I didn't mind. By now, Susan had met and fallen in love with a lovely young man called Rex, so she was never at home anyway. Soon, I moved up to junior school, where I settled in well. I was even allowed to join the Brownies. When I wasn't at Brownies, I was usually found in the back of the shop, peeling onions so they could be pickled and sold. For the first time in years I felt happy. That was until one day when Marion turned up at the shop.

"Here," she said, thrusting a confused-looking Stephen towards Edna. "I need you to look after him for a while."

I looked down at Stephen – he wasn't a baby anymore. He was four years old, and a virtual stranger. At first I didn't understand why Edna had seemed so happy to take him in, and then I realised, now she had two of us Dad would send her twice the money. I found it hard to adapt to my brother living there because part of me resented his close relationship with Dad. But, although I was only eight, I realised Stephen was the closest thing I had to family so I had to protect him. One day, I returned home from school to find Liam standing in the chippy, peeling potatoes.

"Hello, Barbara!" He grinned. His big, kind face lit up as soon as he saw me. "Here," he said, digging a big hand in the front pocket of his trousers. "You wouldn't be a sweetheart and nip to the paper shop to get a paper for me, would you?"

"Keep the change, poppet," he said, holding his finger up to shush me so Edna wouldn't hear.

I ran to the shop and had just turned the corner when I stopped dead in my tracks. There was a man who looked vaguely familiar, but I couldn't quite place him. We'd recently had a school talk about strangers, and this man had unnerved me because I was sure that I knew him from somewhere, only I couldn't place where. My anxiety rose, and every sinew of my body told me to turn and run. The man looked over but I'd already started to sprint, tearing up the street as fast as I could. I was so frightened that I didn't dare look back in case he was following. Panting for breath, I turned the corner and ran right into the fish man, who was making his daily delivery.

"Here, little lady, where's the fire?"

I was so terrified that I didn't have time to stop and chat. I ran into the shop. Liam and Edna were standing behind the counter and they looked startled as I came dashing in.

"Whatever's the matter?"

I was so upset, I couldn't catch my breath.

"There's a man..." I gasped, trying to get the words out.

"Someone must've tried to grab her," the delivery man interrupted. Before I could say a word, both he and Liam went bounding up the street to look for my 'abductor'.

Edna was still trying to calm me down as Susan arrived.

"Whatever's the matter?"

"Take her upstairs," Edna told her.

Susan took me upstairs to my bedroom, where we spent hours making a doll's house. It was only later, when I was tucked up in bed that I remembered who the man was. His face loomed large into my conscience like a sharp, painful slap – my father. I hadn't realised just how frightened I'd been of him until that moment because after I'd seen him playing happy families with Stephen, I'd blocked him out and then it all came flooding back. For a second he and the attic monster of my childhood had merged into a man I couldn't immediately recognise as my own dad. After that day, I tried to look after my little brother and be the best sister I could. We remained that way for the best part of a year, until one day Edna told me we'd be moving again.

"It's too much, managing a chip shop and looking after you two," she said by way of explanation.

Before I knew it, boxes had been packed and we were on the move. Thankfully, they'd rented a house only five minutes' walk from the shop so I didn't have to change school.

The weather soon turned cold as Christmas approached. Edna spent her winter evenings in front of the fire, poring over the pages of her catalogue, looking for presents.

"Look," she said, pointing at something. "I've ordered you that, that and that."

She was pointing at a picture of a doll's highchair, a play iron and ironing board. I gasped, because I couldn't believe I'd be getting all those lovely toys for Christmas. A few days later, I returned home from school starving hungry. I wasn't supposed to eat before dinner, but I was ravenous. I spotted some grapes in the fruit bowl and I checked over my shoulder.

She'll never notice one missing, I thought as I plucked one off the bunch and popped it inside my mouth. I closed my eyes as the sweet juice exploded against my tongue.

"Hungry are you?" A voice called from the kitchen doorway. It was Edna.

"I... I..." I stammered. With her breath stinking of drink, she marched across the kitchen and picked something up. I couldn't make out what it was until she'd smashed it hard against my face – it was a raw egg.

"I'll show you, fucking tinker!"

I was sent to my bedroom. An hour later, I heard her shouting at me to come downstairs. I'd wondered what my punishment would be and was surprised when she asked me to run an errand to the local shop to fetch a loaf of bread.

"But don't go to the shop on the corner. Go to the other one. The one a few streets away."

I took the money and left. By the time I'd returned her mood seemed to have lifted.

"You can go and play by the canal, if you like? But you're only allowed by the bridge. You mustn't move from there, do you understand?"

I nodded, relieved to have escaped Edna and her moods. I walked down to the canal but as I neared the water, I saw something sticking up out of it. I craned my neck to try and get a better look and then froze to the spot – it was my doll's high chair.

What was it doing in the canal?

I took a tentative step forward and peered in. My doll was floating face down in the water, bobbing along the surface. I gasped as I spotted some fabric shifting against the current. It was the cover of the ironing board. The play iron that Edna had ordered from the catalogue had been dumped there, too, alongside all my Christmas presents. I was devastated.

Tears pricked at the back of my eyes. I raced home because I had to tell Edna – she'd know what to do. But as soon as I told her what I'd seen, her face had clouded over.

"You've done what?"

I gasped and shook my head.

"No, no, you don't understand," I said, trying to calm her down. "I didn't put them there. They were there when…"

It was no good, Edna refused to listen. Her right hand swiped through the air and connected with the side of my face.

"After all I've done for you!"

"No, no, it wasn't me!"

Edna had exploded. She continued to punch and slap me until I was a shivering wreck on the kitchen floor. I cowered beneath her as blow after blow rained down. As I lay there, something occurred to me – it'd been Edna who'd thrown my toys in the water. She'd done it just so she could give me a good

46

hiding. Finally, when she'd exhausted herself, she banished me to my bedroom for the rest of the day and night. I was told I'd go without dinner. I'd not eaten a thing for hours, so by the next morning my stomach felt hollowed out with hunger. I opened my bedroom door, and peered out onto the landing – everyone was still fast asleep. I sneaked downstairs and padded into the kitchen, looking for something – anything – to eat. That's when I spotted the fresh loaf of bread on the side. I took out a knife and cut myself a slice before walking to the fridge to look for butter. The bread had tasted heavenly and I desperately wanted another slice but didn't want to push my luck. Scooping up the loose breadcrumbs, I wrapped it back in its brown paper bag and gave the kitchen a quick check over. Happy there was no trace, I sneaked upstairs to my bedroom and closed the door. I must have fallen asleep because the next thing I knew I was being pulled roughly out of my bed by Edna.

"Starved, are you?" She bellowed, her eyes wild with fury.

It was clear she knew what I'd done.

"Thought you'd been clever, did you? Well, you're not clever," she said, giving me a slap. "'Cos you left the butter dish out."

She slapped me again.

"Now get ready for school!"

With trembling hands, I pulled on my clothes, grabbed my bag and went downstairs. Stephen was already sat at the table having breakfast, but even he jumped in his seat as Edna threw my plate on the table with a clatter. I was relieved when I saw it because she'd cooked me bacon, eggs, sausage and beans. Steam rose up from the plate – the aroma making my stomach rumble.

"Go on," Edna said, looming over me.

I picked up my knife and fork ready to eat, but she snatched the plate and rubbed the breakfast into my face.

"Starving, are we? I'll show you starving," she cackled.

I whimpered as the gooey egg slid down my face and hair, followed by the beans. Edna snatched back the plate and threw it into the sink in a temper.

"Now, go and get washed!"

I fled the kitchen and ran to the bathroom to wash. By the time I'd finished I was late for school. Not only that, but I also had a blue bruise on my left cheek where she'd slammed the plate against it. Edna took me to see the doctor.

"She's got a tooth infection. That's why her face is all swollen," she lied.

He believed every word, just like everyone else. Edna was a respectable woman. She had a nice husband, house, TV and car. *Why would she hurt a child?*

Christmas came and went, and Stephen was delighted when Santa brought him a commando bike. I wasn't as fortunate. All my toys had been left to rot in their watery grave and all I was given was a small doll and a selection box. It was a miserable day. I decided from that moment on that I hated Edna with every fibre of my being. I didn't realise it then, but worse was yet to come.

Chapter 4

The Lost Children

Before long we were on the move again, this time to a bigger house. Even though I was nine, I didn't recall much of the move apart from a big white van being parked up outside and a trail of men lifting out boxes and furniture. Edna didn't want us under her feet, so Stephen and I were sent to play outside in the new garden. Unlike the previous one, this property was large and had a pink rose tree growing up and along a wooden archway that led to a small unkempt lawn with an old air raid shelter at the bottom. The shelter made the perfect den, and Stephen and I spent the entire first day lost in our own world of adventure. Every so often Edna would pop her head out of the back door and call me in to help carry a box upstairs, but otherwise she pretty much left us alone. As she handed me a plate of sandwiches she'd made for lunch, I felt a small glimmer of hope.

Maybe things would be better?

The house was ancient, but not as old as the last place. There was a coal fire in the living room and the kitchen was at the back of the house, along with a bathroom that faced the back door. There was a small gate in the back garden that led to an alleyway at the side, but the fences were so low that everyone could see in. I noticed a group of children peering over, so I smiled back and they came to say hello.

"Want to play?" the eldest boy asked.

I nodded, delighted that we'd been accepted into their gang. I dared to hope it'd be a new start. No one knew I was a tinker here. Everyone thought I was just like them. The older boy was called Jamie and he was one of a gang of seven.

"See you tomorrow?" he said.

"Yes." I grinned, happy that I not only had a new house but a new set of friends too.

The move meant I had to start at a new school but I wasn't worried because I'd already met the gang, so I knew I'd have friends.

"I can't wait to get started on this place," Liam remarked later that day, eyeing up the walls with a paintbrush.

Stephen and I had to share a room at the back of the house. It was a small plain room that overlooked the garden. It had contained bunk beds, but Liam had dismantled them so they became two single beds, perched underneath the window. Although it was grander than the last place, there was still no carpet. At the top of our new street was a pub, and it wasn't long before Edna and Liam became regulars. They would be found drinking there every Friday night, and all day Saturday and Sunday, and they didn't return until it had shut.

Thankfully, Edna's mood had seemed to lighten a little and, for the first time, I was allowed to wear trousers and get my hair tangled in knots as I played outside. She didn't even complain when I climbed trees, played football or built dens with the boys. But, the more she drank, the more her personality seemed to darken, and before long she started to view us as a burden. She realised if we played outside we might get hurt, meaning she'd have to leave the pub early, so she soon put a stop to our new-found freedom. Instead, she locked us inside the house. But she was clever, because she'd remove our shoes so the neighbours wouldn't hear us moving around. I began to have flashbacks to before, waiting in the darkness, hoping the monster wouldn't emerge. It wasn't as bad for Stephen because he had me there with him but he soon started to struggle with the constant hunger, so I stole biscuits from the kitchen. I'd take them when Edna wasn't looking and stockpile them in our bedroom.

"Don't go near the window," she'd warned me the first evening she left us alone.

I didn't need telling and she knew it. It was difficult, but I tried to keep Stephen entertained with long games of I Spy. We'd play it for hours until the days turned into darkness and we could no longer see our hands in front of our faces. Sometimes, Edna would call me down late at night and ask me to regale her with tales of my suffering before she'd "saved me".

"You're lucky to 'av me," she slurred after I'd finished. She swayed around and struggled to focus as she delivered her lecture. "An' I'll tell yer another thing. I've done nothin' but ssshow you bothhhh kindnessss. Your mothhher didn't want you."

Her words made me sick to my stomach. Edna was lying. She wasn't kind, she was sadistic. But I didn't say a word. I listened to her telling me what a wonderful person she was as I thought of my toys submerged and rotting in the canal.

One evening, I was just dozing off when I heard the latch shut on the front door. Edna and Liam were home.

"Barbara, get down theeees sssstairs now," she slurred.

I wearily climbed out of bed and made my way downstairs to find Edna standing in her usual place, warming her legs in front of the fire.

"Now," she said, swaying. "Tell me thissss. Do I, or do I not, treat you well?"

I was stumped. Of course she didn't, but I couldn't say it because I knew I'd be beaten.

"Err, yes," I mumbled.

"Sssso, why do you continue to sssssteal from me? Go on, anssswer me that."

I looked at the floor – she'd noticed the missing biscuits. I was unsure what to do when she lunged forward and slapped me hard.

"You're lucky to 'av me and not yer dad. I'm only doing this for yer own good. I have to punish yer so yer learn. Do yer understand?"

But I didn't understand, not at all. If anything, she was worse.

"Ssso, who sssstole the biscuits? Was it you or Ssstephen?"

My heart pounded. I desperately tried to think of an answer. I didn't want to get Stephen into trouble but I didn't want to get a beating. My silence only served to infuriate her more.

"Come on, tell me. And tell me the truth; otherwissse you're going across my lap," she said, flopping down into her usual fireside chair.

Liam was on the sofa, but I noticed his eyes looking at me, pleading with me to tell her the truth and keep the peace.

"It was me. I took the biscuits. I was hungry."

"I knew it!" she exclaimed, jumping to her feet.

She dragged me by my hair, bent me over her knee and smacked me as hard as her temper would allow. With a stinging arse and red legs, I was ordered back to my bedroom.

"Things need to change around here, my girl," she called as I pelted upstairs.

One day, I was sitting in her favourite chair when she walked into the room. She dropped the towels she'd been carrying and began to scream. I jumped up, but it was too late. She'd seen me.

"Come 'ere," she screamed, grabbing my hair as she spanked me raw.

The front door opened and Liam walked in.

"For God's sake woman, leave the poor girl alone. Enough is enough!"

But Edna refused to stop. Finally, after what had seemed like hours, she gave me a hard shove and I fell to the ground.

"Bed. Now!"

As I ran upstairs, I realised Stephen was behind me – he'd seen it all and was petrified. I crawled into bed and tried to lie on my opposite side so it wouldn't hurt as much. The following morning I awoke fearful and tear-stained. I loved my new school and the new house; I loved being able to start again. Everything had changed, and most of it for the better, everything apart from Edna. To the outside world, she was a saint who'd taken in two lost children and had saved them from a life of misery. If only they'd known the truth. Liam, on the other hand, was a decent and hard-working man. He taught me to box so that I could defend myself against school bullies.

"That's right, protect your face, keep your fists high and always keep an eye on your opponent."

Every Friday, Liam would return home with two bars of mint chocolate – one for me and one for Stephen. On Saturdays, he'd give us enough money to go to the swimming baths. Stephen was a good boy but he was timid and small for his age, so he became a prime target for the local bullies. One day, we were walking to the swimming baths when two lads approached.

"Where are you two going?" the bigger one asked, shoving Stephen in the chest.

"Swimming."

The older boy held out his hand.

"Okay, if you're going swimming then you must have money. Come on, hand it over."

I refused so they dragged Stephen to the ground and started to kick him. I tried to drag them off, but there were two of them and only one of me. I'd wanted to protect my half-brother, but I couldn't. By the time they'd finished, a trickle of blood seeped from Stephen's nose. Once I'd seen the blood I handed over the money and cradled Stephen in my arms.

"And we'll be here next Saturday and the one after, so you better make sure you bring us your money."

They walked away laughing and counting out the money in their hands, but they didn't realise I knew where they lived. I vowed to get revenge. That day, Edna and Liam were down the pub as usual. Thankfully, they'd left the door unlocked, so I slipped into the house and began to clean Stephen.

"Oww," he said, wincing.

"Hold still. I can't clean it up if you don't stay still and Edna will go mad if she sees you."

The following day, Stephen and I were dressed in our finest clothes, ready for church. Edna and Liam didn't go to church, but she'd asked Lorraine to keep an eye on us.

"She'll tell me if you don't behave," she warned as we headed out the back door.

My heart thudded because I had other plans.

Edna had dressed me in a beautiful green dress with matching cape. It was a hollow gesture. She'd only dressed me up so that she could show me off to the neighbours.

As soon as we were out of sight, I turned a corner and told Stephen to follow.

"But this isn't the way to church. Where are we going?"

"Just follow me," I said, taking his hand to try and hurry him up.

We turned into an unfamiliar street and headed towards a park, where I led him to the swings and told him to wait for me.

"And whatever you do, don't wander off. I won't be long."

"But where are you going?" he asked.

"Never you mind. Just wait for me here and don't leave until I come back."

I set off through the park, down the road and along an alleyway that led to the street where the two bullies lived opposite one another. Grabbing the button of my cape, I fumbled with it, laid it on the ground and filled it with stones. I collected the biggest and sharpest stones I could find until the cape was bulging. I sneaked along the road and climbed into a tree. The cape was heavy and I almost dropped it but somehow I managed to shin myself up. I pulled out a stone and chucked it at the main bully's house. It thudded against the back wooden door, sending the dog inside crazy. Moments later, the door opened and a woman peered out, but the backyard was deserted so she went inside. I threw another. This time one of the bullies appeared so I bombarded him with stones. He held his hands up to try and shield himself as he shouted to his mate for backup.

"Keith!"

Keith came running out of his house, but now I had them both in my sight. I pelted them until I'd run out of stones. They started to pick up the stones I'd thrown and fight back. That's when it dawned on me – I didn't have an escape route. I felt a thud above my right eye as a stone cut my skin, splitting it apart. Blood streamed from my face and soaked my best dress. I can't remember how I climbed down from the tree and managed to escape, but, with the adrenalin pumping, my legs carried me faster than I ever thought possible. As soon as I ran in through the back door, Edna screamed.

"What the…!"

She grabbed me and pulled me towards the sink.

"Get the dress off, get it off, quick!"

I pulled it down until it was a puddle around my ankles. She pushed me aside, grabbed it, and began scrubbing furiously at the neckline.

"Your Sunday best. What the hell have you been doing?"

I didn't know what to say because I knew she'd beat me. Just then, Liam came rushing in and as soon as he saw the state of my face he ran to the bathroom to fetch a towel. He wrapped it around my head to try and stop the flow of blood.

"This is a hospital job," he said, turning to Edna, who was still angrily scrubbing my dress. "Quick, turn off the oven. We need to get Barbara to hospital."

He packed me in the back of his posh new car – a red Ford Zephyr – as Edna jumped into the passenger seat. The car had a cream leather interior so she'd brought extra towels so I wouldn't bleed all over it. We picked up Stephen from the park en route to the hospital, where I was given five stitches. In spite of my wound, Edna was still furious because my dress was ruined.

"Have you been fighting?" she asked.

I told her the truth, although I left out the fact it had been me who'd started it. Edna was fuming and demanded to be taken to where the bullies lived. As she took a step forward and knocked loudly at the first door, I cowered behind her.

"Your son has been throwing stones at Barbara," she said, turning to point at me. "She was wearing her best dress for church, but now it's ruined. It cost me a small fortune that dress and you're going to have to pay for it."

The woman listened and folded her arms across her chest as she stood in the doorway.

"So she hasn't told yer then?"

I gulped.

"Told me what?" Edna huffed.

"That she started it. She threw the first stone."

She glared at me and back at the woman, but she refused to believe her.

"No she didn't! It's your hooligan son and his friend over there. They're troublemakers."

The woman let out a snort of laughter.

"Well, if that's true, why's her cape still up there in that tree," she retorted, pointing up at it.

She was right: my distinctive green cape was hanging from a branch, blowing gently in the breeze. In my rush to escape, I'd left it behind. My heart stopped, waiting for Edna's reaction.

"She started throwing stones first. So, if anyone should be complaining, it should be me because she whacked the hell out of my back door. Look!" she said, tracing her finger across some small dents.

Edna was so angry I'd shown her up that I swear I saw horns grow out of the top of her head.

"You. Home. Now!" she spat as she dragged me all the way.

My ruined dress had been flung over the back of a chair. I knew I was done for because it was caked in dried blood, and no amount of scrubbing would fix it.

"Bed. Now!"

I flew upstairs and dived underneath my bedcovers. I didn't care how long I had to stay there as long as I was out of her way. An hour or so later, Edna brought Stephen into the bedroom. I was still shaking under the bedcovers but I peeked out and watched as she snatched my shoes up off the floor.

"I'll deal with you later, you dirty little whore! What were you doing in trees with boys anyway? You should've been in church!"

Once the door had closed, I lifted my head out. Stephen blinked at me, a little confused. I put a finger against my lips to shush him. I needed him to be quiet so I could hear where she'd gone. I heard her footsteps downstairs – they were off to the pub. With the house empty, Stephen crept across to my bed. He'd done it dozens of times before because it'd brought him comfort.

"Come on then," I said, patting the side of the bed.

We both fell into a deep slumber. Hours later, I was woken by raised voices, it was Edna and Liam having a huge argument. They often argued, but not like tonight's row which sounded particularly vicious. Edna was saying something that I couldn't quite hear, so I sat up to listen.

"I have to know, I have to know," I heard her say.

Liam mumbled something before Edna replied, "And I will, you know. I will find out."

I wondered what on earth she was talking about as their voices became louder. Stephen shuddered and wrapped his arms around me. We were starving hungry, but we didn't dare move or ask for food because we knew it'd make her worse. Suddenly, there was the sound of heels as she walked from the front room to the bottom of the stairs.

"I'm coming up!" she bellowed.

I shivered and gripped Stephen against me. Edna was drunk, so it could only mean something bad. I trembled as I wondered what weapon she'd bring with her. Whatever it was, I knew I'd be beaten for the trouble I'd caused earlier. Light from the landing flooded the room as the door swung open and she stood as a shadow in the doorway. She gasped when she spotted Stephen in my arms.

"You little whore," she raged. "Get to my room now!"

I was dumbstruck.

I panicked as Edna turned and went back downstairs. I didn't dare disobey her.

"Barbara," Stephen cried, stretching his arms out towards me.

"Don't worry, everything will be alright. You just stay there and keep quiet."

I crossed the landing, walked into her bedroom and stood by the bed. The room was dark as I glanced around anxiously, looking for any weapons she might use on me. My eyes darted across the room, but it was no good, it was too dark to make out any shapes. I heard footsteps on the stairs – Edna was coming. My heart was pumping so furiously that I could hear a rush of blood in my ears. I could hear her anger in her short, sharp steps closing in on me. The door opened and I was momentarily blinded by the light.

"On that bed now!"

I did as she said and obediently sat down on the side of the bed.

"No! Not there. At the end."

As she pointed, I spotted something metal glinting against the light. My body was telling me to run, but I was too busy trying to work out what she was holding. I sat on the end of the bed, all the time watching her hand. She wedged a suitcase against the door to allow more light in, strode over and pushed me back onto the bed. Then she started tearing my knickers off.

"Open your legs!"

I started to cry, but did as she asked.

"Now bend them so they're flat against the bed."

I felt scared. Hot, humiliated tears streamed down my face as I tried to work out what she was going to do to me. As she came closer I saw the metal thing in her hand. I lifted my head off the bed, trying to see as it caught the light coming from the outside landing – it was a serving spoon.

"What have you been doing?" Edna snapped, pinning my legs down. "What have you been doing with your brother?"

Her breath stank as she leaned in and the awful perfume she wore made me feel nauseous. She grabbed each leg and forced them wider. I felt a strange sensation of cold, hard metal scraping against soft skin as she shoved the spoon hard into my vagina. I closed my eyes and winced in pain.

"What have you been doing with Stephen?"

"Nothing. I haven't been doing anything."

But she refused to believe me.

"What about those other boys? The ones you threw stones at. What have you been doing with them?"

I told her I'd done nothing, but she didn't believe me. She grunted as she forced the large spoon in deeper. She used it as a mirror – she was trying to look inside me. I didn't know what to do or what I'd done wrong. My eye was still throbbing from the hospital stitches and a crushing headache gnawed at my skull, but Edna didn't stop. I lay there as she twisted the spoon.

A shadow suddenly appeared in the doorway momentarily blocking out the light. Edna stopped and turned around.

"What the fuck are you doing?" Liam bellowed. "This isn't right. Stop that now!"

She turned back towards me. "No! I have to know and this is the only way I'll find out."

But Liam refused to back down.

"Stop that right now or I'm leaving you. She's just a child, for Christ's sake. Look at what you're doing. You are sick. I'll tell Social Services what you're doing because this is wrong."

Edna sighed and pulled the spoon out of me.

"Barbara," Liam said suddenly. "Get off that bed now."

Realising it was my only chance, I leaped up. I was too frightened to push past Edna, so I remained transfixed like a trapped animal at the side of the bed. I thought of Stephen on the other side of the wall. I desperately wanted to hold him.

I was shell-shocked as the tears flowed down.

"Come here," Liam said softly, holding out his hand.

I was still trembling as I grabbed it, but I couldn't take my eyes off Edna or the spoon. Liam pulled me towards him and rubbed the top of my head fondly.

"Go on, tatty head, go to bed," he whispered. "You're okay now, and I promise you this will never happen again."

He rested his hand on the point of my chin and lifted my face so he could look at me. I couldn't be sure, but I'm certain I saw tears in his eyes.

I wandered back to my room, closed the door and jumped underneath the covers. Stephen was shaking in my bed. He'd not seen anything but he'd heard the shouting. I was trembling too, unable to get the image of Edna and the spoon out of my mind, I held Stephen tight.

What if she decided to attack him too?

I needed to get him away from Edna. He needed to be with his real mum and I needed mine. We had to escape. I knew Liam would keep us safe but he wasn't always there. I had to leave and take Stephen with me. It was the only way. I hatched a plan and decided to wait until the following Sunday, when I knew they'd be at the pub. Over the days that followed, I pilfered food, wrapping it inside an old tablecloth. Then I asked the gang to help me shift a ladder that Liam kept in the garden.

"Where do you want it?" Jamie asked.

"Over there." I pointed at the side of the house.

I knew Edna would presume that Liam had moved it.

"I need you to come by the house on Sunday."

"What for?"

"To help us escape."

Sunday arrived, but instead of feeling excited, I felt sick with nerves. I listened for the sound of the front door, signalling that they'd left for the pub. I peered out of the window, searching for Jamie. Moments later, he appeared along with some other boys. I opened the window and the boys lifted the ladder and rested it against the windowsill. I told Stephen to go first.

"Do I have to?"

"Yes, it'll be an adventure." I smiled, trying to jolly him along.

After a bit of persuasion, he finally climbed down the ladder.

"Here, we'll hold on for you now," Jamie called.

The old tablecloth was bulging with food, so I tied it around my body and began my descent. Once we were both on the ground, I looked at Stephen's feet and then at my own – neither of us had any shoes, Edna had removed them before she'd left. We had little choice – it was now or never.

I thanked Jamie and waved goodbye to the rest of the gang as we crept barefoot along the street, constantly on the lookout for Edna.

"Look, over there." I pointed at a builder's yard. "We could hide in one of those houses."

The red-brick houses were still being built but I knew they'd make the perfect hideout. We spotted some builder's sand and started to make castles. Then I found an old, discarded lemonade bottle that I rinsed out and filled with water. I scoured the room to see what else I could use. I spotted a pair of wellington boots that I pulled on, but they were men's wellies so they were far too big for me and difficult to walk in.

Stephen was barefoot and struggling to walk so I told him to stand on my feet. He didn't like walking backwards so it took us ages to get down the road. I convinced myself that I was Stephen's mammy and I would be until we found his real one. I'd do anything to stop him being taken back to Edna. Soon it turned dark so we hid inside a church doorway. I'd found a workman's jacket that I wrapped around us to keep us warm. It was difficult, but we survived the next few days by stealing milk from people's doorsteps. I loved the cream, but the milk tasted thin. I didn't know it but the police were out looking for us. It was the time of the Moors Murders, and two missing children had sent panic waves through the community. But I was oblivious as I walked along and spotted a park with an outside swimming pool. Taking Stephen's hand, we walked over to it so that we could soak our feet. I was just dipping them in when a policeman appeared.

"Barbara?"

I looked up and noticed his uniform. Grabbing Stephen's hand, we began to run, but the policeman gave chase and soon we were cornered. We were packed into the back of a police car and taken to Edna's house. Our disappearance had made the news so there were lots of newspapers waiting to speak to us and get our photograph. The police didn't want us pictured, so they parked around the corner and asked another police car to meet us. An officer climbed out of the other car and handed us a pair of grey blankets.

"Here, cover your heads with these."

"But we've done nothing wrong," I said.

"No, but you've caused an awful lot of worry," he replied, pulling the blanket over Stephen's head.

I covered my face as we pulled up outside the house. Even through the thick blanket I could hear the flash of photographers' bulbs as they took pictures of the two missing children. Edna was furious and she was dying to beat me but couldn't because the place was swarming with press and police. Over the next few days, we stayed there but there was always a police officer present. Sadly, I never returned to school. Instead, letters continued to fall through Edna's letterbox – hate mail. She was even sent razor blades through the post. The public had realised we'd run because we were frightened and now everyone was calling her a child abuser. Unwittingly, she'd become a marked woman. Social Services later discovered that she had not only been receiving money from them, but also from my father. They needed to put me somewhere away from the media glare. Terrified Social Services would find out what she'd done to me, Edna told them I'd been drawing disturbing images of naked men. She did it to take the spotlight off herself. Shortly afterwards, Stephen was sent to live with Dad and I was placed in a children's home. I should have felt jealous but I was relieved because I knew he'd be safe and away from Edna. I was glad to get away from her too, because now I was free to find my real mother.

Chapter 5

The Doctor

One afternoon, I was talking to a boy in the children's home when we got into an argument and he called me a "bastard".

I'd heard the word before, but I didn't know it meant something.

"You don't know what it means, do you?" he crowed.

I was only 11 years old and I didn't, so I went to ask the teacher.

"It's someone who doesn't have a father," she explained.

I shrugged my shoulders. I definitely had a dad, but I didn't have a mum. Or I did, but I didn't know where she was. I wondered if that made me a "bastard"?

Weekends were the hardest part of living at the children's home because that's when parents would call for their children and take them home. I prayed that my mother would turn up, but she never did. I tried to make sense of the fact that she'd left me behind when I'd been a baby. I convinced myself I'd been stolen from her, not abandoned. That night, I laid out my school uniform at the end of the bed and hatched a plan. The following day, instead of going to school in Coventry, I caught a bus to Nuneaton in Leicestershire. I had a bus pass that enabled me to travel anywhere within the Midlands and, although I was only young, I was determined to use it. I knew which bus to catch because the ones that travelled outside the area were bright yellow, so I took a chance and jumped on board. I didn't have a plan as such; I'd just decided on Nuneaton because I needed to start somewhere. I didn't know what my mother looked like only that she had red hair, so I sat, watched and waited for a lady with red hair to pass by. As soon as one did, I began to follow. As I trailed behind her along the street, she turned to look at me.

"Are you following me?" she asked, eyeing me warily.

I nodded.

"Why? Are you lost?"

I shook my head.

"I'm looking for my mum, but I don't know her name."

The woman looked a little startled as I continued, "I live in a children's home. My name is Barbara."

Her face softened as she rested a hand against my shoulder.

"I'm sorry, Barbara, but I'm not your mother."

My face fell as she walked away. She'd only taken a few steps when she stopped and turned. "But I do hope you find her."

I spent the rest of the day waiting, my eyes scouring the crowds for ladies with red hair. I spotted one. Her head had bobbed up and down as she made her way along the street. I noticed she was holding two carrier bags that looked too heavy for her. My heart was in my mouth as I crossed the road towards her. I followed her until we entered a housing estate. It was clear that she was heading home and I wanted to see where she lived — where my mother lived. As she walked down the garden path, she turned to pull her key from her bag and that's when she spotted me.

"Hello," I mumbled.

"Hello," she replied, smiling warmly.

It was her. I just knew it. I couldn't believe my luck. At last I'd found her!

"My name's Barbara and I'm looking for my mum," I called from the garden gate.

The woman seemed puzzled and I felt a knot of uncertainty twist in the pit of my stomach.

"I… I'm looking for my mum, and I think you're her."

She thought for a moment, put the key in the lock and turned it. I was still standing there, waiting.

"Would you like to come in?" she asked.

I ran up the path and followed her inside. I was delighted when she brought me a glass of orange juice and a fairy cake.

"Sit on the sofa and eat your cake."

I sat there for the rest of the afternoon and I told her all about my life and my search for my mother.

"You do know I'm not her, don't you?" she said finally.

I knew she wasn't, but it didn't mean that I didn't want her to be.

"But you could be," I suggested.

The woman, who was in her late thirties, explained that she was married but had no children of her own.

"Didn't you want any?" I asked, my legs swinging against the sofa as I licked buttercream off my second fairy cake.

Her eyes seemed sad as she clasped her hands together and glanced at the floor.

"Yes, I would've loved children – a little girl like you – but I wasn't blessed with one."

I'd convinced myself that if I sat there long enough then maybe she'd decide to adopt me. But just as my hopes had started to rise, they quickly came crashing back down.

"You do know I'm going to have to call the police pretty soon, don't you? There'll be people out looking for you. They'll be worried about you."

I shook my head.

"No they won't," I answered, shrugging my shoulders.

"Listen," she said, tapping my knee. "If they say I can keep you then I will. How about that?"

A grin spread across my face. The woman wasn't my mother, but she wanted a child, and I was a child without a mother. It seemed perfect. Half an hour later, there was a knock at the door. The two uniformed police officers sat and listened as the woman explained about my ongoing search.

"But if she needs a home then I'm happy to have her here," she told them.

The older policeman shook his head.

"Sorry, Madam, but it doesn't work like that. We'll have to get Barbara back to the children's home as soon as possible, but thank you for ringing in."

She seemed heartbroken and, as the policemen led me towards the door, she came over to give me a hug. She wrapped her arms around me and held me close. As she pulled away, I noticed she had tears in her eyes.

"Today, you've made me a very happy lady."

She grabbed my hand in hers and pressed something into it. I looked down to see a crisp £5 note. It was more money than I'd had in my life.

"I hope you find your real mother, Barbara," she said, planting a tender kiss on my forehead.

The woman's kindness spurred me on. Now that I had some money I decided I'd use it to fund more trips to find my mother. Soon, I was constantly absconding and Mrs Baker, the manager of the children's home, became tired of my antics. Shortly afterwards, I got involved in a fight with another girl. It was the final straw.

"You're being moved," she informed me as I stood in her office.

I watched as she signed a piece of paper and popped it into a file.

"But where am I going?"

"Somewhere they can keep an eye on you."

Sure enough, within days I was shipped out once more, this time to a remand home called The Cedars, that was housed inside a tall and imposing Victorian building. A tarmac driveway led up to property, which had a grand stone entrance and a porchway covered with terracotta tiles. As I pulled up in the social worker's car I noticed a large wooden conservatory pegged onto the left-hand side. I was led inside by a social worker; I couldn't help but crane my neck to take in the full grandeur of the place. There was a set of sweeping stairs to my right and the main office. I was told to sit on a chair and wait to speak to Mrs Brown. Within minutes, she emerged with the social worker, who bade me farewell before Mrs Brown beckoned me inside. Her office was inside a conservatory stuffed full of plants, which made it feel very exotic.

"Hello, Barbara, and welcome to The Cedars. This will be your new home until you see fit to learn how to behave yourself. Now, I'll get a member of staff to show you around, take you to where your bedroom is and run through the rules."

I nodded my head and felt myself blush. It was clear that the thick brown file on her desk told her all she needed to know about me.

"For starters, we don't tolerate girls who run away. Besides, this is a locked unit, so you wouldn't get very far. Now," she said, looking me down from my head to my toes, "a doctor will have to check you over for lice and crabs."

My face crumpled.

Crabs? What was she talking about?

She sat back down behind a huge wooden desk and looked at me as though she couldn't quite believe I was still standing there.

"That is all," she said, waving me away from her. I turned and headed for the door. As I did, she called me back.

"And Barbara," she said, her steely grey eyes peering at me over the frames of her spectacles, "I don't want to see you in my office again. Do I make myself clear?"

"Yes," I said, my voice barely a whisper.

I picked up my small bag of belongings, which contained two changes of clothes, and headed over towards the "sick bay" where the nurse checked my hair with fast-moving fingers.

"You're clean," she announced, pushing me away. She sat back down at her desk and wrote something down on a piece of card with my name on.

Thinking I was free to leave I stood up.

"No," she said. "You're not done here. You need to take your clothes off, even your underwear, and lie on that bed. The doctor will be in to see you soon."

The single metal bed was so uncomfortable that I could feel the mattress springs digging against my back as I lay down and waited for the doctor to arrive. He was a tall, skinny man with a bald head, glasses and a pointy face, and he was wearing a white doctor's coat. He lifted his hands and tapped my belly, and then he put a stethoscope in his ears and listened to my heart and lungs before giving me a clean bill of health. I was allowed to dress before another member of staff, who I discovered was called Pegleg because she wore a calliper, showed me to my dormitory. It contained around ten metal beds similar to the one in the medical room.

"That one's yours," Pegleg said, before leaving the room.

My bed was on the right-hand side of the room beneath a window and by the door. The dormitory looked out onto the back garden with steps leading down to a lawned area that was surrounded by beautiful trees. I was shown where the laundry, classrooms and cellar were. I had to pick up my uniform from the cellar along with another girl, who was a few years older.

The uniform was pretty basic – a white blouse, brown skirt and basic black lace-up shoes, but my heart sank when they handed the other girl a bra and me a vest.

"I'd like a bra, not a vest," I insisted.

The woman looked at my skinny frame.

"You can't have a bra," she sniggered, elbowing her friend, "because you don't have anything to put in it."

I glanced down at my flat chest.

"But I want a bra like the other girl."

The woman leaned forward and looked me directly in the eye.

"We don't have one that'll fit you, so a vest it is."

"But I want one."

"I know you do, but we don't have one that'll fit you, and if I give you one that's too big it'll be uncomfortable."

I shrugged my shoulders because I didn't care. I wanted a bra because I knew the vest would make me a prime target for bullies.

"I *want* a bra."

The woman looked over at her colleague and grabbed something off a pile of clothes.

"Just give her one," her colleague said. "She'll be crying for a vest tomorrow."

But I was happy that I'd won my first battle.

I grabbed my clothes – bra and all – and made for the door.

I went back to the dorm to get dressed. As I pulled on the grey-white bra over my chest I looked down at the empty cups where my breasts should be and sighed. But I refused to give up, even when it crumpled underneath my shirt and rode mercilessly up and down my back, rubbing it raw.

"You can have a vest if you prefer?" the nurse offered.

"No, because this bra will help my tits grow faster."

She stifled a laugh as I stuck my nose in the air and walked off down the corridor, the bra sliding with every step I took.

A few days later, I decided to escape. I confided in another girl called Denise.

"Want to come with me?"

Denise nodded. "As long as I can take my teddy bear," she said, clutching it against her.

In the end, we both took our bears. I planned to abscond during the following morning's break. Once the coast was clear, I grabbed Denise's hand and we ran around the back of the building where I knew the wall was only three-feet tall. I was tall for my age, so I helped Denise shin over first, and then she pulled me over. We found ourselves in a field full of sheep and ran as fast as we could. At one point, Denise slipped and fell over in some sheep shit.

"Look at me," she wailed.

"Shut up! Just keep running."

Soon we'd made it to the main road, where we tried to thumb a lift. A dark-blue car pulled up alongside us.

"Where are you two going?" a man asked.

I looked at Denise and then at the man.

"Our nan's house," I lied.

He nodded and told us to get in the back.

"I'll take you there."

I grinned at my friend as we climbed in, and that's when I spotted it – a police radio. The officer turned in his seat and stared at us.

"I think I better take you two girls back, don't you?"

As the car fired into life, my heart sank. We'd only been gone a few hours but now we were heading back to The Cedars. As soon we pulled up outside, Mrs Brown was standing there waiting.

"Thank you, officer," she said taking control.

I watched glumly as a member of staff led Denise away and along the corridor. I was taken to a room, which looked a bit like a padded cell. It was narrow with dark-green padding stuck to the walls. There was a mattress on the floor, but very little else. There was no light – only what had seeped underneath the door from the corridor outside.

"Bang on the door if you need the toilet," a voice called as the door slammed shut.

The following morning, I was returned to the dormitory. I never saw Denise again. A few days later, Mrs Brown told me another doctor was coming to see me.

"But I've already seen the doctor," I replied.

"No, this is Dr Milner. He's a very important person, so you'd better be on your best behaviour."

I thought no more of it until later that morning when I was told to go to the sick bay.

"Wait here," the nurse instructed.

The room was on the first floor above the entrance hall and was pretty bare, apart from a metal bed and a set of drawers.

As I sat there, my legs swinging beneath me, I thought how much I'd love a room like this – a room of my own. I was still dreaming of my own bedroom, when the door opened and in walked a man with grey hair and black-framed glasses. He was probably only 45 or 50 years old, but to a twelve-year-old girl he looked absolutely ancient.

"Hello, I'm Dr Milner," he said in an authoritative voice.

He walked over and picked up both my hands in his. Then he did something really odd – he started to stroke them. I was embarrassed because it felt strange, intimate somehow, and not what I'd been expecting.

"Let me see your fingernails," he said.

I cringed as he traced his fingertips along mine.

Why did he want to see my fingernails? I wondered. *Was he going to ask me to clean them?*

"Oh," he said, his expression changing. "It looks like you've been biting your nails. You're very nervous, oh, you poor child."

I looked at my fingernails and shook my head. I didn't understand what he was talking about because I didn't bite my nails and I never had. As he leaned in close his stomach strained against his cream shirt and the belt on his corduroy trousers cut in against it. He was wearing a brown tweed jacket with large, dark patches sewn over both elbows. I thought that he looked more like a geography teacher than a doctor. But his voice was posh, and even though I didn't bite my nails, I didn't correct him because I didn't want to end up back in the padded room.

"Oh, you poor, poor child," he muttered as he stroked my hands.

I felt uncomfortable. I wanted to pull them away. I wanted to hide my hands from him, to wedge them underneath my legs and against the bed where he couldn't reach them. I didn't like it. I glanced down at my fingernails.

Did they look bitten?

No, I decided. My nails were dirty but they were fine. I peered at the doctor's hands. His nails had been perfectly filed, like a lady's, only without polish. His skin was soft, much softer than Dad's, and far too soft for a man.

"You obviously suffer with your nerves," the doctor said as he shifted his gaze from my hands to my eyes. I didn't look at him because I felt weird, trapped in a room with him.

After a while, I found my voice.

"I haven't been biting my nails," I insisted.

The doctor stopped stroking me and held his hand aloft to shush me.

"Oh, yes, you have," he said in a voice that warned I shouldn't argue with him.

I shut up. There was no point trying to disagree because I knew I'd be in more trouble. I sat there quietly as Dr Milner continued to stroke my hands. There was an uncomfortable silence until he stopped and patted my hand lightly.

"Would you like to come into hospital?"

Hospital? The word stuck inside my head.

I wasn't sick, so why would I need to go to hospital?

"You'll be taken care of there," he continued.

It was odd because I knew there was nothing wrong with me, and so did the doctor. But the more I thought about lying in a big hospital bed rather than a small, metal one, the more I liked the idea. Although I'd never been inside a hospital, I'd seen them on TV and I thought they seemed like lovely places that were full of happy nurses who looked after you. If I was a patient I'd get to wear fluffy slippers and eat bunches of grapes, instead of sitting inside a locked remand centre. I'd be taken care of and there'd be people to entertain me and the other patients.

I wouldn't be locked up like I am here, I thought. *I'd be able to leave when I wanted. I'd just say I was feeling better. Then I'd be able to find Mum and live with her.*

"Alright," I said, smiling at the doctor. "I think I'd like that."

"Wonderful!"

Although I'd agreed, I tried to shake off a sense of unease and focus on the positive – *hospital would mean freedom.*

I watched as he dipped a hand inside his jacket pocket and pulled out a small bottle. He shook two white tablets into the palm of his hand, walked over to the sink, poured a cup of water and handed it to me along with the tablets.

"Here," he said. "I want you to take two of these three times a day. Two after breakfast, the same after dinner and again after tea. It's very important you take them."

My forehead crumpled. I was confused.

"Why are you giving me tablets?" I asked, looking at them in the centre of my palm.

"Because you bite your nails. I'll start you on your first two now, then tomorrow Mrs Brown will give you them."

I'd never taken a tablet before in my life, so Dr Milner told me to pop them at the back of my tongue and take a big gulp of water.

"That's right!" he smiled. "Now," he said, turning to leave the room. "You need to take the tablets every day. If you don't, you'll be in serious trouble. Do you understand?"

I nodded.

"Good. You'll be in hospital before you know it. I'll have it all arranged. In the meantime, sit tight and wait here."

I glanced over at the clock on the wall. I'd been with the doctor less than ten minutes but he'd given me pills and I'd been admitted to hospital, even though there was absolutely nothing wrong with me.

Chapter 6

Out of Sight, Out of Mind

Monday mornings at The Cedars were always the same. We got up, washed, had breakfast and went to school, which was another room inside the main locked building. But suddenly my routine had changed, because now I had to go to see Mrs Brown and wait in line alongside half a dozen other girls to be given tablets prescribed by Dr Milner. Mrs Brown had a list that she ticked your name off. She was a large, overweight lady with severe black hair pulled off her face and secured in a tight, neat bun. I don't know if it was the sheer size of the woman, but I'd always felt intimidated by her. She glanced down at the list for my name, dispensed two white tablets from a small brown medicine bottle and handed me a glass of water. She sat back and watched me swallow. Although I was too frightened not to, she still made me open my mouth and lift up my tongue to prove I'd done it.

"That's it," she said, marking a small blue tick by my name. She glanced over the top of my shoulder and beckoned the next girl forward.

I wasn't sure which week I'd leave for the hospital, but I knew it'd be a Monday because that's when the call came in.

The phone would ring early, usually before breakfast at eight o'clock. As soon as we heard it we knew someone would be getting shipped out later that morning. But as the days turned into weeks and the weeks passed by, I started to doubt if I'd ever be called up. Soon, Christmas came, yet still no word. As we opened our presents – a toiletry set for each girl – my heart sank as I wondered what the new year would bring.

I'd still see Dr Milner. He'd often call in to visit Mrs Brown in her conservatory office. I'd watch them chatting through the window, sipping their tea politely from china cups. It was easy to spy on them without being noticed because the room was full of pot plants. We always knew when Dr Milner was at The Cedars because the biscuit tin would be brought out. One day, I was peering through the window when he passed by as he walked along the corridor.

"Hello," he said, stopping dead in his tracks. "How are you feeling today?"

I wasn't sure what I should and shouldn't say. I didn't want him to think I was well because I wanted to go to hospital.

Anything had to be better than here, I reasoned.

"Actually, I've not been feeling well," I piped up, hoping it would help rush things along.

Dr Milner glanced down at me. "Well, you'll feel better soon enough because you'll be in hospital."

I can't get there quick enough, I thought.

A few weeks later, I was standing in the queue, waiting for my tablets, when I heard the phone ring in Mrs Brown's office. Moments later, she walked into the room. I looked up expectantly but she didn't say a word. I felt my heart sink and my hopes fade. Instead, I inched forward in the queue until soon I was at the front. Mrs Brown held out my tablets and I swallowed before lifting my tongue for her usual inspection.

"No school for you today, Barbara," she mumbled.

I stared at her, waiting for her to elaborate, as she ticked my name off her list. She lifted her head, looked at me and absent-mindedly circled her pen between her fingers.

"No school because you're going to hospital today."

Yes! I thought. *Today, I'm finally getting out of here!*

It was 1971 and a particularly cold Monday morning in mid-January, but to me it felt like Christmas and my birthday all rolled into one, because today was the day I got to leave The Cedars. After breakfast, I sat waiting in the reception area. I craned my neck to look up through the window. I spotted a red mini pull up outside and watched as a male and a female social worker climbed out. The lady entered the reception area and the nurse pointed her over towards me. She took the carrier bag from my hand and peered inside. It didn't contain much, just the clothes I'd arrived in, a set of pyjamas and a toothbrush.

"I couldn't find any soap," I explained.

"Don't worry; you don't need many toiletries because they've got plenty there."

I felt happy – happy to be leaving the remand centre for good. The air felt cold and crisp on my skin as I climbed into the back of the car. The sun was low in the sky but it was trying its best to warm the frozen earth. The man turned a silver key in the ignition and the car spluttered into life. As I sat alone in the back, I thought how young they looked. They were both in their late twenties, and I assumed from what she'd said earlier that they'd made this trip countless times. I caught my last glimpse of The Cedars' gardens as we followed the winding driveway out towards the front gates and main road. I didn't look back. I didn't even feel tempted – I was just relieved to be leaving. The scenery sped by in a blur as they chatted amongst themselves in the front seats. At one point the woman glanced back to check if I was listening. I was, but I didn't want her to know so I pretended to look out of the car window. As soon as she'd turned around, I glanced back at them. I noticed a thick, brown cardboard folder resting in her lap. In fact, it was so thick that it had a couple of elastic bands wrapped around it just to stop the papers inside from falling out. I guessed all those pieces of paper contained information about me. Although she was trying her best to talk in a quiet voice, I could still make out what the female social worker was saying.

"Well, here goes another one," she sighed, drumming her fingers on the file.

The man turned towards her, momentarily shifting his eyes from the road.

"You know something, Eleanor," he said, gripping the steering wheel tightly. "I don't agree with this. I don't agree with any of it, and one day someone's going to have to pay. There'll be questions asked, you mark my words."

Although I wasn't supposed to be listening, I'd heard every single word.

The woman's eyes darted back at him. "You're right," she agreed. "There'll be questions to ask."

That's odd, I thought. *I wonder what they mean by that. I'm going to remember everything you just said,* I vowed. And I did.

We drove for another half an hour, as they continued to talk in some sort of a code that only they could understand. I knew they were being extra careful with what they said in case I picked up on any of it. Abruptly, the car signalled and turned left. We left the main road and drove in through some gates towards the hospital. As we travelled into the grounds I spotted a blue sign.

Aston Hall Mental Hospital.

Panic overwhelmed me and my heart started beating furiously as I turned to try and read the sign again.

Had I read it wrong? Did it really say mental hospital?

But it had long gone – the sign was way behind us, disappearing off into the distance. I looked out of the left window and noticed a beautiful white mansion with a church opposite. I assumed that we must be going there but we drove straight past it and along a road that was surrounded by red-brick buildings on both sides.

"Why are you taking me to a mental hospital?" I asked suddenly.

The woman glanced over at her colleague, composed herself and then turned to me.

"No," she smiled, patting my hand for reassurance. "We're not taking you there. We're taking you to another part of the hospital. You're not going to the mental hospital, you're going to the other side."

I sighed with relief and flopped back into my seat. But the sign had left me feeling uneasy.

Why would it say mental hospital if it wasn't one?

My gut instinct told me to run, but just as I considered it, the car came to a halt outside a building, similar to the others we'd passed. I looked over at it, trying to make out where we were, and that's when I noticed the windows. They were open, but only by a few inches. It was as though they'd been bolted half-open from the inside. Uncertainty gnawed away in the pit of my stomach – the sign and now the windows. At first glance, it looked and felt like The Cedars, like another prison, even though it was supposed to be a hospital.

"Come on, Barbara," the female social worker said breezily.

She pulled a lever and the front seat flipped forwards, allowing me to climb out. She held out her hand but I knew it wasn't a sign of affection – it was to stop me from running away. I climbed out, took a deep breath and stood in the driveway, taking it all in. There was a blue door to the right of us. We walked over to it, the man pressed a doorbell and we stood there waiting. Moments later, a key scraped in the lock and the main door swung open. A nurse stood in the doorway with a large bunch of keys swinging from a black leather belt that she wore around her waist.

Why would a nurse have so many keys? I wondered. *And why was the door locked?*

Before I knew it, I was asking her the question. The nurse stopped, looked down and considered me for a moment.

"It's because we don't want people getting out and hurting themselves," she said in a voice that was more stern than friendly. "We've got some very sick people in here."

I nodded my head to show that I understood, even though I didn't.

As we walked into the entrance hall, the stillness of the place overwhelmed me. For a children's hospital it seemed eerily quiet. It was *too* quiet. The female social worker broke the silence.

"This is Barbara O'Hare," she said, her voice cold and business-like. "She's come from The Cedars."

I watched as she handed over my file to the nurse.

The social workers said goodbye and left through the same door. I didn't say a word because I was too busy taking it all in. I spotted a pale-blue set of stairs over towards my right and wondered if they led to one of the wards but, before I could ask, the nurse broke my thoughts.

"Take a seat here," she ordered, pointing at a solitary chair. It was perched at the end of a very long corridor. Once I was seated, she marched along the corridor and came to a halt outside a door. I guessed it must have been an office. Holding my file in one hand, she lifted the other and gave the door a light tap. I heard a voice. The nurse opened the door and disappeared off inside. I sat there trying to second guess what would happen next. Suddenly, she reappeared in the corridor.

"The doctor will see you now," she called, beckoning me over.

I almost ran to her and then walked in through the half-open door. The office was plain with a table, a set of cabinet drawers and very little else. The doctor was sitting down behind the desk, reading and filling in a form with a fountain pen. The door closed behind me as the nurse left the room. Now it was just the two of us. I suddenly felt very small, standing in that big room, alone and unsure why I was there. I recognised the man immediately – it was Dr Milner, the man who'd stroked my hand in The Cedars. But this time, he didn't seem as friendly. In fact, he barely looked up as I stood there before him.

"No tea. Treatment tonight," he said with a wave of his hand as though it wasn't up for discussion.

The nurse opened the door and ushered me through. I followed her along the corridor and upstairs into the dormitory. She unlocked and locked a succession of doors as we passed through them.

"That's your bed." She pointed at the first one on the right. "Now put your things in the cabinet."

I did as I was told. I wanted to ask what the treatment was, but the look on her face told me not to. Instead, I followed her downstairs. She led me into another room next to the doctor's office. Again, she used another set of keys from the big bunch on her belt to open and lock the different doors as we passed through them. As the last door swung open, I saw that we'd entered some sort of common room. There were lots of girls wandering around or sitting, watching a TV in the corner. But no one seemed to notice me. Unlike The Cedars, there was no chatter or conversation, just the sound of voices from actors blaring away on the black-and-white screen. A shudder ran down my spine. I couldn't put my finger on it, but it felt wrong.

There was a series of tables lined up along the back of the room. The TV was at the front along with a few old chairs that were dotted about. I walked over to one and sat down. The nurse had left the room but returned moments later, clutching a small container. Inside was a brown medicine bottle. She held out a spoon and poured some thick, brown syrup into it.

"Here," she said, holding it in front of my mouth. "Take this."

I clamped it shut but she remained there, determined that I'd take it.

"But I've already had my tablets today," I said, hoping it'd change her mind.

"Don't mess with me," she snapped, pushing the spoon hard against my mouth.

I knew I wouldn't win so I did as she said and swallowed the medicine. Then she handed me a single tablet. It looked exactly the same as the ones I'd taken at The Cedars.

"Why, am I sick?" I asked, wondering why I needed to take more medicine.

The nurse didn't answer, so I tried again.

"What's wrong with me? Why am I in hospital?"

I was starting to worry that maybe I really was sick, and no one wanted to tell me. But the nurse refused to answer.

"Just sit and wait," she said. "The doctor will be ready for you soon."

With that she left, unlocking and locking the door behind her.

I sat looking at the other patients but no one glanced over. It was as though I was invisible. Even those looking straight ahead seemed to be staring into thin air. A fist of anxiety balled inside my stomach. Something was horribly wrong – this wasn't normal. I sat and waited, not daring to speak. Suddenly, I began to feel extremely drowsy. My eyelids felt heavy and I was battling just to try and keep them open. Although I tried my best to keep myself upright in the chair, my head lolled forwards.

Why did I feel so tired? What had been in that medicine?

These and other thoughts were running through my head when I noticed a pair of shiny black shoes standing right in front of me. My eyes moved up the shoes to a pair of white cotton bobby socks and up a pair of long bare legs. They belonged to a woman – an older lady in her late forties – who was standing in front of me. Although she was much older than the others, she was dressed as though she was still a little girl. With her blue blouse, pink cardigan, white skirt and a large white bow in her hair she seemed strangely out of time.

"Hello, would you like to dance?" she asked.

I shook my head. I felt so odd that I wasn't sure if I was dreaming. As I looked again I realised she had lots of teeth missing and her hair was a mess of matted, grey strands. In my semi-comatose state, I tried to reply.

"Daaaance?" I slurred.

I was shocked by my voice. I sounded drunk, like Edna.

"Yes," the woman laughed, swirling around in front of me. "I'm a tap dancer. I've danced everywhere – all over the country. I used to be a big star."

She threw her hands across the air in front of her as though she could still picture herself up on stage. Even though I was young, I realised that the woman was quite mad but, at the same time, I was grateful that someone had talked to me.

"Whaaaat's yourrrr naaaame?" I said. My slurred voice sounded alien to me.

"Jane."

"Mmmine's Barrrbrrraaa."

Jane garbled as I struggled to stay awake. My head felt heavy and awkward, like trying to balance a bowling ball on my shoulders. I must've dozed off, although I couldn't remember doing so. I'm not sure how long I was asleep, but when I awoke Jane had disappeared and a nurse was gently shaking my arm to try and rouse me from my slumber.

"Come on. Come on," she said. "The doctor's ready for you."

I opened my eyes and glanced across the room. I noticed that Jane was sitting with the other girls at a long line of dining tables. Everyone was eating silently, staring out into space. The only noise was the occasional scrape of cutlery against plate as they ate their food. I spotted a clock on the wall – it was five o'clock. I had no idea how long I'd been asleep, but I knew this nurse was different to the last one. She was wearing a different hat, although I had no idea what it meant or if she was more senior or junior than the last. She helped me to my feet but I felt woozy and unsteady on my legs. I still felt wobbly as I placed one uncertain foot in front of the other and followed her upstairs into a bathroom.

"Strip off," she ordered, "you need to bathe."

The room was cold and unfamiliar. I felt out of it. The last thing I wanted to do was to strip off in front of a complete stranger – nurse or no nurse. I looked around. There were two baths and both had different types of weird hospital equipment attached to them.

"Come on, hurry up," she snapped.

I did as I was told although I took my time because I'd hoped she'd leave the room. She didn't. Instead, as I removed my top, revealing my baggy white bra, she began to laugh.

"Why are you wearing a bra," she smirked, pointing at it.

"Because I don't want to be picked on."

The words left my mouth as though I had no filter. It was the truth – I'd just told her the real reason I was wearing the bra. The words had come trickling out as though I'd lost the ability to lie. I felt exposed. I didn't want to be locked up in this stupid hospital where all the nurses had keys and acted like jailers.

"Come on, get in the bath," she instructed, waving a hand towards it.

I peered over the edge. The water was only a few inches deep – barely enough to cover me – and, as I dipped my foot in I realised it was tepid to the touch. I was handed a bar of green soap that smelt of disinfectant and told to wash myself quickly.

"We don't want to keep the doctor waiting," she said, searching through a cupboard for a towel.

Her words chilled me more than the lukewarm water.

What did the doctor want with me and what was the treatment?

I washed myself but had to be helped out by the nurse, who handed me the towel and told me to dry.

"Hurry up, I need to weigh you."

I stepped on the scales as she moved something across a long bar and made a note of my weight. Then she asked me to hold my arms out, slipped an old, grey gown onto me and secured it at the back with ties. The fabric felt thick and heavy, as if I was wearing cardboard. It was far too big for me and there was a draft at the back where the fabric fell apart like a half-opened mouth.

"Can I put my underwear back on?"

But she ignored me. I wanted to cry because I felt so naked.

"Can I please put my underwear back on?" I begged. "Why do I have to wear this thing?"

"Because Dr Milner said so."

I knew she was getting annoyed because she tugged angrily at the last of the straps as she tied them together. I used a hand to try and clamp the open bit of the gown together but it was impossible. The fabric was so thick that I could barely bend my arms.

"Come on, follow me."

She walked out of the bathroom and across the landing into a room opposite. As I followed her I noticed a trolley parked up outside. On top was a kidney-shaped dish that contained a long needle, a roll of greying bandage and various white packets.

"Come on." She ushered me inside the room.

I looked around but all I could see was a single rubber mattress on the floor. There were no pillows or sheets, or anything else, only a small window with shutters on the opposite wall that let a bit of daylight in. But as soon as we entered the room the nurse closed them, blocking out all natural light.

"Lie down." She pointed at the bed.

I did as I was told. She went outside and wheeled in the trolley, parking it up against the mattress. I watched as she picked up the old bandage that looked as though it'd been used countless times before.

"Right," she said, bending down towards me. "I need you to cross your right hand over your left."

I did as she said and she knelt down and began to bind my hands tightly together. My heart was thudding so loud inside my chest that I was certain she would hear it.

"Please," I begged. "I don't bite my nails. I promise. I've never bitten my nails and I never will. You don't need to do this. Please don't tie my hands up."

"Shush!" she scolded. "The doctor will hear you and you don't want to upset him, do you?"

I shook my head defiantly. I'd fight this if I had to.

"I don't care!" I shouted. I began to kick my legs out to try and stop her, but they felt heavy from the medicine so my protest didn't last long.

Once my hands were bound, the nurse perched herself at the end of the mattress.

"Open and close your hand, like this," she said demonstrating.

The bandages were tight and they felt as though they were cutting off my circulation.

"It hurts," I mumbled, but she wasn't listening. Instead, she rubbed a finger up and down my arm. She took the needle out of the dish and turned towards me. I'd never been inside a hospital or had a single injection before so I was simply terrified.

"I don't need that," I said beginning to panic. I scrambled against the mattress, trying to back away from her. "I'm not sick. I want to go back to The Cedars."

She ignored me.

"You'd better calm down. You'd better calm down or you will end up having electric shock treatment."

But I couldn't help it. I was frightened and angry – angry that I'd been tricked into coming here. Hot tears streamed down my face as I begged her not to inject me. I felt a sharp, stinging pain in my arm. I looked at her but she seemed totally detached from the situation and me. The cold and determined look in her eyes scared me half to death. For a split second I actually wondered if the injection would kill me. In many ways, I hoped it would then at least I wouldn't feel frightened anymore. A coldness flooded through my veins as I fell back onto the bed. I was trapped. I wanted to move but couldn't. Instead, I remained there, watching and waiting, as still and as cold as a statue. The wheels of the trolley squeaked as the nurse headed towards the door. She turned to speak to someone standing by the doorway, just out of sight.

"Alright, doctor, she's all yours."

I gasped. Dr Milner was here.

Even though I couldn't move a muscle I was totally aware of what was happening. I watched as the doctor came into the room, he was carrying three seat cushions under one arm. Instead of his usual tweed jacket, he was wearing a short white doctor's coat with a breast pocket at the top and two at his waist. His silhouette was lit from behind by a bulb in the corridor – the only source of light in the now darkened room. He placed the cushions on the floor in a line to form a make-shift bed and lay down on them. I felt his breath against my skin, hot and urgent. I tried not to breathe in because I didn't want to swallow his breath. He placed something across my mouth. It felt hard and sharp, as though it were a mask made of wire. Then he put something white over my mouth. It felt soft and ticklish against my skin. There was a strange sensation of something being dripped against it. My mouth felt wet and my skin cold as the foul-smelling liquid evaporated against the cotton.

Drip, drip, drip.

I felt myself falling backwards and suddenly everything went black. I don't know how long I was unconscious but as I came to I heard Dr Milner's voice. He was asking me one question after another.

"What is your name? How old are you?"

But before I could answer he poured more liquid onto the mask.

Drip, drip, drip.

I slipped under again. I blinked as I came to once more, only this time I'd been moved. Now I was on my side, facing him. The doctor was so close that I could smell his breath.

"How old is your brother?"

I opened my mouth to try and answer.

Drip, drip, drip.

I momentarily felt the coldness of liquid against my skin, my nostrils flared and everything faded. I awoke again. This time I was facing the wall. He asked me something but as soon as I tried to answer my voice was drowned by more liquid being poured onto the mask.

Drip, drip, drip.

I came around, but this time I was on my back. I spotted another silhouette, one that wasn't the doctor. It was a man. He was wearing a short brown technician's coat that rested against his hips. He lifted a square-shaped object in front of his face and a light flashed as a bulb crackled. My gown had been pulled up around my waist, exposing my private parts as the camera flashed again and again. The light burned into my eyes, but I couldn't move or shout out.

Drip, drip, drip.

More wetness, more darkness. Another question, but no time to answer. Instead, the chemical smell filled my senses as I slipped into unconsciousness once more. I came to. This time I was laid face down and on my stomach. I felt a sharp stabbing pain in my buttocks – another injection. The room went dark and my mind blank. When I finally came round, I was lying in my bed back in the dormitory. I felt groggy and my mouth was bone dry. I cried out for a glass of water, but the dorm was empty apart from me. Every bed had been neatly turned under and topped off with a matching blue bedspread. My body ached as though it'd been kicked all over. I felt a shooting pain in my wrists. They felt bruised and sprained, as though all the bending and pulling had stolen the strength from them. I tried to put both hands underneath to hoist myself up to a sitting position but they were weak, so it took me a couple of goes before I was fully upright. As I sat, a sharp stinging pain seared up my body from in-between my legs. The pain was so sudden and unexpected that it stole my breath away. I screwed up my eyes and winced. I felt damp below, as though I'd wet myself. My face flushed hot with embarrassment as I patted a hand against the sheet. It was dry. Something was wrong.

A nurse appeared.

"Oh, you're awake," she said.

I tried to look at her but my head felt heavy as the room began to spin.

"Well, you'll have to stay in bed till after dinner," she was saying, as she plumped up the pillows beneath me. "But I'll go and bring you some marmalade sandwiches."

She had disappeared almost as quickly as she'd arrived and I was alone in the dormitory once more. Moments later, she reappeared and was carrying a hospital tray. She balanced it across my lap. It contained marmalade sandwiches, my two white tablets and a paper cup measure of the awful brown syrup.

"Come on." She handed me a glass of water. "Take your tablets."

I took them and then gulped down the horrible brown medicine. I wanted to argue but I had no fight left in me. Instead, I ate the sandwiches and drank the water. I needed to go for a wee but felt dizzy as I made my way to the bathroom. I put out a hand and grabbed hold of the bed to try and steady myself. I still had a strange sensation down below. I felt swollen too, as though something had been put inside me. My whole body felt messed up somehow. My stomach started to cramp below my bellybutton. Although the toilet was yards from my bed it might as well have been miles. As I tried to turn around I spotted the nurse, who'd popped back onto the ward.

"What are you doing? Get back in that bed now!"

"But I need the toilet."

"No, you will get back in that bed now. I'll bring you a bed pan."

She turned and left the room. I didn't know what a bed pan was or how long she'd be, so I continued to the bathroom. It took me a while, but I made it. After I'd finished, I pulled off some sheets of toilet paper to wipe myself, and that's when I saw it – blood. It was a watery pink colour but there was no mistaking it – I was bleeding from down below. Someone had done something to me in that room. Even my wee stung against my insides like acid. It was as though someone had taken a blowtorch and had burnt me internally. I flushed the loo and opened the toilet door to find the nurse standing outside with her arms folded angrily across her chest.

"Stay in bed until you're told otherwise," she snapped.

By now the medication had kicked in and my eyelids felt heavy as sleep gripped me. Within moments, I'd slipped into a deep slumber. My last thoughts were this was no ordinary hospital.

Chapter 7

The Hospital

Hours later, I was awoken by another nurse, one with glossy, black hair. I felt her tap me lightly on my shoulder.

"Wakey, wakey," she sang in a jolly voice.

Her voice had sounded so friendly that for a moment I'd almost forgotten where I was. But as soon as I opened my eyes, the realisation I was inside the hospital dorm hit me.

"Come on," she said, holding out an open palm. "It's medication time."

I'd barely lifted myself up when I felt her hand against my mouth as the pills flew in and landed at the back of my tongue, making me gag.

"Here." She handed me a glass of water. I took a grateful gulp. As I did, I spotted a paper medicine cup in her hand. The pleated white tiny paper cup was a quarter full with the sickly brown syrup, which I had to force myself to drink.

"That's better. Now it's time to get up. You can go downstairs and have your tea."

I watched as she began to pull out some clothes from my bedside cabinet.

"Come on, get dressed."

Although I still felt groggy from the medication, as soon as I saw my underwear I wanted to weep with gratitude because I'd felt so exposed. Sitting on the bed, I began to dress. The soft fabric comforted me as it brushed against my skin. But my wrists were hurting where the nurse had bound them together. They felt so sprained that I was struggling to put on my underwear. I stood to try and pull up my knickers, and as I did I noticed blood on my bedsheet. I checked my wrists. They weren't bleeding and neither were my arms or legs. I spotted the nurse on the other side of the dorm and called her over.

"Can you look on my back? I think it's bleeding," I said, turning it towards her.

The nurse's eyes scanned me.

"It's not," she replied, sounding puzzled. "Why would you think that?"

"Because there's blood on the sheet."

"Oh, that's just a stain that hasn't come out in the wash."

She was wrong. I knew it wasn't a stain.

"But there was blood… when I went to the toilet and I wiped myself. There was blood. I saw it."

"Less of this rubbish. Now, hurry up and get dressed. You're going downstairs to have your tea."

And then she'd gone. I was left standing there wondering why I was bleeding but, more importantly, why the nurse hadn't believed me. I looked at the mark on the sheet and rested a hand against it. As I lifted my palm, I noticed it was now stained red. It was blood and it was fresh because it was still wet to the touch. I wanted to show her, to shout after her, but the nurse had already left. I tried to pull on the rest of my clothes but no matter how hard I tried I just couldn't fasten the buttons on my blouse. Eventually, she wandered back into the room and sighed heavily when she saw I was only half-dressed.

"I can't fasten the buttons," I explained. "It's my wrists."

She turned my arms in her hands to examine them. The angry red marks had deepened in colour, turning into dark purple and blue bruises. I glanced up. She seemed alarmed. Although she didn't say a word, her whole demeanour changed towards me.

"Here, let me help you with those buttons," she said, fastening them.

Then she picked up my socks off the bed and helped me with those, too. I knew my hair was a mess so I picked up a brush to smooth it but my wrists hurt too much. I did the best I could and turned to face the nurse.

"You'll do as you are," she decided. "Now come on, I knock off soon, so it's time to take you downstairs."

My legs still felt wobbly as I made my way along the corridor. As we passed the bathroom my heart froze. I turned to see the treatment room. Thankfully, the door was closed but I knew what happened in there. The palms of my hand began to sweat and my heart pounded. Instinct told me to bolt downstairs, tear open the front door and run as fast and as far away as I could get. But it was no good, all the doors were locked – there was no way out. Instead, I followed the nurse. She unlocked the final door and pushed me inside the communal room. There were dozens of girls and, although I was tall for my age, they all looked a few years older than me. I felt self-conscious and out of place. I didn't know a soul and no one seemed to want to know me, apart from tap-dancing Jane. Some girls were sitting down watching television. Others were standing to the side, staring out of the main window but no one was talking. At the previous homes I'd been to all the kids would crowd around the new girl. They'd want to know your name and where you'd come from. But no one had any questions here. No one wanted to know. Instead, they seemed locked away, trapped inside their own worlds. I looked across the room and spotted two girls playing a game of cards. Even though they were playing a game, they had no expression. It was as if they were just going through the motions, as though they were there physically, but mentally they were somewhere else. A figure was twirling away behind one of the seated girls, it was Jane. She looked over and a big, toothless grin spread across her face. I smiled back, comforted that someone was pleased to see me, even if it was Jane.

I suddenly felt very tired. I spotted an empty chair, wandered over and sat down in it. Something moved out of the corner of my eye – it was a nurse on the far side of the room. There was a loud clatter of cutlery as she picked it up and placed a cutlery tray down on the table. She looked over at the two girls who were playing cards and asked them to put their chairs back at the dining table. Then she started to clap her hands.

"Head count," she called out.

Everyone stopped in their tracks and waited to be accounted for. I wondered what on earth was happening, but as soon as she'd finished counting the girls started to mill around the room once more. I watched as a small crowd wandered over towards the window. It looked out onto the same front tarmac drive that I'd travelled up the day before. It was as though they were all watching or waiting for something or someone. Unlike the others, I remained seated. I wasn't sure what to do, so I decided to sit it out until I knew how things worked. The silence in the room unnerved me because I wasn't used to it. I was used to lots of swearing and girls arguing. I was used to noise, bad tempers and tellings off. I was used to all of that, but not this.

Someone crouched down at the side of my chair. She was a teenager – around 14 – her dark hair fell down around her face as she began to whisper.

"Are you new here, on Laburnum Ward?"

"Laburnum Ward?" I repeated.

"Yes, that's where you are. That's what this is called."

"Oh," I sighed, and then I nodded. "Yes, I'm new."

The girl lifted herself up and perched her bum on the wooden arm of my chair. But I felt wary because I wasn't sure who she was or what she wanted from me.

"What's your name?"

"Barbara. Why? What's yours?"

"Christine."

Christine looked over her shoulder to check the coast was clear and dipped her head so that she couldn't be heard by anyone but me.

"Did you have treatment?" she asked.

I felt the blood drain from me.

How did she know?

I paused for a moment and then answered.

"Yes, I did."

Christine smiled and patted my hand kindly. It immediately made me feel better. We were still deep in conversation when I was startled by a noise. It sounded like a collective gasp and it was coming from the girls over by the window.

"Here he is," one said, sounding petrified.

"Yes," another gasped. "That's his car."

Fear filled the room as everyone began to panic.

"I hope it's not me," another cried, her voice cracking with emotion as she mouthed the words.

"Or me."

I heard a quiet sobbing and turned to see another girl crying to herself. Her head was bowed as she tried to wipe away tears using the sleeve of her cardigan. It was obvious she was utterly terrified.

Christine spoke.

"I hope it's not me… again."

Fear rose up my throat and I had to gulp it down. I felt nauseous, as though I might vomit right there and then because it hit me – all these girls had received the same treatment as me, we'd all been 'treated' by the doctor. My hands began to tremble and soon I couldn't stop my whole body from shaking. It was like being caught up in the middle of a nightmare. Panic filled the room as the small crowd of girls ran away from the window. The beam of headlights from the doctor's car streamed inside and pooled against the opposite wall. Everyone darted as they shone, the golden light picking out frightened faces as girls scattered like skittles to the far corners of the room. The headlights indicated he was here. Dr Milner was back.

"What's happening?" I asked Christine, who told me to be quiet because someone was coming.

A key scraped in the lock, and the nurse who'd clapped her hands earlier suddenly emerged.

"Okay, girls. Calm down," she said, clapping her hands again.

The room fell silent. Through the silence I heard a car door slam. Everyone was looking at one another, half-expectant, but all utterly terrified. I didn't know what was happening, but I guessed from the panic that it must have something to do with the treatment.

"Have you had the treatment?" I whispered to Christine.

"Yes," she said. I watched as her large, dark eyes clouded over with sadness and she looked down. "I've had it about seven times now."

I gasped.

"Seven?"

Christine nodded.

"Why, how long have you been here?"

"About a year. I came here from a remand home called The Cedars in Derby."

I gasped again.

"But that's where I came from."

My heart plummeted. The words banging loudly inside my head.

Seven times in one year.

Don't worry, I told myself. *Dad will come and get me out of here as soon as he knows. He'll knock that stupid doctor out.*

I knew my father was my only hope because he was all I had. I also knew he was busy, working away on the oil rigs. He wasn't due back for another three months, and I hadn't seen him for about six.

But he'll come. I told myself. *He'll come for me.*

He had *to.*

I glanced across the room and noticed a small, odd-looking window in the middle of a wall by the door. It was the window to the nurses' office. Christine told me they used it to keep watch and to sometimes dispense medicine through. There was a lank net curtain hanging on the office side, which made it almost impossible to see through.

The girls in the room stood suddenly still as though they'd been turned into statues. Even Jane stopped dancing and twirling.

"What's happening?" I asked.

"Shush," Christine said, putting a finger up against her lips. "Milner's here. Don't speak. You don't want him to pick you. Just stay still."

I stared at my hands. They were trembling against my lap.

The little window in the nurses' office. Of course! That's what Milner must use to look through. That's how he'd choose his next victim.

I followed the other girls and remained as still as I could. It was as though we were all playing some kind of weird game of musical statues. No one moved a muscle. No one stirred. The room was as silent as a morgue. I noticed a hand brush against the net curtain and lift it up. It was a man's hand, not a nurse's. A head appeared, bobbing underneath as someone looked out into the room. As soon as I saw the grey hair and dark-rimmed glasses I knew it was him. It was Milner. My heart was in my mouth. He was searching for his next victim. The terror in the room was palpable. My ears pricked up at the sound of wood scraping against wood. Milner had opened the window and was looking into the room. The window slid shut and the net curtain pulled down. He'd chosen. I just hoped and prayed it wasn't me. No one said a word. A nurse walked and glanced around.

"Emily Thompson," she said beckoning towards a blonde-haired girl, who looked about 13.

"No!" Emily gasped. "Please, not me!"

The nurse tried to grab her, but Emily was fast and had managed to claw her fingers against the side of a chair and was hanging onto it as if her life depended on it.

"No. I'm not going to do it!" she screamed.

"Come on, Emily. Calm down. The doctor is waiting to see you."

"But I don't want treatment!"

The nurse lost her patience and pulled at Emily's hands to try and loosen her grip.

"Come on now. Don't make it worse for yourself."

"Please, please!" Emily was wailing now, begging to stay in the room.

The net curtain shifted and Milner's head appeared as he looked through the glass again. Fear stole my breath and

I turned away quickly. I didn't want him to see me looking because he might change his mind and choose me.

Emily continued to wail as a couple of nurses led her sobbing from the room. We could still hear her pitiful cries out in the corridor long after the door had closed. I realised then that bad things happened here. Bad things happened to naughty children. No one cared, because no one wanted us. My thoughts were broken by the sound of the nurse clapping. The room seemed to return to normal as she patted her hands together as though she was herding sheep.

"Come on, girls. Tea time."

I watched as the crowd who'd been standing near the window took their places at the dinner table. It was as though the past five minutes just hadn't happened. I got to my feet and followed Christine towards the table, but there were hardly any seats left and those that were weren't together. I felt awkward because I didn't know where I should sit. I spotted an empty chair. I realised if I sat in it my back would face towards the nurse's window which meant I wouldn't be able to see Milner. It made me nervous because I wanted, *no, I needed* to keep my wits about me, to see where he was at all times so that I wouldn't be chosen. Through the fog of the medication and confusion in my mind I thought I heard counting. I looked over at the nurse.

"16, 17, 18, 19," she chanted.

For a second I thought she was doing another head count, but then I noticed she wasn't looking up but down at the cutlery tray. She counted the forks and wiped each one as she put them inside the tray.

"20, 21, 22…" She continued until she'd reached over 50. Then she picked up the knives and started to count them.

With my back to the window, I felt extremely vulnerable. I turned my head slightly and noticed a shape through the weave of the white lace curtain. It was Milner. I could tell it was him by his brown tweed jacket. He was moving around inside the room. I wasn't sure if he was looking out, but I turned away and looked at the table. My heart was pumping so fast that I could hear blood rushing inside my ears.

The nurse continued to count.

"31, 32, 33," she mouthed methodically.

I felt glued to my seat, unable to move. Even in my medicated state, every sinew in my body was telling me to run as far away as I could from the doctor and the horrible dining room.

"39, 40, 41…"

I looked down and tried to make out patterns on the surface of the table. I heard the scraping of chair legs against the floor. Moments later, someone was by my side and a small, delicate hand tapped gently on my shoulder.

"Come and dance with me."

It was Jane.

In a dreamlike state she extended her arm and tried to take my hand in hers. I grimaced and held mine firmly in my lap.

"Look, I can do this dance," she laughed as she began to tap and twirl around in front of me.

"45, 46, 47…"

"Go away," I hissed. I was terrified that she'd draw unwanted attention to me or, more importantly, pick me out for Milner.

I knew he was only feet away in the other room and I didn't want to be next. I refused to hold her hand. Jane ignored me, threw her head back and laughed. She began to tap her shoes against the polished floor. The sound was so loud that it momentarily drowned out the cutlery count.

"Look, I can teach you," she was saying. "I was a famous dancer, you know."

Tap, tap, tap.

She tried to grab my hand but I snatched it away angrily.

"I danced at the Royal Albert Hall," she continued.

"49, 50, 51…"

"Here, let me teach you… then you can be a famous dancer as well."

I couldn't contain myself any longer.

"Go away… leave me alone," I hissed through gritted teeth.

Jane stopped twirling, gasped and held a hand against her chest as though I'd just plunged a dagger into her heart. I felt horrible, but I couldn't help myself. I couldn't risk it. I couldn't risk Milner singling me out for the next treatment.

"Come on, girls. Sit down," the cutlery nurse called.

Jane looked around and realised that she wasn't sitting down. Without a second glance, she wandered off to look for an empty seat at another table. I was relieved to see her go. I remained seated, my eyes staring hard at the grey Formica table in front of me. I heard the nurse call out two names. For a moment, I wondered if they were being called for treatment, but she handed them some cutlery and they began to pass it around. One girl put down the forks whilst the other lay the knives in front of each person. As soon as she reached me she stopped.

"Don't even bother," she said gesturing towards the knife with a cursory glance. "All the knives and forks are counted, so please don't try to take them."

I was baffled. The thought hadn't even crossed my mind. Once the cutlery had been laid, a nurse wheeled in a trolley that contained plates of food. My mouth watered as soon as she put the hot plate of mashed potato, stewing steak, onions and peas down in front of me. The others picked up their knives and forks and began to dig in. I followed them, but as soon as I grabbed my cutlery an agonising pain ripped through both sprained wrists. I was starving hungry but it was impossible to use the cutlery. Every time I tried to stab at the food, my wrist buckled, making it more painful. I could barely grip my knife, never mind cut with it. The food smelled lovely and my stomach felt hollowed out with hunger, but the cutlery had defeated me. I dropped it angrily onto the table and sat there envious as I watched everyone else stuff their faces. It was agonising to watch, but it was less painful to go hungry.

An overweight girl called Emma was sitting opposite. She looked up at me and then down at my plate.

"Don't you want that?" she asked, her mouth already full of mashed potato.

I didn't reply.

"Hey, you, are you deaf?" she hissed. "If you don't want it then pass it over to me when the nurse isn't looking."

I ignored her again, which only seemed to enrage her more.

"Hey, new girl," she said, spitting particles of mash and stewing steak across the table. "Don't ignore me or you'll get it."

I glanced up at her for the first time and nodded to show that I understood. She could have my food because looking at Emma – her fat face smeared with mashed potato and gravy – I'd suddenly lost my appetite. Also, I didn't want trouble or any unwanted attention, so I passed my plate over. The only problem was I didn't realise how heavy it was and soon my wrists had given way.

CRASH!

The plate clattered loudly against the table, scattering food across both it and me. The noise had brought the nurse running over. She was at my side glaring down.

"Get up!" she hollered.

I turned and looked back at the window. I was terrified that Milner would hear and come rushing out for me. I didn't want to stand up for the nurse because I didn't want to be noticed. It seemed to make her angrier as she swooped down and grabbed a handful of my hair. Twisting my blonde curls in her fist, she pulled me up to my feet.

"Oww!" I yelped, trying to loosen her grip.

She pulled me over towards the wall and window of the office where I knew Milner was standing. I was scared stiff. My instinct told me to escape, so I began to kick and lash out, using both my arms and legs. I realised I was fighting a losing battle; the medicine had rendered my limbs useless. Hearing the commotion, another nurse came running over to try and restrain me. She pulled both my arms behind my back so hard that I thought they'd snap.

"Oww!" I screamed as they dragged me past the window.

"Do you want treatment?" the first nurse threatened.

By now my temper had reached boiling point and I could contain it no more.

"I don't care!" I screamed.

Deep down, I did. I was terrified that Milner would appear at any moment.

The girls sitting at the table suddenly became animated and started banging their cutlery loudly against the table like a pack of wild animals.

"Fight, fight, fight!"

The noise had startled me, because up until then the room had been almost silent. Now someone was fighting back, and that someone was me. The nurse let go of my hair and forced my face up against the wall. I felt the coldness of the painted plaster as it pressed hard against my skin.

"Do you want Dr Milner to come out?" a voice behind me called. But I didn't care, not even about Milner. I was as good as dead anyway.

"You'll get treatment," the nurse hissed.

"I don't fucking care about treatment!"

"Well, maybe electric shock treatment will get the better of you," she whispered.

I was 12 years old and I didn't have a clue what electric shock treatment was, but it sounded terrifying. Suddenly, a third nurse approached and the others pinned me harder against the wall.

"Hold her tight," I heard the third nurse say.

I felt the prick of a needle and a coldness spreading through my veins.

"Night, night," the first nurse whispered.

Everything went blank as my mind shut down.

Chapter 8

Human Guinea Pigs

My head felt like lead as I tried, but failed, to lift it from the rubber mattress. As I opened my eyes I was consumed with a sudden and overwhelming sense of dread – I was back in the treatment room. Every bone in my body groaned with pain as my eyes scoured the darkness, trying to make out a shape, any shape. I blinked to make sure I was awake and not asleep because the room was so black. I felt drunk with exhaustion, but as I tried to move my legs, a sharp pain shot up my back. I was in agony. The blackness was so oppressive that I somehow managed to drift back off to sleep. I awoke sometime later to the sound of the door opening. As the light flooded in from the corridor, I realised I was in a treatment room but it wasn't the same one as last time because the mattress was against the opposite wall and the room had a different layout. I was facing the wall but I could sense someone standing behind me. I was terrified it was Dr Milner and that he'd come back to give me more treatment. I didn't dare move. Instead, I breathed in deeply, as though I was fast asleep. A light scent of perfume had filled the room. It wasn't Milner, it was a nurse. The breath I'd been holding in came rushing out as a sigh of relief. But then it struck me, maybe she'd come with another injection?

"Are you listening?" a female voice said.

I pretended to be asleep.

"I know you're awake," she insisted. Her voice sounded distorted – as heavy as the weight inside my head.

I heard footsteps. She walked over towards the shutters and undid the brass catch. As she pulled them open, daylight came flooding in. I blinked; the bright light from outside felt sharp and unexpected. I closed my eyes once more. I didn't want to be in that room with her. I didn't want to hear what she had to say.

"You're in here for a reason," she continued. "You've been a very bad girl, just like the others, but Dr Milner is going to cure you. He'll cure you of your badness."

I took a gulp of air. The sheer mention of his name was enough to send terror coursing through my veins.

"Dr Milner will arrange electric shock treatment. Do you know what that is?" she asked.

"Nnnnnoooo," I stammered. I was too terrified to turn around in case the doctor was standing right beside her.

"It's where they put a metal hat on your head and connect it to the electric. Then they put electric shocks through your brain. They do it again and again, and they don't stop until your behaviour improves."

I was rigid with fear.

Electricity through my brain?

"Listen, I don't want or need to know why you violently threw your dinner. The fact is, you were violent to another patient and we can't tolerate such behaviour. Now, we can keep you in this side room for as long as we want. We can keep you in this hospital for as long as we want. Everything is your choice – it's up to you. However, with that kind of nasty and aggressive behaviour you're more than likely going to be kept in this side room for a very long time."

My fuzzy brain was trying to process what she was saying. The words scrambled around like marbles in a glass bowl.

Maybe they'd keep me here forever?

"Now sit up and look at me," she ordered.

But I didn't want to sit up. I wasn't even sure I could. Also, I was frightened what she'd do to me if I did.

If you sit up then at least you can try to fight, a voice inside my head whispered.

I tried to raise myself but it was too painful. I refused to be beaten. I knew from the sound of her voice that I'd get no sympathy from her. The light from the doorway and open shutters was blinding, so I closed my eyes.

"Open them," she demanded. "The sooner you open them, the sooner they will stop hurting."

I began to open them and tried to focus. A blurry image slowly came into view. I realised she was holding something in her hand.

"Medication time. Come on, take your medicine."

"I don't waannt it. It'ssshh maaking me worrsse," I slurred.

The figure straightened up.

"Okay. I'll close the shutters and lock the door. You can come out when you've decided to cooperate."

But I didn't want to stay inside the room. I wanted to be back on the ward with Christine and the others. Reluctantly, I stretched out my hand to take it from her. I gulped down the brown syrup, threw the tablets to the back of my throat and swallowed hard.

"Good girl. Now you can come downstairs, if you're prepared to behave yourself. You can have your tea. But no throwing plates, do you understand?"

I nodded.

"We'll be watching you. The first sign of trouble and you'll be back in here, okay?"

The nurse bent forwards and grabbed at my wrist. She didn't mean to hurt me, but I winced in pain as she did. She helped me to my feet, but almost immediately the room began to spin. I felt sick with dizziness. Something rough brushed against my skin and my heart sank as I looked down and realised I was wearing the horrible grey hospital gown. Although my brain felt foggy I couldn't remember getting changed out of my clothes.

"Hhhhavvve I 'ad treatment again?" I slurred as I tried to look at her and focus.

A smirk spread across her face.

"Why do you think that?"

"Beccauussse where's my cllllothes? I don't rrrremember gettin' chhhanged or coming into thissss rooooom… I want my cllllothes," I wailed. "I don't wwwant this horrible gown."

As I moved and felt a draft and I realised that I wasn't wearing any underwear.

"That gown," she said, pointing down at it, "is for your own protection."

But I didn't understand. How could a gown protect me when I was naked underneath?

Even in my confused state I realised I had to comply just to get out of the room. The longer I was in there, the higher the risk of having treatment. I clambered to my feet. Although her perfume had initially masked it, now I was standing I could detect a faint chemical smell. It smelled familiar. Panic over-whelmed me and I wanted to vomit.

"Cccan I please get drrresssed?"

The nurse nodded.

"Follow me," she said as she turned and left the room. She led me down the corridor towards the dormitory. I was so relieved to be out of the room that I followed as fast as my feet and the brain-numbing medication would let me. I heard the rattle of keys as she put one in the lock, turned it and ushered me inside.

"Hurry up, now. Get dressed, then straight downstairs."

But I was dying for a wee, so I headed to the bathroom.

"Where do you think you're going?"

I pointed towards the toilet.

"Don't be holding me up. Get in and get dressed. I'm finishing soon, and I don't want a mental defective holding me up and ruining my weekend."

I was in and out of the bathroom as fast as I could and then I started to get dressed. I picked out a jumper and skirt so there'd be no tricky buttons to delay me. I felt grateful to finally pull on my underwear. To me, it felt like a cloth shield covering my body. I didn't bother with socks because I knew they'd only delay me and I didn't want to make her angry or run the risk of being sent back to the room. The nurse popped her head around the dormitory door.

"You ready? Good." She led me back out into the corridor. She pulled out the bunch of keys and locked the door behind us.

"Go and wait by the stairs."

I walked along the corridor, but my heartbeat quickened when I realised the door to the treatment room was wide open.

Was it a trick? Was she taking me back for treatment?

A sickening dread washed over me and my breath became shallow and rapid.

"Do you want your tea, or not?"

It was the nurse. She'd brushed past me and was heading down the stairs. I hurried behind her, grateful that I was heading to the safety of the others. I had to get to the bottom of the stairs as fast as I could. My feet quickened with every step until I'd reached the bottom. I noticed the main door I'd come through on my very first day at Aston Hall. I knew better than to try and escape. Instead, I waited for the nurse. I felt more in control when I could see her. At least I knew there'd be no nasty surprises. As we reached the communal room, she fumbled with her keys once more. With the silver key in her hand, she shot me a sideways glance.

"I knew you were trouble from the first moment I saw you," she remarked, wagging the key in front of my face. "Now, any more trouble from you and you're straight back in that side room and it's the electric shock treatment. Do I make myself clear?"

I nodded. I just wanted her to unlock the door and let me in so that I could join the others.

Finally, the door clicked open.

I stepped inside and let out a sigh of relief. In that moment, I decided I'd never answer back again. From now on, I'd be a model patient – as good as gold – then I'd never get electric shock treatment. The door slammed behind me loudly as I looked across the room. As usual, the TV was blaring away in the corner watched by the same staring eyes. One girl's eyes were yellow where they should have been white. I looked away and shuddered.

I was trying to decide what to do.

Should I stand or sit? Should I sit at the table early, or would I get into trouble if I did?

The thoughts whirred around inside my head until I spotted someone beckoning me over. As her hand patted the wooden arm of the chair, I realised it was Christine.

"Did you get treatment?" She asked, leaning forward so that she could whisper in my ear.

"I don't know," I replied honestly. "I don't think so."

My voice still sounded odd and disjointed, but at least I'd stopped slurring.

"You're a good fighter," she smiled. "You gave them hell yesterday. And when you threw your dinner at big Emma, well," she laughed. "That was great!"

I shook my head.

"Yesterday?"

Christine nodded.

"Yes, tea time, yesterday."

I was confused. Where had the rest of that day gone?

"Yes," she said. "You've been up there since tea time yesterday. But it's the weekend now, and they always let you out at the weekend."

I was confused.

"But I came here on Monday and it's Saturday now?"

Christine nodded.

"That's right."

But how had I lost so many days? I thought I'd had my treatment over one day, not four?

My head hurt too much to try and fathom it, so I decided I'd work it out later when the fog had cleared.

Suddenly, there was a panic in the room as girls fled from the window. The tell-tale beam of headlights picked out frightened faces across the room.

"Here he is," a voice called out as girls scattered into the far corners.

My body trembled as I turned my back towards the main window.

Please don't pick me. I prayed.

I glanced over to my right. I was looking for Emily – the last girl he'd picked – but she was nowhere to be seen.

"Where's Emily?" I asked Christine.

"She hasn't come back yet. Sometimes they don't come back."

"What do you mean?"

"Oh, I don't know. Maybe they get shipped out of here. Sometimes treatment can take a long time."

I was desperate to know but too frightened to ask. But there was one question I had to ask.

"Have you ever had electric shock treatment?" I mumbled.

I'd said the words so softly that Christine hadn't heard me.

"What did you say?"

But my courage had failed me.

"It doesn't matter," I said, casting my eyes to the ground.

Tension hung over the room like a black fog as everyone waited for a girl to be chosen. The net curtain to the nurses' office began to twitch and a face peered through the glass. I didn't move. I didn't dare breathe or swallow because I didn't want it to be me. The door opened and in stepped a nurse.

"Christine Smith," she called.

It took me a few seconds to register it was Christine. *My Christine.*

"That's me," she sighed as tears filled her eyes. "I hate treatment."

My heart ached as I watched my new friend walk over towards the nurse. Unlike Emily, she didn't protest, she accepted that tonight it was her turn to be Milner's human guinea pig. The nurse said something and Christine turned back and threw her arms around me, pulling me close.

"We'll be best friends forever," she whispered. Then, with tears streaming down her face, she held me at arms' length. "Wish me luck."

"I will," I said, choking back my emotion.

"Come on, hurry up now, Christine."

I watched as she crossed two fingers and began to wave. I did the same, even though I felt a deep sadness that I'd made and lost a friend in a heartbeat.

Would I ever see her again?

The door slammed and Christine had gone. She'd left for the treatment room with its bare rubber mattress. A room without light or sound. A room where time escaped you and there were questions that were impossible to answer. A hidden room, with hidden patients.

But in that single hug, Christine had managed to pierce through my hardened shell. It was the first time I'd experienced physical human contact outside the treatment room. I'd finally made a friend inside this hellhole and I was determined to keep her. I'd protect Christine and she me. If we were going to survive this ordeal, then we had to look out for one another. But at that moment, I was powerless. I couldn't help Christine. I shuddered as I thought of her journey and the long walk down the corridor towards the treatment room. I was still thinking about it when a nurse appeared. She was holding two small paper cups. One contained the brown syrup, the other two white tablets. I didn't argue. I put them both inside my mouth and swallowed. As the medication began to take hold, my head slumped forward as I flopped down like a ragdoll into Christine's chair.

21, 22, 23…

The nurse was counting the cutlery again. With each number came a clatter as a knife dropped into the tray below. I must have fallen asleep while the count continued. I was woken a short time later by the sound of someone clapping their hands.

"Right, head count," she called.

We remained where we were until she'd counted each and every one of us.

"Come on, girls, its tea time. Everyone take their seats."

The word 'seat' jolted me back to reality. I looked up at the table and the empty chairs. I focused on one and stumbled across the room before anyone else took it. My chair had a perfect view of the little window and of Dr Milner. I sat down. I was still watching the window when I felt a sharp tug as someone pulled my hair. I turned to see Emma. She turned away. A few moments later, she pulled it again. I glared at her. She pulled a sarcastic face and some of the other girls sniggered. But I didn't want to fight. I didn't want a repeat of yesterday. I didn't want to be locked in the side room. I just wanted to be left alone – to keep out of trouble. Emma pulled my hair again.

"Stop it," I hissed through gritted teeth.

"Why?" She sneered. "What are you gonna do about it?"

I remembered Liam and how he'd once taught me to box. I knew how to look after myself.

"I'll show you," I threatened.

"You? You're gonna fight me?"

Emma had spotted a loose chink in my armour and now she wouldn't let it go. She continued to pull my hair and torment me. The nurse approached with food, so I didn't dare fight back. Instead, I thanked her as she placed the plate of fish, chips and peas on the table in front of me.

"Thank you," I smiled.

"You're welcome."

It made me feel better. I needed to stay calm. I needed to be good so that I didn't get electric shock treatment. My wrists were sore and I found it difficult to hold my fork, so I started to eat the chips with my fingers.

"Don't you know what a knife and fork are for?" Emma sneered, looking across the table at the others.

Anger bubbled up inside me.

Don't bite. Don't hit back.

I strained my eyes against the net curtain, searching for the shape of Milner, but there was no sign of him. I looked over through the main window. His car had gone.

He must have left. If he has, then who is with Christine?

Emma continued to hurl insults at me, but I was starving and I wanted to eat. The only meal I'd eaten had been the marmalade sandwiches the nurse had given me after treatment. I desperately wanted to finish my chips before finishing off Emma. Her friends continued to laugh and jeer and it was clear that she ruled the roost.

Once my plate was almost clean, I pushed back my chair so that it knocked against hers.

"What you doing?" she grunted.

I turned to her.

"You're nothing but a bully, and I'm not scared of you."

I got to my feet and walked over to the nurse.

"Excuse me, Miss." I felt Emma's eyes boring into my back. "I have a problem with Emma," I said, looking over at her. I watched as she guiltily dipped her head and continued to eat. "She's trying to start a fight with me, but I don't want to fight. I just want to be left alone."

The nurse looked at me and then at Emma.

"Alright," she said with a wave of her hand. "Go and sit down and I'll keep an eye on the situation."

Emma glared as I took my seat. I looked down at my plate. I'd left a small piece of fish but it'd been smothered in salt. She threw back her head and snorted with laughter. I didn't say a word because I knew the nurse would be watching. Instead, I knocked my chair against hers again.

"Stupid bitch," she spat the words out.

I didn't reply. Emma looked over at her friends, who were following her every word. I leaned back in my seat and put my mouth against her ear, but I spoke loud enough for the others to hear.

"I'm gonna rip your head off. Do you hear me? I'm gonna damage you badly."

She seemed shocked but knew she couldn't lose face, not in front of her followers.

"I can box, you know. I was taught how to deal with bullies like you," I continued.

I watched her reaction. She looked shocked, as though I'd slapped her across her face.

"We'll get you, won't we girls?" she boasted.

"Well," I sighed. "We'll see. But you're not going to hurt me. I'm not scared of you, you fat cow."

Everyone gasped as Emma spun to face me, her face purple with rage.

"Fat twat," I added.

I wanted to punish her just like I'd been punished in that side room. I wanted her to suffer as I had.

The nurse appeared.

"Are we all finished here?" she asked, picking up the plates and cutlery.

The counting started up again as everyone remained in their places.

45, 46, 47...

Emma continued to taunt me. By now it was a game of wits to see whose nerve broke first. I was determined it wouldn't be mine.

51, 52, 53...

"I've something for you, little boxer," she whispered. "But you're not gonna like it. You see, you're a cheeky twat and I'm gonna teach you."

But by now I didn't care. Nothing could be worse than treatment, not even Emma. I clenched both fists.

"I've got something for you, too," I said showing her.

The nurse clapped her hands.

"No one move," she shouted as she ran past us and over towards the nurses' window. She rapped a hand hard against the glass and stood with her back against it so that she could see us all. I didn't have a clue what was happening. Then three nurses came rushing into the room.

"What's happening?" one asked.

"We're a knife short," the first nurse gasped. "One of them has a knife."

There was panic in her voice as the room fell silent and everyone eyed each other with suspicion. The head nurse, who'd been in the office, strode across the room and immediately took control.

"Right, no one move. You are all going to be strip-searched unless the person who has the knife stands up and returns it."

She glanced across the tables but no one uttered a word.

"If the one who has the knife does not give it up then all girls will be punished."

There was silence again.

"So make it easy on yourself," the nurse continued. "Give it back."

My eyes scoured each and every face, but no one flinched. Everyone looked guilty.

"Right," the head nurse said, beginning to lose her patience. "I'm giving you five minutes to hand it back."

The silence was deafening.

"Okay, let's play this your way." She stepped forward and pointed at the table nearest to her. "You, you, you and you," she said, picking out four girls from the table. "Come here."

The girls stood up and walked over to her.

"Stand in line."

The girls did as they were told.

"Hands up, legs spread apart," she ordered as she checked them all. Satisfied they didn't have the knife, she told them to line up against the back wall before calling another four girls forward and resuming her search. The nurse continued to frisk each girl, patting down clothes and turning up sleeves. Then she stopped picking girls from each table and began to choose at random.

"You," she said, pointing at me. I got to my feet and went over towards her. She chose three girls, but because I had my back to the rest of the room I didn't know who else she'd picked. I heard the scrape of chair legs against the floor as the others stood up.

"No, not you," her voice sounded panicked. "You stay exactly where you are."

I was desperate to turn around but I didn't dare disobey the head nurse. Suddenly, her face and stern manner began to crumble.

"Emma, do not move!"

I felt sick with fear.

Emma had the knife and I had my back to her.

Suddenly, I forgot the rules and turned to see Emma sat with her back facing towards me.

"All you other girls come over here. Every girl on every table, come here. Emma, you stay exactly where you are," the nurse said calmly.

Other girls ran over and soon Emma was alone. She was hunched over the table because she knew she'd been caught. Without warning, she got to her feet, grabbed a chair, and threw it across the room. Three nurses ran to try and restrain her but she was like a wild animal. She overturned tables and chairs, and faced the staff with a look of pure evil in her eyes.

"Come on, bitches," she screamed as though possessed.

I glanced over at her right hand and saw the missing knife. The metal edge of it glinted against the light. I was standing at the back wall along with the others, watching as the situation unfolded. Emma started to lash out with the knife.

"Stay away from me, you fucking bitches," she yelled.

The room was in utter chaos. Suddenly, Jane tiptoed out into the middle of the room – the no man's land between us, Emma, and the nurses – and began to tap dance.

"By the light, of the silvery moon," she sang, as she tapped and clicked her heels together daintily.

It was bizarre. I felt as though I was caught in the middle of a warped dream. Jane continued to dance while the others stamped their feet against the vinyl floor.

"Fight, fight, fight…" they chanted.

All the time my eyes were flitting between Emma, the nurses and Jane, who seemed oblivious to the unfolding drama around her.

This is a madhouse… a voice inside my head screamed.

The nurses formed a circle around Emma, who was lunging forward and still trying to fend them off. They inched forward until Emma had her back up against a wall. Now she was cornered.

Meanwhile, Jane continued to sing.

"We're sending for the police," a nurse warned Emma. "We're sending for the police and for Dr Milner."

The mention of his name sent shockwaves through the room and everyone quietened down.

"I don't fucking care!" Emma roared.

"Calm down!" the nurse tried to reason. "We can talk this through."

But she lashed out again, this time kicking another chair. She glared over at me as though she wanted to kill me. I should have felt frightened, and I had been, but suddenly I felt sorry for her. She looked pathetic, holding the nurses off with a blunt dinner knife. I glared back at her and noticed she had spittle dangling from her mouth.

"Put the knife down. Drop it to the floor before the police and Dr Milner come," the nurse warned.

The room was silent, apart from Jane's singing.

"By the light of the silvery moon…"

All eyes were on Emma. She lunged forward, tripped and landed hard against the floor, smashing her face as she went down. The nurses jumped onto her, pinning her down, and pulling her hands behind her back, just as they'd done with me. Emma raised her head slightly and I noticed a trickle of blood coming from her nose. A nurse appeared with a hypodermic needle in her hand.

"Hold her steady," she called as she plunged the needle into Emma's backside. We watched as she went limp in their hands.

I felt a pang of regret because I knew what it felt like. The nurses grabbed Emma by her arms and legs and began to drag her across the floor like a dead animal. Even though she was sleeping, she looked as though she was dead. They unlocked the main door and pulled her lifeless body through it. The door slammed and then she was gone.

A nurse clapped her hands loudly to try and bring order back to the room.

"Listen, girls. You've just seen what happens when you play up. Understand this. We always win. Now all of you, go over, pick up those tables and chairs, and put them back where they belong."

Everyone began to mill around the room, picking up debris, as Jane continued to sing and dance, trapped in a world of her own. I felt envious. She lived in her own mind where nothing or no one ever bothered her. In many ways, although she was mad, I almost wished I was her. We worked while Jane sang the same song over and over again. Once the furniture had been tidied, everyone began to settle down and talk about what had just happened. The three girls who'd backed Emma earlier approached me.

"You're to blame," the eldest one said, poking me hard against the chest with her finger. "And you'll be in for it when Emma gets out."

Even though she was three or four years older than me, I looked her square in the eye.

"Listen, I'm not scared of Emma or any of you. No one's going to do anything to me, now leave me alone."

They scowled back at me but eventually peeled away to another corner of the room. Seconds later, two other girls approached.

"Hey, aren't you scared of Emma?" one asked.

"Me?" I replied. "I'm scared of no one."

Inside, I was shaking, but I wasn't going to let them or anyone else know it. I'd learned that you had to stand up to bullies, especially inside children's homes, otherwise your life wouldn't be worth living.

"Can we be your friend?" they asked.

I was taken aback.

"Of course you can, I'm not scared of that fat bitch."

We laughed and began to chat. It turned out the two girls had also come from The Cedars. Soon we were swopping stories and gossip about our time there. It felt good to find new friends but I couldn't stop thinking about Christine and what she was going through upstairs. We chatted a little more until the main door swung open. A nurse stepped in with Christine close behind. I jumped up and ran over to her. I couldn't help myself. I was so pleased to see her that I flung my arms around her shoulders and hugged her for all I was worth. She was smiling like a Cheshire cat, so I took a step back.

"How was the treatment?" I asked, searching her eyes.

"I didn't have it," she smiled as she clutched my hand. "They didn't even give me the needle, because they needed the room for someone else."

I was baffled, and then it hit me. Emma.

"See," Christine said, gripping my hand tight in hers. "Your good luck fingers worked."

We both laughed, as I pulled her over towards the chair. We sat down and talked long into the afternoon.

Jane continued to sing her song, but by now it was beginning to drive us all mad.

"Don't you know any other songs?" I asked.

But she didn't reply because she couldn't hear me or anyone else for that matter.

"Barbara," Christine said, clutching my arm. "Emily is up there, in the other room. I was talking to her through the wall."

I sat up straight.

"So she's alright? You mean she didn't get shipped out?"

"No, she's fine. Even better, she thinks she might be back down tonight or tomorrow."

The nurse walked in front of us and turned the dial on the front of the TV set. It took a moment, but it warmed up and fired into life, the noise drowning out the sound of Jane's singing. The nurse went over and gently put her arm around the old lady's shoulder.

"Come on now, Jane," she coaxed. "The television is on and you might be on it."

Jane stopped singing and looked at the nurse. She allowed herself to be led towards an old leather armchair that was her chair. She sat down and stared at the black-and-white image, totally transfixed.

"I'm going to be on television," she repeated over and over again.

But no one was listening.

Chapter 9

The Queen of Farts

For the first time since I'd arrived at the hospital, I felt happy. Not entirely happy – I hated the place with a vengeance – but with Christine back by my side, I felt safe for the first time. I knew that she would protect the both of us. We vowed to be best friends, and best friends looked out for one another. The tense atmosphere in the room had also seemed to lift with her return. It was clear Milner had left the building as his car had disappeared from outside, which meant we were safe, at least for the time being.

We sat down in the same armchair as Christine told me all about her father and how wonderful he was.

"He'll come for me," she said, without faltering. "As soon as he realises what's going on, he'll come for me."

"Mine, too," I insisted.

"The thing is, I'm a bit of a daddy's girl," Christine said, smiling to herself. "My dad buys me everything. Anything I want, I just have to say the word, and he'll go and get it for me. That's what he's like, that's how much he loves me."

I nodded.

"Mine's the same. He'd do anything for me. He buys me everything. You name it; I've got it at home," I lied.

Christine grinned, continuing with her story as I did with mine. We embellished even the smallest details to make our fathers sound like the best dads ever. Of course, I could see through her lies and she through mine. We both knew the truth – the fact that neither of them cared about us or where we were. If they had, then how had we ended up in a place like Aston Hall hospital? Although they were just children's stories, I prayed that they'd come true – that my dad would save me from Dr Milner's treatments. As we chatted, I discovered that Christine's bed was right next to mine.

"But I've not seen you."

"That's because you've either had treatment or been locked in the side room."

Of course, it made perfect sense.

I've been here a week and not spent a single night in my bed on the dormitory.

"I can't believe we're next to each other."

Christine extended a hand and grabbed hold of mine. She was 14 years old, but she seemed so much more knowledgeable than I was.

"Best friends," she said.

My eyes flooded with grateful tears.

"Yes, best friends forever," I whispered.

Moments later a nurse stepped forward with a medicine tray strapped to her. She held out a paper cup containing syrup and a couple of pills in another.

"Medication time," she chirped.

I'd learned my lesson. From now on I'd take my medication and do whatever the nurses said without fuss or argument. I realised, from watching Christine that the less you said the easier life would be. I swallowed my pills and glanced over at Jane. For once she wasn't singing or dancing, but was fast asleep in her chair. She was snoring and her mouth was half-open as though she was catching flies. The nurse gave Christine her drugs and then wandered over towards Jane. She patted her lightly against her arm to try and rouse her. It took a while, but eventually she opened her eyes. She blinked a few times and smiled warmly up at the nurse.

"Hang on a moment nurse," Jane said.

She planted both hands firmly against the arms of her chair, and, for a moment, I thought she was going to stand up. Then she lifted up her right leg high into the air and let out the biggest fart I'd ever heard. The room was silent, but as Jane started to howl with laughter everyone joined in. Soon, the whole place was in an uproar because the noise of the fart had reverberated against the leather armchair and had sounded across to the back of the room. Even the nurse had a smirk on her face. The laughter had just started to die down when Jane screwed up her face tight, lifted her left leg up and let an even louder fart go. Everyone fell about again; even the nurse couldn't contain herself.

"All right, girls," she giggled. She waved her hands around as though she was trying to control an audience. "Calm down."

Somehow it made it even funnier. The nurse was trying her best to keep a straight face and order in the room, but it was impossible.

"I'll be back in a minute," she said, turning towards the door. She lifted the bunch of keys hanging from her belt and let herself out.

We'd just started to calm down when the awful smell hit us. It had drifted across the room from Jane, who was sitting there totally unabashed. In fact, she almost seemed proud of herself, proud she'd reduced the whole room into a fit of giggles. Christine and I moved to the far end of the room and waved our hands like fans to try and get rid of the awful eggy smell. As it crept across the room, other girls held their hands over their noses and streamed over towards the back wall. The two girls who'd been playing cards were annoyed because their game had been rudely interrupted.

"I only needed one more card and I would have won that game," one complained. She glared over at Jane, who couldn't care less.

"What did you need?" I asked.

"What?"

"What card? What card did you need? Was it the Queen of Farts?"

Suddenly, everyone fell about laughing once more, including Jane. Even the girl who'd forfeited her game found it funny, and it wasn't long before Jane's new nickname became the Queen of Farts.

"You're so funny, Barbara," Christine giggled.

But our merriment was broken by the nurse who stepped back into the room clapping her hands sharply.

"Come on, girls. Put everything in order," she said, pointing towards the dining chairs.

We were still giggling away as we tidied up. The laughter was infectious, even in such a bleak environment. But the nurse no longer seemed amused.

"Calm down, and get in line for bed."

By now the medication had started to kick in. My body felt heavy and I began to feel extremely sleepy. The thought of climbing into a warm bed made me hurry along as I fell in line and followed the group out into the corridor and upstairs. I was so busy chatting to Christine that I'd almost forgotten the treatment room. As we neared it a hush descended on the group. I scanned the look on their faces; it was obvious I wasn't the only one frightened of the room. Walking past it was enough to put the fear of God into me. My pulse and footsteps quickened as I dashed past. I felt my stomach flip and I swallowed down bile rising up at the back of my throat. Christine realised I was terrified and grabbed my arm to comfort me. Once we'd passed, the tension lifted.

Not tonight. No one was getting treatment tonight. We were safe – all of us – safe from Dr Milner.

My heartbeat slowed as the nurse unlocked the dormitory door and we poured into the room. I climbed into bed and sighed as the cotton sheets enveloped me, making me feel secure.

"Goodnight, girls," the nurse called as she strode along the ward doing her final head count.

She traced her fingers against the wall and flicked off the light, leaving the ward bathed in a silvery moonlight. Although I was exhausted, I did one last check around the room before I closed my eyes and noticed that three of the beds were empty.

"Christine, why are those beds empty?"

She pulled back the covers from her face, blinked and glanced over.

"One's Emily's, one's Emma's and the other girl must've been shipped out," she replied in a sleepy voice.

"Shipped out?"

"Yeah, sometimes they don't come back."

Chapter 10

Tears and Toothbrushes

I slept soundly, but woke early the following morning. Light streamed in through the tall windows of the ward, the brightness jolting me into the present. I rubbed my eyes and glanced over at Christine, who was still fast asleep. My eyes hovered above her and over towards the end of the ward. One of the three empty beds had been filled overnight. There was a lump-shaped figure sleeping beneath the covers – someone had been brought in. This had often happened at The Cedars, and the children's home before that, but at least at those places I wasn't left wondering if it was someone new or someone returning from treatment. The hospital had its own set of rules. I tried to work out whose bed it was so that I could identify the lump within it, but I couldn't remember whose bed was whose. I considered the figure – it was far too petite to be Emma.

Who was it?

The question burned inside my brain until curiosity got the better of me. Tiptoeing over, I held my breath and lifted back the blanket to take a peak. As I did, Emily opened her eyes but she looked so startled that I put a finger against my lips to try and shush her. I knew I'd be in trouble if I was caught out of bed.

"Hi," I whispered.

Emily continued to stare; her eyes were wide but glazed over from treatment. Although she was facing me, she looked straight through me.

"Drink. I need a drink," she suddenly gasped.

"Okay," I replied.

I turned to look for a cup and remembered the half-full one on top of my bedside locker. I turned and padded across the ward to fetch it. Picking it up, I dashed back over towards Emily. I was halfway across the room when I heard a key in the lock and I froze as the door suddenly opened and a nurse stepped in.

"Wakey, wakey," she called as her hand stretched along the wall, feeling for the light switch.

Light flooded the room as I stood in the middle of it, holding the cup in my hand. The nurse saw me and scowled, but I didn't know what to say, so I remained motionless.

"What are you doing?" she asked, her voice boomed across the ward, waking everyone up.

I pointed towards the tumbler of water.

"I was getting Emily a drink."

Everyone sat up in their beds, watching the floor show begin with me the centre of it all. My face flushed with hot embarrassment.

"Put that back now, girl. You must never, ever, give girls drinks, do you understand?"

I nodded, ran and put the glass of water back on top of my locker. As I did, I felt my head being pulled back as though someone was tugging my hair. It was the nurse.

"I could lose my job through you," she hissed. "You're getting the toothbrush today, do you understand?"

The toothbrush? I didn't have a clue what she was talking about.

The others were sat up in their beds, watching and wondering what the hell I'd done wrong. I wasn't even sure myself.

I was just trying to help, Emily, I thought bitterly.

The nurse tightened her grip, pulling at every strand of hair, but I didn't dare cry out or complain because I didn't want to end up in the side room. Eventually, she let go and threw me against my bed.

"Wait there."

I did as I was told because I didn't want to make things worse. The nurse told the others to get out of bed and brush their teeth, and I wondered if that's what I should do, but she made it clear that she had other plans for me. Another nurse appeared and began clapping her hands.

"Come on, girls. Chop, chop. Get washed, dressed and then it's medication time."

I watched her as she stood there in the doorway. The medicine tray was attached to her as though she was selling ice cream at the cinema. She glanced over and realised that I wasn't moving.

"Come on, bed number one. Get a move on!"

I grabbed my toothbrush and followed the others into the bathroom before the other nurse noticed and tried to stop me. I wanted to be part of the crowd, to follow the herd. I didn't want to stand out – that was the last thing I wanted. As I walked into the bathroom I spotted Christine over by the sinks.

"You did right not to fight," she whispered. "Don't ever fight back, Barbara, or you'll end up in the side room until Monday. If no new girl arrives on Monday, you'll get the treatment."

My heart thudded with panic.

"But," she added, "Dr Milner is always happy if a new girl comes in, and one will arrive."

I wanted to ask her more but our conversation was cut short by the nurse, who was standing in the doorway.

"Hurry up!"

I washed and dressed as fast as I could, eager to catch the others up. We were told to strip our beds and remake them in a particular fashion – the corners had to be enveloped so they were neat and identical. I'd learned how to make my bed during my time at The Cedars, but I still followed Christine because I didn't want to put a foot wrong. Once the beds had been made we each lined up to get our medication. Then we went back to our beds so that the nurse could inspect them. Once she was satisfied, she released the brake and we pushed our beds and lockers against the back wall. I wasn't sure what was happening, but it was too quiet to try and ask Christine, so I followed everyone else. Some girls left the room and reappeared moments later with cleaning stuff and tins of floor wax. Others wheeled in two big floor buffers that had large flat blocks – the width of two house bricks – on the end of them. They each had an edge of sharp metal teeth that we attached old bits of prison blankets to so we could buff the floor.

"Okay, girls," the nurse said, clapping her hands once more. "Let's brush, strip, wax and buff the floor."

I looked across the room and realised that although her bed had been pushed against the back wall, Emily was still asleep in it.

"She's been drugged," one of the girls whispered. "Don't worry, she won't hear a thing."

Some girls brushed the floor, whilst others tried to strip away the old polish. Another group applied wax, while the rest of us followed behind with the buffers. They were so heavy that they needed more than one pair of hands. I was given one, but I couldn't move it because of the weight. Christine noticed and came rushing over to help, but she didn't dare say a word, in fact, no one spoke. Instead, we worked in complete silence, apart from the whirring noise of the machines. I wasn't sure how clean the floor had to be, but I soon realised that the nurse wasn't satisfied unless she could see her reflection in it.

"Not clean enough. Do it again," she ordered.

It was back-breaking work and all before we'd even had breakfast.

After moving the beds and cabinets back to their original positions we were finally allowed downstairs to eat. As the nurse led us along the corridor, I heard the sound of a girl crying behind the locked door.

"Someone talk to me. I'm here, I'm in here. Can anyone hear me?" she called.

Although her cries were pitiful, everyone ignored her. To my shame, I did too. I was in enough trouble as it was. The nurse led us downstairs, unlocked the door to the communal room and herded us in. The counting of cutlery started up like clockwork.

12, 13, 14...

The table had been filled with cereal and slices of buttered toast. I tucked in heartily, hoping that my earlier misdemeanour had been forgotten. But it hadn't.

"Barbara O'Hare," a voice called out.

I gulped down my mouthful and turned to see the nurse standing with her arms folded.

"Haven't you forgotten something? It's toothbrush treatment."

Christine grabbed at my arm.

"Don't fight," she whispered.

I followed the nurse out of the room and up to the dormitory door where she handed me a toothbrush and told me to start scrubbing.

"You can start with the skirting boards," she said, pointing at them. "I want them clean all along the corridor, from here to over there."

My heart sank down to my boots – it would take all day.

"And when you've done this side, you can start on that one."

She began to walk away but stopped and turned to face me.

"And it'd better be perfect, otherwise you'll have to do it again."

And then she left.

I sighed as I weighed up the task before me. A single toothbrush to clean an entire hallway – it seemed an impossible task. I knelt down against the skirting board and began to scrub away. As I did, I heard a small voice cry out.

"Hello, is anyone there?"

It was the girl in the treatment room. I glanced over each shoulder to check that the coast was clear and walked over towards the side door.

"Hello," I whispered. "What's your name?"

"Emma," the voice replied.

I froze to the spot, worried what she'd do to me when she did get out. She'd stolen a knife, so I knew she was capable of anything, but I also realised it was my chance to sort things out. I remembered a survival trick I'd used in the other children's homes.

"It's Barbara," I replied, cupping a hand against my mouth so that she could hear me through the door. "My big sister is coming soon, so you better watch your back."

It was a lie, but Emma didn't know that.

But her voice sounded different, broken somehow.

"No trouble, I promise."

I realised then that she didn't need an enemy but a friend. I decided to change tack.

"Did you have treatment?" I whispered.

There was a moment's pause before she spoke.

"Yes," she said, dissolving into tears.

I was shocked.

"Are you okay?"

"Yes," she sobbed. "But I think my dad did some bad things to me."

"Like what?"

Emma was sobbing heavily, and for a moment I didn't think she'd reply, but then she spoke.

"Rude things… he did rude things to me."

I had no idea what she was talking about so I didn't know what to say, but it was Emma who broke the silence.

"But he didn't do it. I know he didn't do it."

There was more silence as she continued to sob her heart out.

"Maybe he did," she said, her voice wobbling with emotion. "I really don't know."

My mind was racing.

Why would her dad do rude things to her? And who would have said such a thing? Was it Dr Milner? I wondered. *He's the one with all the questions, the mask and the dripping stuff that made you feel funny.*

I was just about to ask more when I heard the jangle of keys – the nurse was on her way. I ran over to the other side of the room and scrubbed at the skirting board with the tooth-brush. I heard metal scrape in the lock as the door flew open and she appeared at the top of the stairs. She approached the side room and unlocked the door. Emma stepped out wearing the horrible grey cotton gown. She seemed frightened and was blinking, trying to shield the light from her eyes.

"Emma, was anyone talking to you?" the nurse asked. "It's just that I thought I heard voices from the bottom of the stairs."

My heart plummeted as I stared hard at the skirting board and continued to scrub. I waited for Emma's damning reply.

Please God, I prayed. *Please don't let her tell on me. Please don't take her out of the side room and put me in.*

"No. I wasn't talking to anyone," she answered.

The nurse sniffed as though she didn't believe a word of it, but allowed Emma to use the toilet. Afterwards, she was put back in the side room, as the nurse locked the door and came over to inspect my work.

"Not good enough," she decided. "Start again."

I didn't complain because I knew it was a test to see if she could break me, and I refused to be beaten. The nurse watched as I went back to the beginning, got down on my knees and started to scrub it again. Eventually, her footsteps sounded along the corridor as she walked away.

"Come here," it was Emma, whispering through the locked door.

"What?"

"I could've got you into some real trouble, but I didn't, so don't tell your big sister about me, okay? Me and you will be friends."

"Okay," I replied. I couldn't help but smile because my imaginary sister had just saved the day.

I carried on cleaning until Emma called out to say she was going to sleep. I continued to work for the best part of an hour until the nurse came back to do a second inspection.

"Okay, that'll do. You can put the mop back in the bathroom and come downstairs."

I felt relieved as she unlocked the door and I walked back into the communal room. It was midday, so more medication was dispensed to keep us quiet. I noticed Christine and wandered over. The TV was on and Jane was dancing, twirling away, lost in her own world. The atmosphere felt relaxed because it was the weekend, and Dr Milner didn't come at the weekends.

"How did you get on?" Christine asked.

"Oh, okay. She made me do it twice, but it wasn't too bad," I said, flopping down next to her.

We chatted for a while and soon I'd told her how I'd run away from The Cedars. I watched her eyes widen with respect.

"But I was caught soon after," I sighed. "If only there was a way out of here, but it's impossible because they keep every door locked. Even if there was a way of avoiding treatment, at least that'd make things a bit easier."

Christine glanced up.

"But there is."

I sat up. Now she had my full attention.

"There is? How?"

Christine pulled her chair closer and began to whisper.

"Have you started your periods yet?"

"No," I said, shaking my head. I was only 12 and I didn't know the first thing about periods.

She shook her head in pity.

"Well, you're in trouble then."

"Why?"

"Because that's how you avoid treatment."

I was confused, so she began to elaborate.

"A few days after treatment, go and tell the nurse you need a sanitary towel because you have some bleeding."

"Why a few days?" I asked, interrupting her.

"Because we always bleed after treatment."

I suddenly remembered something.

"But I did bleed," I gasped. "After treatment. There was blood on the sheets but the nurse said it was an old stain. I knew it wasn't because I hadn't cut myself."

Christine nodded.

"Yes. That happens to everyone."

"But what do I do, with the sanitary towel?"

"Just keep them… and keep asking for them three times a day for a week. You get them, wrap them in loo roll, and put them in the bin in the toilet, okay?"

I nodded my head, although I didn't understand.

Christine continued, "When you're called up for treatment, tell the nurses you need the toilet. That's when you take a used towel out of the bin and put it inside your knickers."

"Yuk!"

"Yes, it's not nice and there'll be lots of other people's sanitary towels in there too, but you'll start your periods soon."

I pushed my hair away from my face and checked over my shoulder to make sure no one was listening.

"But why would I put it inside my knickers, if I'm not bleeding?"

Christine smiled.

"Because Milner doesn't give you treatment if you're on your period, and if you have a sanitary towel in your knickers, you'll be okay."

I was shocked and it obviously showed because Christine cupped my chin in the palm of her hand.

"Barbara, have you ever done it with a boy?" she asked.

"Done what?"

"You know, shagged a boy?"

I'd heard other girls talking about shagging back at The Cedars, but I hadn't joined in the conversation because I'd never been near a boy.

"I've never done anything like that in my life," I gasped, slightly appalled.

Christine laughed.

"Why, have you?" I asked.

"I have. I've been with most of the boys on my estate – that's why they put me in here. All my friends have as well, but they're not in here."

Christine began to tell me about different boys and what she'd done with them. Then, noticing my horrified expression, she leaned forward and grabbed my arm.

"Don't tell the others in here that you've never done it because they'll think you're a scaredy cat. Don't let them know you're a virgin because they'll laugh at you."

I decided to change the subject. Instead, I told her how I'd kidded Emma that I had a big sister.

"So you've got to promise me that you'll tell her you and my big sister are friends," I insisted. "That way she'll leave you alone, too."

Christine threw her head back and laughed.

"Brilliant!"

Suddenly a nurse loomed into view with the medication tray strapped to her. We both took our pills and syrup without fuss. As I swallowed, the nurse looked down and smiled at me.

"Guess what? Your dad has rung and he's booked a visit to come and see you next weekend. Isn't that exciting, Barbara?"

My whole face broke into a huge smile for the first time. I couldn't believe it – I was buzzing with excitement as my eyes brimmed with tears of happiness. I gripped Christine's hand.

"He'll get me out of this place – just you watch – especially when I tell him about the treatment."

The nurse overheard and had turned back to give me a stern look. But I didn't care, not anymore, because my dad was coming. As she walked away, I raised my voice loud enough for her to hear.

"My dad will knock Milner out with one punch, just you wait and see. I've seen him fight before, and he'll kill Milner when he finds out what he's done to me."

Chapter 11

The Night Has a Thousand Eyes

After dinner and the obligatory cutlery count, it was relaxation time. It was hard to relax in a place where Dr Milner picked off his patients one by one for treatment around eight o'clock every single night. However, I was comforted by the fact that no matter how grim things became I knew my father was on his way to take me home.

After medication time, most girls drifted around the room like zombies, but Jane always danced and sang the same 'By the Light of the Silvery Moon' tune. Although I'm sure it'd been written as a happy-go-lucky song, at Aston Hall the lyrics took on a whole new meaning. As did one of the only records the girls from our ward were allowed to play. Dr Milner had donated the record to the hospital, so it was treated like gold dust, and only a nurse was ever allowed to put it on the record player in case it got scratched. The song was 'The Night Has a Thousand Eyes' by Bobby Vee. It was played over and over again, on a kind of warped loop as our medication made time stretch like elastic. The song was played so much that it remained locked there inside my head over the years that followed. Looking back, its lyrics were foreboding, sinister and strangely prophetic when played inside that locked and oppressive unit, filled with dozens of frightened and lonely little girls. In fact, the more I heard the words, the more the song made me feel sick. When it played, I thought of Milner and his beady dark eyes, watching us through the net curtain in that strange little window. Watching and waiting, like a predator waiting to pounce.

The nurse walked over towards the record player with the vinyl in her hand. She pulled a switch and the single dropped down and crackled away as the needle made contact and amplified it through the speaker until it filled the room. The song and catchy chorus chimed again and again until the end of the song was almost near.

"'Cause the night has a thousand eyes…"

Once it had finished the nurse went over, lifted it up and put it on again. It circled around, the chorus repeating over and over again. When it played, even Jane stopped singing. She'd smile and tap along, her black tap shoes picking up the beat as they clicked across the polished floor. The little girl's bow in her grey hair would bob up and down as she tapped and twirled her way through another routine.

After dinner, Christine and I sat down in our usual chair. I'd wanted to ask her about electric shock treatment and if anyone had ever been given it. I was determined that my dad would get me out before they gave it to me. Inside, I felt stronger than I'd ever felt because I knew Dad was coming. I just prayed it would happen before my next treatment.

Christine wanted to talk about sex and all the boys she'd done it with. She knew I was a virgin, so she insisted on telling me all about the birds and the bees. I let her chatter on until she'd finally run out of things to say.

"Christine," I said, looking over at her. "Have you ever had electric shock treatment?"

I'd finally plucked up the courage to ask her. She looked at me with widened eyes.

"No, but there was a girl in here that did, but she got shipped out straight after."

I gulped.

"Why? What is it?"

"Well," she began, leaning forward in the chair. She grabbed a handful of my hair with her hand. "See this," she said, gesturing towards it.

I nodded.

"They cut most of it off because it's static. Then they put wet sponges on your head and a big metal cap that's connected to some wires, which are plugged into the electric. They flick a switch, and the electric goes down through the wires, through the sponges, and into your brain."

I slumped back against the arm of the chair.

"They put electricity into your brain?"

"Yes, they have burn marks here afterwards." She placed both hands against her temples. "They have them for life."

"But why, what happens to them after they've had it?"

She looked at me, her face deadly serious.

"It makes them crazy. Afterwards they lose their memory and their hearing. All they can hear is the buzz of electricity ringing in their ears."

"But what happens then?"

She sat back in the chair and gazed out into open space.

"They never talk again. They spend the rest of their lives in a wheelchair."

Dr Milner's treatments had been terrifying, but electric shock treatment sounded a million times worse.

I have to get out of this place, I thought.

Christine began to tell me about a girl at Aston Hall hospital, who'd had electric shock treatment.

"I saw her briefly afterwards. All her hair had been chopped off, and she was just sitting there in a wheelchair, her mouth hanging wide open with dribbles of spit hanging from it. She never spoke again."

I wasn't sure how true the story was, but Christine had sounded convincing. I decided I'd never upset the nurses again because I had to keep myself safe and the only way I thought I could do that was to pray. Only God and our Lord Jesus could keep me safe until the following week until Dad arrived.

Seven days. Just seven days, then Dad will get me out of this place for good. But could I even last a week? I wasn't sure.

Tears filled my eyes and I started to sob.

"Hey," Christine said, wrapping an arm around my shoulder. "Don't cry. You have to be strong. If the others know you're a crier they'll pick on you."

She hugged me, which made me feel a bit better.

"Shush. You're asking for trouble if they see you like this. You're a virgin and you cry. The other girls would love that. They'd make things really hard for you."

I used the sleeve of my jumper to wipe away my tears before anyone saw.

She was right. I needed to be strong. Only seven more days.

"Christine," I said, pulling away from her embrace. "Have you ever run away?"

She shook her head.

"And don't even try it. Some people have, but there's a big lake outside and some sinking sand," she said, her eyes widening with the drama of it all. "I even heard a few people drowned before I came here."

"But how, how do you know?"

"Because some of the others told me."

That was that, I thought. *My father is my only hope because there's no other way out.*

That evening, before I climbed into bed, I knelt down at the side of it and said a whole rosary and three our fathers. Prayer and Dad were my only hope.

Forgive me, God, for whatever I have done to end up here at Aston Hall... I whispered. *If you cannot find it in your heart to forgive me, then please let me die and go up to heaven with you, because it would be so much nicer than being here...*

I crossed myself and climbed into bed. As I did, I glanced out of the window and spotted three tall chimney stacks, the sort that belonged to a power station. Outside, people were living normal lives and going about their daily business. Other children would be climbing into bed at the same time as me, but they'd wake up to two parents in a happy family home. Here, all I had to look forward to were talks with Christine, meal times and the visit from my father. The Cedars had once felt bleak but it was a holiday camp compared to this place.

Why had I agreed to come here? I cursed. *How could I have been so stupid?*

But I wasn't stupid because I had an escape plan – Dad. He'd get me out of this hellhole and far away from Milner.

Just wait till I tell him what that doctor's done to me. He'll sort him out, I thought as I shut my eyes and fell asleep.

Only six more sleeps. Six, then I'd be out of this place for good.

Chapter 12

The Hospital School

Sundays were more relaxed than the other days because we didn't have to strip, wax and buff the floor. It was a day of rest, not that you were ever able to truly relax. Most of our day was spent inside the communal room with Jane dancing, but Sunday was also the day for visitors. I knew Dad wasn't coming because the nurse had told me when his visit would be, and now it was only five more sleeps away. I couldn't wait.

The top of the dining room was out of bounds on Sunday because that's where the visitors would sit. The nurses were totally different when the visitors were around; they were all smiles. We all knew it was an act. Although we were only children, we could see through it. We lived there so we knew what really went on inside the hospital. The girls who did get a visitor would be over the moon, but the visits would usually end in tears as they were reminded how happy they once were only to have it taken away from them again. At the end of visiting time, a few girls had started to kick off, so the nurses pinned them down, injected them and dragged them off to the side rooms. The only good thing about Sunday was that Dr Milner never came to the hospital. I'd been told that occasionally someone would get treatment at the weekend, but it was always a Saturday, not a Sunday. I wondered what it was he did on a Sunday that stopped him from coming.

Maybe he spent time with his family? Maybe he played golf? Maybe he went to church?

I shook my head. *Surely not. No man who believed in God could do these things, could he? I wasn't sure. Dr Milner certainly acted as though he was God inside the hospital.*

To the outside world there was no clue that Aston Hall housed children at all. We weren't allowed to play outside in the grounds, and there were no swings or slides.

Mondays were exciting because although we felt sorry for her, whoever she was, we knew that someone new would be coming in. I discovered that most of the girls had come from The Cedars. The remand home seemed to supply children directly to the hospital. I noticed something else, we were all white – there were no black or Asian children, even though I'd seen them inside other homes. In the hospital, every girl was a similar age, too, usually teenagers, so I was an exception. Chatting to the others, I realised the only thing we all had in common was the fact we had no mother, so no one to listen to us. There was no one to fight our corner.

I started school the following Monday, a week after I'd arrived at the hospital. I was excited about school because I'd hoped to meet new children. Our routine would be a bath on Sunday night so that we'd be ready for school the following morning. The bathroom had two baths so two girls got to bathe together. I went in with Christine. We only had time to have a quick dip, in and out, before the next girls came along, but it was precious time to ourselves.

"What's school like?" I asked Christine as she sat in the other bath.

She looked over and shrugged her shoulders.

"I dunno. I don't go."

I was shocked.

"But you're 14!"

She nodded.

"I know, but they don't make me go, so I don't ask."

I heard the nurse at the door with two other girls.

"Come on, girls. Don't dilly dally; everyone's got to take a bath."

Christine and I had planned to have a pillow fight, but following our medication we felt so drowsy that the best we could do was throw a sock at one another. We thought it was hilarious, but as soon as we'd started to giggle, the drugs took hold and we fell asleep. At six o'clock sharp, the nurse came into the dormitory and flicked on the light.

"Rise and shine girls!"

We washed, dressed, and stripped, waxed and buffed the floor. The dorm was spotless as we each swallowed our medication and headed down for breakfast. I felt a rush of excitement wondering what school would be like. I'd assumed it'd be in another building somewhere, not inside Aston Hall. It was a hospital, and they didn't have schools inside hospitals. After breakfast, I waited inside the communal room until nine o'clock, when the nurse called me forward and we headed out into the corridor. I was convinced I'd be leaving and had even considered making a run for it, but I knew Dad was coming and I didn't want to get any bad reports. The nurse handed me my jacket, something I'd not seen since I'd arrived, and led me over to the main door that she unlocked. My feet were itching to run, but I told myself to stay calm. I couldn't risk it. It was only five more sleeps until Dad arrived.

I'll soon be gone. "I won't run, I promise," I told the nurse.

She glanced down.

"Oh, I know you won't."

The door opened and I felt the crisp January air hit my skin and lungs. I gasped and took a huge breath of air. I felt exhilarated by the smells, sights and sounds of winter. There was a silver shimmer of frost on the grass and glittering against the tarmac. I stood and exhaled while the pitiful cries of crows, nestling in barren trees, filled my ears. I'd been so busy taking it all in that I'd not noticed the tall man waiting outside the door. He was wearing some sort of uniform – dark trousers and a dark navy jumper with lapels and a breast pocket. He looked like a security guard.

"Meet Frank," the nurse said, nodding over at him. "He is going to take you to school and bring you back again."

My heart sank. I had a guard, even outside. The hospital was no better than a prison.

"If you try and run, then Frank will have to hold your hand, and you don't want that, do you?"

I shook my head.

"I promise I won't run."

Frank was a giant of a man with fair hair that had been combed into a side parting. He was tall with a broad chest and he was extremely imposing.

"Alright then, we'll see you for dinner," the nurse said as she shut the door and locked it from the inside.

Frank started to walk so I followed. I didn't wear a school uniform, and we didn't make conversation. Instead, I took in my surroundings, making mental notes of possible escape routes in case my plan with Dad didn't work out. We walked in silence along a grey concrete pathway that led us right outside Cherry Ward, where the boys were. There were empty fields to my left and in the distance I could see the three big chimneys I'd spotted through my bedroom window, billowing out their white-grey smoke. I wished I was on the other side of those chimneys looking at the hospital grounds rather than within them. I wondered what ordinary families were doing outside in the normal world.

What if the other children were walking to school, looking over at the hospital, wondering what we did all day?

A shiver ran down my spine.

I hated this place.

Soon we'd arrived at a modern building.

"This is it," Frank pressed a buzzer and we waited for someone to answer the door. Moments later, a man opened it and beckoned me inside.

"Hello," he said cheerily. "I'm Mr Hope. I suppose you must be Barbara."

"Yes," I smiled. I wanted to get a good school report for when Dad came, so I tried to be on my best behaviour. "Good morning, Mr Hope."

He smiled at me warmly, said goodbye to Frank and locked the door.

"This way, follow me."

We walked along a corridor and then through a door that led into a huge assembly hall. There were around 30 children of all ages, sitting in wheelchairs and on the ground. There were children with all sorts of disabilities. Some were severely disabled and couldn't speak, while others were physically handicapped. There were boys of all ages from Cherry Ward, but it was hard to tell how old they were because the boys always looked younger than the girls. As soon as we entered the room, the teacher who'd been giving the assembly broke off and asked the children to welcome me.

"This is Barbara," she said, pointing over. "Let's all say welcome Barbara."

Welcome, Barbara, they chanted in unison.

I wasn't expecting it and I momentarily froze to the spot.

"Barbara, would you like to take a seat over there, next to Hannah." She pointed over towards a girl in a wheelchair. Hannah had beautiful long black hair, but her tiny body was badly twisted and deformed. She blinked over at me, so I smiled at her and she grinned back. I decided that I liked her immediately.

The school seemed so much more relaxed than the ward, and although the teacher carried on with her speech, I had no idea what she was talking about. I was too busy looking around at everyone. Eventually, she stopped speaking and we said a prayer. Then we picked up our hymn books. Some of the other children looked over and smiled at me. A few even gave me friendly little waves, but the severely disabled ones were unable to hold their books, so they sat as the teacher picked up a guitar and began to play. As the music began, Hannah, who'd been sitting next to me in her wheelchair, began to sing *Ave Maria*. I turned towards her utterly dumbstruck because she had the most beautiful voice I'd ever heard. It was so pure and powerful that the sound of it brought tears to my eyes. The emotion in her singing stirred up all the feelings I'd desperately been trying to keep locked away. Hannah's angelic voice soared up into the air, rising above us, as I sat there open-mouthed staring at her. She was simply spellbinding and I could've listened to her sing all day. After she'd finished, I was so caught up in it that I wanted to jump to my feet and applaud her. But I didn't. Instead, I sat and looked on in wonder.

How could someone – anyone – sing like that?

Soon it was time for lessons, and everyone who could stand up was told to.

"I'd like each of you that is able to walk to go and stand by a wheelchair," the teacher told us.

I immediately positioned myself behind Hannah, who looked up and beamed. I knew I'd made another friend and it felt good. We were told it was our duty as able-bodied children to push around the ones who couldn't walk and help them for the rest of the day.

Mr Hope appeared and took Hannah's wheelchair so that he could show me how to push and apply the brakes.

"So, you see it's pretty simple. I'm sure you'll soon get the hang of it."

School had felt like a breath of fresh air. We got to do lessons in maths and English, although it was all pretty basic. The best thing was the relaxed atmosphere, with no threat or mention of treatment. I'd learned to be on high alert, watching and waiting in case Dr Milner appeared, but he never did.

The day passed and soon it was playtime, something I'd not experienced in a long time. I smiled as I pushed Hannah out into a small playground outside. We were within the hospital grounds and we only had 30 minutes, but it was still a short burst of freedom. Hannah didn't talk much so I read to her. She loved to listen to fairy tales and I discovered that *Rapunzel* was her favourite. With her long black hair, she imagined herself as the princess, trapped in an ivory tower. She was trapped, not in a tower, but inside her own body and the hospital, along with the rest of us. My other duty was to take her to the bathroom. A member of staff showed me how to remove the arm of her wheelchair, pull down her underwear, and slide her across and onto the toilet. Then I had to wipe her, pull up her underwear and slide her back into her chair. I didn't mind helping Hannah because she was seriously ill. She had brittle bone disease so she was unable to do anything for herself and was in constant pain, yet she never once complained. Hannah was only seven years old, and a pretty and lovely girl. Although she hardly spoke, she loved to sing. It was as if it was the only thing that brought her joy.

Before I knew it, it was dinner time and Frank had arrived, ready to take me back to Laburnum Ward. We followed the same path we'd trodden earlier. A skinny boy with bright red hair came over and started to walk along with us. His name was James.

"Hello, where have you just been?" he asked.

"School. Where have you been?" I replied, curious why he was able to walk freely around the hospital.

"Oh, I help the gardener."

"So you work here?"

James smiled as though I'd said something funny.

"What?" I said, slightly annoyed that he was laughing at me.

"No." He grinned. "I don't work here. Well, I suppose I do – I help the gardener out, but I'm on Cherry Ward."

I was shocked – James was a patient too.

Frank followed a few steps behind us, and although he occasionally looked up to check we were still there, he allowed us to talk.

"Do you get treatment?" James asked suddenly.

The blood drained from me.

How did he know about the treatment and Dr Milner? I felt myself blush and I stared hard at the ground.

"We get it, too," he whispered. "The boys, over at Cherry Ward. We've all had it."

I was stunned, and James had realised because he saw the look on my face.

The boys get treatment, too. I repeated it over inside my head. I could barely believe it. Dr Milner was treating both boys and girls. *Wait until I tell Christine about this.*

James looked up, stopped in his tracks and pointed up at a window.

"That's where you get treatment, isn't it?" he said.

I followed his gaze, and to my horror I realised that our short walk was over and we were standing in front of Laburnum Ward. Frank rang the doorbell as James cheerily waved goodbye and disappeared. The door swung open and standing inside was the nurse, the keys still swinging on her belt. Frank left and the nurse led me towards the communal room door. I'd expected her to unlock it, but she disappeared off into Dr Milner's office. I froze.

Was he in there?

Moments later, she reappeared with my usual medication in two small paper cups and told me to swallow. She unlocked the door and I found myself back inside the room just in time for the cutlery count.

51, 52, 53…

Jane was over by the television, twirling away, while the others were sitting staring into space. I spotted Christine, who waved me over.

"I've got something to tell you," she began.

"Me, too," I replied, flopping down in the seat next to her. Christine looked at me expectantly.

"No, go on," I said. "You first."

"The new girl has arrived."

"How do you know, have you seen her?"

She shook her head.

"No, but one of the other girls has, and guess what?" She paused for extra effect.

"What?"

"She's from The Cedars."

A bubble of excitement rose up inside me.

I wonder if it's someone I know?

"So, come on then," Christine said with a nudge of her elbow. "What have you got to tell me?"

Just then the nurse clapped her hands to shush us all and two girls started laying cutlery on the table.

"It's James," I began. "He's a boy I met on my way back from school."

Christine grinned and nudged me as though he was my boyfriend.

"No, I said shaking my head, it's nothing like that."

"Barbara O'Hare, could you please stop talking," the nurse shouted.

I dipped my head down. I didn't want any unwanted attention, not now. Not after what James had said.

"I'll tell you later," I whispered.

Chapter 13

Bodies

It soon became normal for me to walk to school every day with Frank. He didn't hold my hand because I'd promised I wouldn't run away. James would join us most days, walking alongside, chattering away, and it wasn't long before we became good friends. Frank would be there, but he allowed us to talk as long as he followed close behind.

"I know this area well," James told me. "I'm from Nottingham, you see. My dad used to take me camping all around here."

Soon he was telling me about all the places he'd been on holiday, including the Yorkshire Dales, where he'd seen the most beautiful waterfall.

"You should've seen it, Barbara; it was the most incredible thing."

However our conversations began, they always turned back to one subject – the hospital.

"I haven't seen my mother since I was little," James told me.

"Me neither. I don't even know her name, because no one will tell me. All everyone ever says are nasty things about her. I don't even remember what she looks like because she left when

173

I was just a baby. My foster mother once told me my mum didn't want me."

James shook his head in pity.

"That's awful," he sighed.

I wiped away a stray tear that had suddenly filled my eye.

"But I don't believe it because Edna was a cow, and she's jealous. My mum's a lovely lady, and she's out there right now, searching for me."

James looked over and smiled.

"I bet she is," he agreed.

"One day, she'll find me and I'll have a mother just like other children. I'll have a mother who braids my hair and looks after me. She'll be proud of me, too," I insisted. "Not like my foster mum. She wasn't my real mum, she's a fake. Only real mums can be proud of their daughters. That's why I was put in here, to stop me from running away. I kept running away, you see, running away to find my real mum."

James was quiet as he listened to my story.

"Hey, maybe we should both run away so we can find our mums together."

I grinned. It sounded like a great idea. The only problem was Dad would be coming in a few days and I knew he'd take me out of the hospital, so I had no reason to go.

James looked up because we'd reached the school.

"Well, I guess this is you," he said as he began to walk away. "See you later?"

I nodded.

"Yes see you later."

We had the usual assembly, I helped Hannah go to the toilet and then pushed her around at break time. A few more lessons followed, and then it was time to head back to Laburnum for dinner. The days passed by in a blur until one morning when James met me on my usual walk; he seemed very withdrawn and quiet.

"What's wrong?" I asked, giving him a nudge, as Frank followed us close behind.

James didn't answer, he just stared out into space as though he was lost in thought.

"Why are you so quiet?" I whispered.

He turned, his eyes searching mine as he grabbed my arm.

"I've got something to tell you."

I watched as he turned his head to check that Frank couldn't hear.

I laughed because he looked so serious.

"Whatever it is, it can't be that bad," I smirked.

James's face clouded over as though he was carrying the whole weight of the world on his shoulders. I realised then that whatever it was, it was something very serious indeed.

"Is it something to do with the treatment?" I asked.

He shook his head.

"It's bad."

"God, what is it?"

James inched up close so that he could whisper in my ear.

"Have you ever seen a dead body?" he asked suddenly.

My heart missed a beat.

A dead body? What on earth was he talking about?

"Because I saw one… on the ward last night. It was covered with a sheet."

I gasped.

"What did it look like? Who was it?" I demanded.

"It was a lad on my ward. He went for treatment, but never came back…" James whispered as his voice trailed off.

I wasn't sure if the story was real or not, but he was clearly shaken.

"But when did you see him?" I asked. I was desperate to know.

"I couldn't sleep, so I was looking out of the window. That's when I saw it – a black van. It pulled up and two men got out. The next thing I knew, they'd brought a body out wrapped in white sheets."

"But who are they?" I interrupted.

"The two men? I don't know, but it's not the first time I've seen them or that van driving around the wards. It's usually parked up at the old people's ward."

I was both scared and completely fascinated by James's story of a dead body and a black van. I'd never had any dealings with death before, so I was naturally curious.

"So how do you know it was him? I mean, how do you know it was the boy from your ward?"

He ran a trembling hand through his red hair and sighed.

"Because he never came back. His bed was empty after that, and no one saw him again."

Before I knew it, we'd reached the school, but my head was all over the place. All the talk of dead bodies and black vans had left me fearful.

James said goodbye as I peeled away towards the school door. I spent the rest of the day thinking about him and what he'd said.

What if there were dead bodies? What if children had died during treatment? I shuddered. It didn't bear thinking about.

I couldn't wait for dinner time so that I could ask him more. As soon as the bell sounded I was first at the door, waiting with Hannah. I was desperate to see James and ask him more. But as I headed to the main door there was only Frank waiting.

"Where's James?"

Frank shrugged.

"All I know is he's not here today and he won't be here tomorrow."

"Why?" I asked, thinking about the bodies and the black van.

"All I know is he was called back to the ward and then I saw him being taken out of the hospital."

"In what? What did they take him away in?" I asked, my heart pounding.

Frank looked at me oddly. "Oh, I don't know. It was a car, a car being driven by a social worker. Anyway, he's gone, so it's just you and me from now on."

My heart sank, because I knew then I'd never see James again. I wondered whether Frank had overheard us speaking and had reported it to the nurses. Maybe he'd heard us plotting to run away? Maybe he'd heard James tell me about the black van and the bodies. Maybe James knew too much. These thoughts scrambled around inside my head until I didn't know what to think anymore.

Frank took me back to Laburnum where I was medicated and taken inside the communal room. Jane was there, dancing and twirling away as the endless cutlery count continued in the background.

21, 22, 23…

"Hello," Christine said as she plonked herself down in the chair next to mine at dinner. "How was school?"

Right now she felt like my only friend in the world.

"Remember when I said I had something to tell you about a boy called James? Well, he told me that boys on Cherry Ward had treatment."

Christine's eyes widened with surprise.

"That's not all," I said, dipping my head. "He told me he's seen bodies, dead bodies, taken from the hospital by two men in a black van."

I watched as Christine nodded knowingly.

"But aren't you shocked? About the bodies, I mean."

She shrugged.

"People die here all the time and the black van comes to collect them. I see the van all the time."

"You do?"

"Yep."

"But what about James?" I asked.

"What about him?"

"Well, he's gone," I said, looking over at her. "James has gone."

Christine sat up in her seat.

"But where? Where has he gone?"

I shrugged.

"I don't know. Frank said a social worker took him away."

Christine shook her head. I could tell she wasn't convinced.

"You don't think anything's happened to him, do you?"

Anxiety rose up inside me, and for a split second I actually wondered whether James was dead.

"You mean the black van?"

She looked at the table and said nothing.

"What if James died and the black van came to collect him?" I said, voicing my fears out loud.

As soon as I'd said the words I realised how ridiculous they sounded. "No, he can't be dead because Frank saw him leave with a social worker in a car," I said, beginning to backtrack.

Christine stayed quiet. She arched her eyebrows in a way that told me, in here anything was possible.

Thoughts of Frank and James filled my head as Jane continued to twirl and the nurse started counting the knives.

1, 2, 3…

I decided that whatever happened, I didn't want to go back to school that afternoon. I had to get out of it. I felt sick; sick at the thought of James being shipped out or even worse. I was so upset that I couldn't eat my meal. A nurse had noticed and came over to speak with me.

"Why aren't you eating, Barbara?"

"I don't know. I just feel sick," I said, rubbing my hand against my stomach.

She removed my plate and took me back to the dormitory. I was relieved because it meant I'd get out of school for the rest of the day. At tea time the same nurse came to look for me. She held out my medication; only this time there was a double dose of the syrup. I'd wanted to argue, but all the fight had gone from me so I took it without question. I was led downstairs, where I sat in Christine's chair. A small crowd of girls was standing at the window, looking out for Milner. The atmosphere felt as black as my mood.

"By the light, of the silvery moon," Jane sang, as she danced and tapped her way around the room.

12, 13, 14…

The count continued, filling the room with background noise.

I sat there staring into space. My body felt numb. In my head, I wanted to stand up and scream. I wanted to stand up and smash up furniture. But I couldn't. I'd been given some sort of liquid cosh and I couldn't move. Instead, I screamed silently inside my head. My mind felt as if it'd been caught inside an invisible net. I couldn't move or think straight – I wanted to die. Death had to be better than this. Dad was coming, but what if he didn't turn up? What then? At least if I was dead then I wouldn't have to endure this anymore because death had to be better than this. It was my only real escape. I glanced up at the girls standing by the window. They were scared – frightened of what the night would bring. But I'd been anaesthetised – my emotions blunted by a double dose of the dark brown syrup – so my fear had vanished. I felt dead inside.

You have nothing left to live for, the voice in my head screamed.

It was right, I didn't. No one wanted me and I'd be stuck inside the hospital for the rest of my life. I looked at Jane and pictured myself an old woman, trapped in a hospital with girls young enough to be my granddaughters. I shook my head. I didn't want that. I couldn't bear the thought of it. An image of the black van flashed through my mind. I pictured the coldness of the sheets as they wrapped my body in them. I'd be dead but at least I'd be free from the daily torture.

35, 36, 37…

If I was dead then Milner couldn't carry out any more treatments on me. I'd disappear off into the back of the black van, they'd close the door and I'd never be seen again. I'd be at peace.

That was it. I decided *I needed to die – it was my only escape.*

I opened my eyes and found myself standing in front of the window. The crowd of girls had parted to each side and were watching as I pressed my face up against the cool glass.

42, 43, 44…

Time stood still. My forehead and nose flattened as my breath formed clouds of steam against the glass. I breathed harder and harder, the condensation spreading like a silver blood across the smooth surface. I was standing in the window, but I wasn't frightened anymore. I was sick of the fear.

I wanted him to see me. I wanted him to pick me. I wanted him to treat me with so much medicine that I died. Then I'd be able to leave the hospital for good.

48, 49, 50…

I thought of Dad. Only two more sleeps and he'd be here, but that would take too long.

I wanted to sleep now. I wanted to lie down and go to sleep and never wake up. I'd not be a burden to anyone, because I'd be in a hole in the ground. The dirty tinker swallowed up by the dark, cold earth.

Everyone held their breath.

Familiar headlights flashed, dipped down and tilted upwards as the car drove along the drive. The other girls screamed and scattered like confetti blown away into the dark corners of the room. He was here. Milner had arrived. Fear flooded through the room. Everyone moved; everyone apart from me. I remained there, staring defiantly, burning with rage as he swung into his usual parking bay. I watched as he pulled on the handbrake and turned something near the steering wheel, snuffing out the beam of headlights. He calmly climbed out of the car, wearing his usual brown tweed jacket, as though he didn't have a care in the world. I remained rooted to the spot, glaring at him through the glass.

Milner looked surprised when he spotted me, but his eyes refused to meet mine. Instead, he arrogantly glanced past as though I wasn't there.

51, 52, 53…

Anger flooded through me, until I couldn't contain it anymore.

Bang, bang, bang!

I hammered my fists against the window. I was telling the world I was here. I was letting him know, offering myself up to him – a willing victim. A 12-year-old girl begging to die.

Bang, bang, bang!

I screamed and thumped my fists against the glass to try and get his attention. I was only a child, but I'd never felt such white, hot rage.

Bang, bang, bang!

"Pick meeeee," I screamed, the words slurring slightly as hot, angry tears streamed down my face.

It was the fear. I couldn't cope with the fear. At least if I offered myself to him I was in control, not him.

I hit the glass harder as it shuddered and vibrated underneath my white-knuckled rage. I wanted him to look me in the eye. I was a sacrificial lamb to the slaughter, but the cold bastard had cut me dead, turned and walked towards the main entrance.

Bang, bang, bang!

"Pick meee," I shouted myself hoarse.

I watched as Milner strolled through the blue entrance door of his kingdom. I turned and marched over towards the small nurses' window. I knew exactly where he was going. I waited to give him enough time to reach the office. I pictured him, his long legs, striding along the corridor, cold and calculating. I imagined him holding out his hand, turning the handle... walking inside.

Bang, bang, bang!

Pressing my face against the glass of the nurses' station, I began to shout and scream as the room held its breath and time stood still.

"Pick meee," I screamed a third time, my voice giving way.

My face was so flattened against the glass that I could see through the complex threads of the net curtain. There were shadows moving around inside. My eyes frantically scoured them all, looking for the shape of Milner.

"You hear me, Milner? I want treatment."

There was the touch of a hand against my shoulder. I turned expecting to see a nurse, but it was Jane.

"Do you want to dance?"

It was the last thing I wanted or needed to hear.

"Fuck off!" I yelled, as she backed away like a frightened child. "Fuck off, you fucking freak, and stay away from me."

A door swung open and the nurse stepped in as though it was business as usual.

"Sarah Fleming," she called.

I marched over to her.

"Me. Pick me," I said, thumping my chest hard.

But the nurse glanced over my shoulder as Sarah approached with tears streaming down her face. They disappeared off into the corridor and the door closed. I turned and realised that everyone in the room was staring in open-mouthed silence at me. Even Christine was standing there, but no one said a word because no one knew what to say. Just then the door opened a second time and another nurse appeared. Everyone held their breath. This never happened; they never came twice.

"Barbara O'Hare," she said, looking directly at me.

At last! I'd been chosen. Milner would drug me, but hopefully this time I'd never wake up. I'd be like all those other dead bodies in the back of the black van. This is it. The torment is finally over…

I marched towards the nurse and followed her outside. I started to stride along the corridor towards the stairs that led to the treatment room. I felt relieved; relieved that I'd die and head to a better place; relieved I wouldn't have to spend another moment inside the hospital.

"No, Barbara," the nurse called me back.

She was standing outside his office and I was certain he was inside it waiting, just behind the door.

"Go and sit over there," she said, pointing to the solitary chair that I'd first sat in when I'd arrived at the hospital. She disappeared off into Milner's office and came out clutching a paper medication cup.

"Take these," she said handing me two small, yellow tablets.

I eyed them with suspicion.

"What are they for?"

"Dr Milner said to give you these because you've been upset."

I wondered if the tablets would kill me. In that split second I hoped that they would. I grabbed the cup, threw them to the back of my throat, and swallowed them hard and defiantly.

"Good girl," the nurse said, taking the cup from my hand. "Now, you wait here. I'll be back in 15 minutes."

"But I'm going for treatment, aren't I?"

She seemed shocked.

"No. Why? Do you want treatment?"

"Yes, and I want it now."

The nurse seemed perplexed.

"But why do you want treatment?"

The medication had blunted my emotions as the truth came spilling out of my mouth.

"Because I want to die and go inside the back of the black van, wrapped in sheets. Then I won't have to go into any more homes. It's the black van," I sobbed. "It's the only way I'll ever get out of here."

The nurse shook her head and placed a gentle hand against my shoulder.

"Don't be silly," she said. "Your dad's coming in a few days. Aren't you looking forward to seeing him?"

I tried to nod, but I felt the medication beginning to grip me, taking hold once more. I slumped forward in the chair. The nurse glanced down at her watch and anchored her hand underneath my left armpit.

"Come on, I'll take you up to the dormitory now."

I don't remember climbing into bed, but my body seemed to melt against the mattress as I sank down into it and the darkest sleep I'd ever known.

Chapter 14

The Visit

At last, it was Saturday and Dad was coming. I could barely contain my excitement as I gathered up my school drawings. I wanted to tell him how good I'd been and what had been going on with the drugs and treatment so that he'd get me out of this place. I glanced up at the clock – it was midday – only two more hours until he arrived.

It was medication time, but for some reason I wasn't given the brown syrup, only the tablets. At first I thought they must've forgotten, and then I realised something; Dad was coming, I suspected they wouldn't want me to be drugged up for his visit. After dinner, I sat chatting to Christine. I checked the clock again – one o'clock, only another hour until I escaped this place for good.

"Let's go over to the window so we can look out for your dad coming," she suggested as I followed her across the room.

"Yes, he might come early," I shrieked, the butterflies rising inside my stomach.

"Are you excited?"

I grinned and nodded.

"But I promise, whatever goodies my dad brings I'll share with you."

"Me, too," she insisted, as we shook on the deal.

I told her how my father would bring me new clothes, underwear, books and records to play.

"He always buys me records, usually Elvis Presley ones."

Christine continued to stare out of the window.

"Will your dad be in a car?"

I nodded my head. "Yeah, but I'm not sure which one, because he has lots of different cars."

As we continued to watch the outside world, a storm broke and rain patted softly against the glass, making it difficult to see out.

We passed the time by playing a game of I Spy.

"I spy with my little eye something beginning with r," I began.

Christine scratched her head and thought. She guessed every word she could think of beginning with the letter r.

"Give up?" I asked.

"Yes."

"Rain," I smirked, pointing at it running down the glass outside.

Christine giggled and pushed me playfully. For the first time in weeks I felt happy. Soon, it was half-past one. No more hours to count, only minutes. The headlights of a car twinkled as they approached, travelling slowly along the tarmac driveway. My heart skipped a beat. It was Dad.

"Does my hair look alright, Christine?" I asked, jumping down off the windowsill.

"You look great," she said, handing me my school work to show him.

We watched as the lights of the car came closer. I looked at Christine and back at the car. It needed to turn right for Laburnum Ward but it headed straight on, towards the school. The headlights passed until all we could see were the red tail lights as they disappeared off into the distance.

"Maybe he's lost?" Christine said kindly.

We waited for the car to turn around and come back, but it never did.

The clocked ticked to quarter to two, but there was still no sign.

"What will I do if my dad doesn't come?" I asked, my eyes filling with tears.

Christine sighed and looked over at me, full of pity.

"Don't be silly, Barbara," I said out loud, trying to be brave and hide my disappointment. "He always turns up in the end."

The clock ticked two o'clock and more headlights appeared.

"I bet this is him," she said, suddenly sitting up straight. It was a dark, dreary day as we looked out and I prayed that the car would turn right. When it did, I felt my heart skip a beat.

This is it. Dad's here!

I jumped off the window ledge and grabbed my school work, watching and waiting to see his familiar figure climb out of the car and slope off towards the main door. I was staring so hard through the rain that my eyes hurt. I felt Christine tug against my sleeve.

"Barbara, I don't think it's your dad. Two ladies just got out of that car."

I pressed my face against the glass. She was right; it wasn't Dad, but two older ladies standing by the main door, ringing the bell.

Surely the next car would be Dad?

But inside my heart was already broken because I knew he wasn't coming.

"Never be late for an appointment," he always said, "unless it's your wedding day."

Soon it was quarter past two, and still no sign.

"How about another game of I Spy?" Christine suggested.

But all the excitement had gone from me.

The clock ticked half past two.

"A game of cards?" Christine offered.

I sighed and reluctantly joined in. We played snap until three o'clock, but still no word.

"Has my dad rung?" I asked a passing nurse. She offered to go and ask in the office for me, but soon returned, saying there'd been no word or phone call.

The clock ticked four o'clock, and still no sign. Visiting was over and my heart was well and truly broken.

"Are you sure he's not rung?" I asked the nurse again, but she shook her head sadly.

I was heartbroken and humiliated. I wanted to die.

The nurse reappeared and handed me more tablets, which I took without fuss.

If I don't have Dad, then I have nothing, I thought.

Christine had tried her best to comfort me, but I wanted to cry. I'd waited so long for him to come, and now that he hadn't I realised I'd been left to my own fate.

32, 33, 34...

The count started up again.

"Are you going to dance with me?" It was Jane – the last person I wanted to see.

"Go away," I snapped. "Just go away."

It was dinner time, but I had no appetite. My throat felt closed up, as though my body was too upset to swallow food.

"Here, have mine," I said, passing my plate to Christine.

"You sure?"

I nodded.

After dinner, the cutlery nurse called my name and handed me two more yellow tablets – the same ones I'd been given when I'd banged at the window. I swallowed them robotically. I was still thinking about Dad, when I realised the nurse was speaking to me.

"Do you want to go to bed now, Barbara?" she asked.

I looked up at her, numb and utterly heartbroken.

"Can I please be locked in the side room?"

The nurse looked at me oddly.

"That's a strange thing to ask."

I was fighting back the tears, but they came tumbling down my face.

"I want, I... I... I want," I stammered, unable to get the words out. I looked down at the floor – all the hope had been knocked from me. "...I want to be on my own," I whispered.

My shoulders shook up and down as I began to sob.

"Come on, Barbara," the nurse coaxed. "I'm sure your dad will come soon. Don't be upset. Anything could've happened. Listen, his car could've broken down or anything. He'll come, otherwise he would've rung to tell us."

I wanted to believe her but I couldn't. My father worked on the oil rigs and I knew when he left he was gone for months at a time.

"Can I go in the side room?" I begged. "I just want to be alone."

"Are you going to cause trouble?"

"No," I sobbed.

"Well, you don't need to be in the side room then, do you?" The nurse reached out her hand and wrapped it around my shoulder.

"Come on, I'm taking you to the dorm. Your tablets will be kicking in by now."

She was right, I suddenly felt extremely sleepy. I allowed myself to be led to the dormitory. The medication had flattened my emotions and I didn't even flinch as we passed the treatment room.

I'm worthless. I'm nothing but a dirty tinker, who deserves to be in this hospital.

As soon as my head hit the pillow I sank into a deep sleep. I awoke the following morning, my face pressed against a wet pillowcase. My tears had soaked it through the night. At breakfast, Christine sat next to me and asked if there was anything she could do to cheer me up. I grabbed her hand gratefully, but even she couldn't lift my mood – nothing could. The smell of breakfast made me feel sick and I pushed my plate away.

"Could you eat it for me?" I asked her.

Afterwards, Christine fetched some crayons over and started to draw. She was a fantastic artist and she taught me how to colour in and shade, using a pencil. At least it stopped me from thinking about Dad. Before we knew it, the morning had passed and the nurse was standing in front of us with our medication. I was given two extra tablets. I knew it must have had something to do with my low mood because Dad hadn't showed.

23, 24, 25…

Dinner was served, but I couldn't stomach it. Instead, I pushed the food around my plate. I was just about to offer it to Christine when a nurse approached.

"Barbara, you have two options," she said, looming over me. "You either eat or you don't. If you don't then you will be force fed. Do you know what force fed means?" She asked, as everyone at the table turned to look at me.

I shook my head.

"It's where we put a tube down your throat and force you to take food."

I felt Christine kick me under the table, reminding me to stay calm.

"Okay, Nurse. I'll eat." I picked up my fork and stabbed at a few carrots. She watched as I put them inside my mouth, chewed and swallowed.

"Good girl," she smiled, satisfied that I was on the mend.

I knew they were watching me, so I had to eat, even if I didn't want to. After dinner, we carried on drawing. I was still tired, but I felt better for having eaten something. The afternoon passed slowly, but I started to talk once more. We were sitting over towards the back of the room. I had my back towards the door and the nurses' window when I noticed Christine look up. She was staring at someone over my shoulder. I turned and followed her gaze.

It couldn't be.

"Dad!" I shouted, as I ran across the room and into his arms.

"Hey, calm down, calm down!" he chuckled as he hugged me. "No need to get so excited," he said, smiling at one of the nurses.

"I'm sorry," I gushed, my heart still racing. "I'm just so pleased to see you."

The nurse approached with my coat in her hands.

Oh, my God! I thought. I was barely able to contain myself. *I'm finally getting out of this place.*

I looked at Christine.

"I knew he'd come and get me. I hate to leave you, but I'll write," I said, hugging her goodbye.

"Wow, slow down," Dad said taking my coat from the nurse. "I'm only taking you for the afternoon, you'll be back later."

My heart sank, but then I remembered – he didn't know.

Yes, but when I tell you what's going on here, you won't bring me back, I thought.

Dad helped me on with my coat, pulling my arms in the sleeves, and then I waved at Christine with my fingers crossed and my heart dancing for joy. Christine crossed her fingers and waved back as we closed the door behind us. It was pouring with rain as we headed outside to Dad's new van. It was a Transit van with large sliding doors. I went around to the passenger door and Dad opened it. Even though I'd only been in the rain a few moments, I was dripping wet. But I couldn't wait to tell him, tell him what'd been going on.

"Dad, Dad," I started, talking quickly. "I've got something to tell you."

He looked ahead, turned the key in the ignition as the car fired into life.

"What?" he asked. His hand dipped down, to release the handbrake, and then we set off.

"Listen, Dad, they're injecting me with needles. They're taking me to a side room and stripping me off. They're putting a mask over my face," I said, barely pausing for breath. "They're making me take disabled kids to the loo, and I've got to wipe them…"

Dad's face changed as his eyes left the road and he turned to face me. But I hadn't finished.

"Dad, a boy called James told me about the bodies, and now he's gone. Dad, you've got to help me… you've got to help me before they give me electric shock treatment."

In a temper, he pulled the gear stick forward and started to reverse back towards the entrance of the hospital. It was so shocked and unexpected that I fell silent. The van screeched to a halt as he slammed his hand hard against the dashboard. He was furious – I could see it in his eyes. He turned and pointed a finger at me.

"Listen, tinker. You're a liar," he said, spitting out the words. "What's wrong? Can't you run from this place, or something? You're nothing but a dirty, rotten tinker, and this place will get those tinker ways out of you."

I felt the blood drain from my face.

He didn't believe me.

"I'll not be driving all this way to listen to your tinker lies no more, understand?"

"B… b… but Dad," I said, trying to protest.

"Shush! I know you're lying because I've signed no consent forms. You're a liar. What are you?"

"A dirty tinker of a liar," I replied, tears welling in my eyes.

"Right," he said, slamming the gear stick back into first, "Don't ever try that one again. I'm sick of you."

The engine fired up as the van lurched forward and we drove out of the hospital grounds. I was devastated because he hadn't believed me – devastated because I knew he was my only hope.

"Yes, Dad," I whispered as we sat through the rest of the journey in silence.

Countryside rolled past in a windy and wet blur, as the rain pattered softly against the side windows, mirroring my misery. We passed the three chimneys I'd seen from my bedroom window. I glanced up at them, curious to finally see them up close. I had no idea where we were going until Dad parked the van up outside a pub.

"Wait here," he said as he climbed out of the van, covered his hair with his jacket, and ran through the rain into the pub.

I sat waiting for 20 minutes, watching the rain; until I spotted two figures emerge. It was Dad and he had his arm around the shoulder of a woman I'd never seen before. She had black hair, heavy make-up, a black dress and wore a black fur coat. The passenger door creaked open and Dad introduced us.

"You need to get out, Barbara," he told me. "This is Janice."

I got out as Janice perched herself in the passenger seat next to Dad.

"Hello," she smiled, shaking my hand. "I've heard so much about you."

I scowled at her because I hated being on the end of the seat. *I want to sit next to Dad. This is my day out, not hers*, I thought bitterly.

With his girlfriend in the van, Dad was extra nice. He drove me to a corner shop and bought me everything I asked for. I chose more than usual because I'd planned to give half to Christine. We went back to the van and I tried to push in the middle to be next to Dad, but he was having none of it.

"No," he said shooing me out. "Janice sits next to me."

Janice was actually a nice lady, who was trying her best to make conversation. But I still resented her being there, encroaching on my time with my father. We drove back to the same pub.

"Let Janice out," Dad told me.

Janice lifted up my chin and planted a lipsticked kiss on my cheek.

"Lovely to meet you, Barbara," she said before heading back towards the pub. But then she stopped and turned to my father.

"We forgot the stuff we brought for Barbara. It's in the back of the van."

Dad slapped a hand against his forehead as though it'd skipped his mind.

"Oh, yes!"

He slid open the side door and I peered inside. There was a suitcase, vanity case and my Dad's going away bag. There was also a carrier bag of clothes from C&A.

"These are for you," he said, handing them to me. "Now, get in the van. I won't be long."

He reappeared five minutes later, holding a bottle of Coke and a bag of crisps.

"Thank you." I grinned.

He nodded and was about to close the door when he paused.

"Never, ever mention that hospital to Janice, do you understand?"

I nodded.

"Good," he said, slamming the door. With that he disappeared off inside.

Around half an hour later, the door opened and he told me to climb into the passenger seat.

"I have to get you back now," he said, turning the ignition key.

My heart sank to my knees.

"Please don't take me back there. Everything I said is true," I pleaded.

But he refused to listen.

"Please, please don't take me back…" I wailed.

Dad slammed on his brakes.

"You can't run from there, so you're going to say anything to get out. You're staying there."

I started to cry. Huge sobs ripping inside my chest as it heaved up and down, gasping for breath.

"I'd sooner die than go back there. Please, Dad, you can put me anywhere but there. They really are giving me injections, Dad. I swear."

He sighed heavily.

"Do you think I'm a fool? They're not, and you know they're not."

It was his final word on the matter.

It was no good, I was powerless. I was going back to the hospital.

We drove the rest of the way in silence, apart from the swishing sound of his windscreen wipers as they cleared the rain away. He parked up the van and pulled on the handbrake, but by now his mood seemed to have softened.

"Listen, I'm going away to work, but when I get back I'll get you home for the weekend."

But I couldn't even look at him, I was too devastated.

"Thank you," I mumbled as I climbed out.

I saw Christine sitting in the window, waiting for me. She lifted her hand to wave. I couldn't see if her fingers were crossed or not, but I crossed mine because, right now, I needed all the luck I could get. Dad walked me over towards the main entrance and pressed the bell. A nurse unlocked it and opened the door. I turned to him, but he didn't come inside.

He smiled, raised his hand and rubbed it against my head, messing my hair up.

"See you soon," he said. "Be good."

I lifted my bag and stepped inside the hospital. I turned and watched as my dad – my only hope – got back in his van and drove away.

"Bye, Dad."

Chapter 15

Midnight Feast

Once the nurse had checked my bag, she took me upstairs to the dormitory and told me to put away my new clothing. Inside the C&A bag were underwear, a dress, a cardigan and a hairbrush. Janice and Dad had also bought me a bottle of perfume, but the nurse had taken it off me.

"I don't think you'll be needing this in here," she said, swiping the bottle from my hand.

Dad had also given me money, which he'd told me to spend, because decimal currency was coming. He'd said there'd soon be no more ten bobs, half a crown, tanners or sixpences. The thought of new money concerned me because I was worried I wouldn't understand it.

The nurse reappeared in the dormitory.

"All unpacked?"

I nodded.

"Good, now let's get you downstairs."

Although I had bags of sweets, new clothes and money to my name it didn't make up for the fact I'd lost my dad again. He seemed more interested in his girlfriend and, if it wasn't a woman, it was my half-brother, Stephen. I always felt as though I was at the bottom of the pile. I thought it strange that Dad never mentioned Stephen, just as he never mentioned my mother. I had no idea where either of them were and I knew better than to ask. I'd asked Dad a few times over the years about Mum, but it was always met with the same response.

"She's a dirty tinker, like you."

So, I stopped asking, but I still ached to find her. I wondered why no one would tell me her name – just her name. It made me feel sad, but then I reasoned I'd call her 'Mum' anyway, so why would I need to know her name? It was my way of coping. I'd often sit and daydream about her. I wondered what she was doing, and I often pictured her searching for me.

Maybe she was in a far-flung country like America or Australia, and she couldn't get back to find me? When I'm old enough I'll travel to Australia to find her, I decided.

I'd once seen the film *Gone with the Wind*, starring Scarlett O'Hara, and I pictured my mother to be just like her, even though the only similarity was in the surname.

"You okay?" It was Christine.

"Yes," I mumbled.

"Good," she said, plonking herself down next to me in a chair. "It's just that you seemed miles away."

I sighed.

"I was thinking about my mum."

Christine raised her eyes and nodded her head. She knew all about my mum and how much I missed her.

"What's it like to have a real mum?" I asked.

"Oh, it's okay. I suppose it depends on who your mum is."

I felt I was the only kid in the world who didn't know her mother's name. I'd always thought that if I caused enough trouble my father would send me back to Mum to be rid of me, but all that had done was land me in Aston Hall. I was still thinking about things when I heard my name being called.

"Barbara."

My mind bolted back into the moment. The nurse was standing in front of me, holding out my medication. "Wow, you were miles away," she said.

She handed me to two small paper cups, containing my medicine and tablets. I took them without a word. "Penny for your thoughts?" she asked.

I looked at her, my eyes brimming with tears.

"I just want my mum."

Tears spilled down my cheeks and I began to weep. I didn't care if the others saw me. I didn't care about anything anymore, I just wanted my mum.

"Come on now," she coaxed. "I'm sure you'll hear from her soon."

I gasped and looked up at her.

Did she know something that I didn't?

"Why, has she rung?" I asked, my heart full of hope.

The nurse looked uncomfortable. It was clear that she knew nothing about my personal situation.

"Er, I don't think so," she mumbled.

My face fell and she'd noticed.

"But it doesn't mean she won't."

203

She took the paper cups from my hand, gave Christine her medication and stepped away. I sensed she wanted to get away from me and my questions as quickly as possible.

"So," Christine said, watching the nurse disappear. "How did it go with your dad?"

I knew it was a gentle reminder to share my stash of goodies with her.

"Oh, he took me everywhere," I lied. "We went to see some narrowboats, and he was so sorry that he couldn't come earlier, but he's a very busy man, you see. He's got a very important job."

Christine nodded, although I could tell she didn't believe me.

"Anyway, he said he's going to get me out of here, but Milner isn't here today, otherwise Dad would've killed him. But he's going to come back – to sort Milner out."

I knew it was untrue but it made me feel better just saying the words.

23, 24, 25…

The count continued in the background.

Jane was over in the corner, singing away to herself, while the others sat staring blankly at the TV screen. Jane moved, dancing and twirling between them but no one complained. It was as though she was so much part of the furniture that she'd become invisible.

After tea, I told Christine about my stash of sweets in my locker upstairs.

"Guess what?" I said, imagining myself to be in an Enid Blyton story. "We're going to have a midnight feast tonight."

She grabbed my hand, gave it a squeeze and squealed with excitement.

"It's a good job Emma isn't here, she'd eat them all!"

"Yeah," I laughed. "I bet she'd love to be here right now."

But Christine's face clouded over.

"I know where she is," she whispered.

"Where?"

I'd expected her to tell me Emma was back at The Cedars, but it was worse than that.

"She's on Rowan Ward," she said, her voice trailing off.

"Why, what happens there and where is it?"

"Rowan Ward? Well, let's just say, when they go there they never come back."

I turned to her.

"You mean it's worse than here? It's worse than Laburnum Ward?"

"Yes, that's where they get electric shock treatment, so don't fight with anyone or cause the nurses any trouble; otherwise you'll end up on Rowan Ward."

Her words sent a chill down my spine. Electric shock treatment – poor Emma. Even though she was a bully, my heart went out to her because no one deserved that. To try and take our minds off it, Christine and I planned our midnight feast and, for once, we couldn't wait to get to bed. Once we'd been given our medication and the ward lights had been turned off, we crept out of bed and put our pillows on the floor to form a makeshift table. It was awkward, trying to remove the rustling wrappers quietly so no one else would hear, but it was made doubly difficult because our only source of light was the moonlight, streaming in through the window. Sadly, our midnight feast didn't last long because the medication had started to kick in and it took all our strength to keep our eyes open.

"Shall we eat the rest tomorrow night?" Christine suggested.

"Yeah, I'm really sleepy," I yawned.

We packed away our treasure, pushed it to the back of my cabinet, and climbed back into bed.

"Night, Christine," I whispered.

"Night, Barbara."

I was awoken by the sound of clapping hands before the main ward light snapped on.

"Wakey, wakey, girls. Come on, chop, chop," called the nurse, who was striding along the bottom of our beds. She stopped as soon as she reached me. "What on earth have you been up to?"

I was shocked. How did she know? I looked at my bedside cabinet – it was closed and there wasn't a sweet wrapper in sight.

The other girls looked over at me. Soon, they were all laughing and pointing. Christine heard the commotion and lifted herself up. As she did, I realised why everyone was looking – her face, and mine, were smothered in milk chocolate. I couldn't help myself. I took one look at her and cracked up laughing. As soon as she saw me, she did the same. Although we both knew we were in big trouble, we couldn't help it.

But the nurse didn't see the funny side.

"Right, you two," she said, her hands on both hips, "get up and cleaned. I'll deal with you both later."

As we legged it over towards the bathroom, I looked down at Christine's nightie. It had chocolate and toffee stuck across the back of it and she looked as though she'd messed herself. There were tears of mirth rolling down my face.

"What?" she asked, but I couldn't tell her for laughing.

"Well, whatever it is, it can't be as bad as your hair."

I pushed myself onto my tiptoes and glanced at my reflection in the bathroom mirror. She was right – I had chocolate caked in it. Soon, we were laughing so hard that I was bent over double.

"Don't," I gasped. "I think I'll wet myself."

"I think I already have," Christine quipped as we both dissolved into a fit of the giggles.

"Get washed and dressed. You're both on toothbrush duty – for the whole day." It was the nurse, standing in the doorway. She had both arms folded angrily across her pinched little chest.

We stripped, waxed and buffed the floor afterwards, and then we had breakfast. But I was called out for school, so I escaped my toothbrush punishment. As I walked to school with Frank, my thoughts returned to my mother. I thought how I'd have given the world just to have a photograph of her. I decided that I'd pray for her every night – that God would keep her safe and bring her to me. I thought of her pushing me on a swing in a park, taking me shopping or just plaiting my hair, but these thoughts did little to comfort me. Instead, they hurt bit by bit, like a plaster being slowly ripped from an open wound. At least when I dreamed of her it was time alone together, even if it was only inside my head.

The Hospital

I had to escape from the hospital – I had to find my mother.

Life at the hospital continued in a daily grind. Hannah and I had become good friends. She didn't talk much, but her singing voice was so lovely that I could've listened to her sing all day. We formed such a good relationship that I didn't even mind cleaning her up after she'd been to the bathroom. Not long afterwards, I arrived at the school to find that Hannah had gone. I asked Mr Hope, my teacher, but he seemed reticent, as though he didn't want to discuss it.

"She's gone, Barbara, and she won't be coming back to school again."

That night I wept for Hannah – the lovely little girl with the beautiful voice – because I knew; I knew that she'd been taken away by the two men in the black van, wrapped in a white sheet. Like James, my mother, in fact anyone I'd ever loved or befriended – she had disappeared. And the worst part was I knew I'd never see her again.

Chapter 16

The Mouse

Winter had passed and soon it was spring and I was still trapped inside the hospital. The birds had started nesting in the trees. They sang sweet songs that reminded me life still existed outside the hospital walls. My brief walk to and from school was my only relief and connection with the outside world. Other than that, I'd become a zombie like the others.

I hadn't had treatment since the first time I'd arrived at Aston Hall, and although other girls had been routinely called up for it, I'd escaped. I wondered if my disruptive behaviour and the fact I'd demanded it that time, beating my fists against the glass window, had helped me avoid it.

Maybe I'd never be called again?

Despite my bravado, I looked up at the treatment room window every day I passed by it, hoping that I'd never be called again.

It was 3 March 1971, and less than three months since I'd arrived at Aston Hall. I came back from school and was chatting to Christine in the communal room when Milner's car pulled up. His tyres screeched as they parked up outside one of the windows, sending the girls scattering away in panic.

I wasn't concerned because I was certain I'd beaten him and the treatment. The nurse handed out doses of medication, which we took without fuss, as the cutlery count began in the background. By now, I'd become so used to it that I barely heard it anymore. Everyone sat still as the net curtain lifted and Milner's head peered underneath. I was just wondering what we were having for dinner, when the nurse appeared inside the door and called out a name.

"Barbara O'Hare," she said, holding a clipboard.

My heart stopped as I felt Christine grab the top of my arm.

"Don't fight, you won't win," she whispered as I struggled to breathe.

Had she really just said my name?

"Come on, Barbara. Hurry up. Dr Milner's waiting for you."

The room seemed to close in on me as I got to my feet. I felt unsteady and for a moment I thought I might pass out.

Breathe, I told myself. *You must breathe.*

My whole body was trembling as I made my way over towards the nurse. She looked down, grabbed the bunch of keys on her belt and unlocked the door. I was so frightened that I forgot to wave back at Christine, who was holding her hand aloft with both fingers crossed. I felt like a dead man walking as the nurse began to lock and unlock doors. Soon, we were standing in the bathroom.

"Get in and wash," she said, while she went in search of a towel.

I sat down in the tepid bath and wrapped both arms around myself protectively. The thought of Milner, the room, the gown and the needle stole my breath away as I tried to concentrate and stop my heart from violently pounding inside my chest. The nurse appeared with a towel in one hand and the horrible grey gown in the other. I wanted to vomit.

"I think I'm going to be sick," I gasped.

She ignored me.

"Come on, up and out," she quipped, holding the towel open for me.

I dried quickly and slipped both arms inside the stiff, grey gown. She led me through to the treatment room and wheeled in the trolley. My eyes darted over towards it and I spotted the greying bandage, kidney-shaped dish and large needle.

"Honestly, I'm going to be sick," I said, clasping a hand against my mouth.

"On the bed," she ordered.

I lowered myself and sat down, the skin of my legs making contact with the cool rubber mattress.

"Lie down."

I did as she said, but the gown gaped, leaving me partly exposed from my back down to my ankles. I physically winced and she shot me a stern look.

"You're not going to cause any trouble are you?"

But I couldn't speak; fear had rendered me mute. Instead, I lay there as tears ran down from my eyes, trailing against the side of my temples, wetting my hair before pooling against the mattress beneath me. I looked at her and shook my head. She bound my hands together and, although it hurt, I knew I was one of the lucky ones. I'd heard of girls who'd had their hands tied to their legs in the crab position, so, in many ways, with mine tied above my head, I felt more fortunate. After she'd finished, she dipped her hand over towards the trolley and pulled a second, longer bandage from it. Panic overwhelmed me. I wondered what she planned to do with it. Without a word, she was at my feet, tying my ankles together. I was completely freaked out and started kicking for all I was worth. But she was stronger than me and, in my drugged-up state, I was no match for her. It was always the same woman – the same hard-faced bitch. I decided that she wasn't a nurse, or a woman, but a monster, a monster with a heart of stone.

"Please, please don't tie my legs together," I begged, finding my voice. "You don't need to do that. You've tied my hands, please leave my feet alone."

She continued to ignore me as my pleas fell against deaf ears.

"Why?" I cried. "Why are you doing this to me?"

She stopped wrapping my legs together and looked at me lying across the mattress.

"It's for your own good." Her voice sounded hard and sharp.

My mind went into overdrive.

She's tying my legs together because they're going to give me electric shock treatment, I thought. I jolted my body to try and untie my legs.

"Calm down," she ordered, trying to keep me still.

My eyes darted around the room, trying to make shapes out in the darkness. The only source of light was coming from the corridor. I looked around, and that's when I saw it – a black,

212

square shape on the floor in a corner of the room. It looked like a big black box.

Was that what they used to give the electric shock?

I was so petrified that I tried to fight, but it was no good – I was trussed up and completely at the mercy of the nurse and Dr Milner.

I thought of Emma and the other girl Christine had told me about. I thought of a life in a wheelchair, like Hannah; a life of being pushed around and wiped after I'd used the toilet. I thought of James, the two men and the black van.

Maybe this treatment would kill me?

In many ways, I hoped it would, then at least the fear would die along with me – at least I wouldn't feel frightened anymore.

Fight. A voice inside my head screamed. *You must fight!*

With all my might, I jolted my body again and this time I sent the nurse flying. As she fell, I got to my feet. The bandages had worked themselves loose as I wobbled over to one side, sending the trolley crashing to the ground.

"Wait!" I screamed as loud as my lungs would let me. "Wait until my dad finds out about this."

I stood on top of the mattress, eyeing the nurse warily as she picked up the overturned trolley. My back was flat against the cool wall – I was trapped, but I felt in control.

"You're horrible. You're a horrible woman," I screamed, as I bounced from one foot to the other, like a boxer, just as Liam had taught me.

Keep an eye on your opponent at all times, Barbara. I heard his voice inside my head.

Christine had always told me not to fight back, but now I had nothing to lose. I was getting electric shock treatment – that's what the black box was for. I was as good as dead. My eyes darted from the nurse to the box on the ground. It had a silver trim that ran along it and two silver catches, like the ones on a suitcase. There was a handle, too, and two big reels with lots of buttons. I was breathless as I continued to dart around, trying to evade the nurse's hands. She realised she was fighting a losing battle because I was too fast for her, so she backed off and tried a different tack.

"Listen, if you calm down we can talk about this."

But I didn't want to talk.

"What's that thing there," I said, pointing over to the box on the floor. "Is it for electric shock treatment?"

She didn't answer.

"Calm down, Barbara. You're going to get treatment, no matter what, so you may as well make it easy on yourself."

"Is it for electric shock treatment?" I demanded.

The nurse stood back.

"No, it's a tape recorder. It's Dr Milner's."

I shook my head. I didn't believe her. But when I looked again, it did look a bit like a tape player.

"Now," she said, trying to reason with me. "Do you want me to lock you in here and ask Dr Milner to give you the injection or are you going to behave?"

"My dad is going to kill Dr Milner," I sobbed. "You do know that, don't you?"

The nurse smirked as though she found it amusing.

"Now you know and I know your dad doesn't care. If he did, you wouldn't be in here. He can come and get you any time he wants, but he doesn't care because he doesn't want you... just like your mother."

The words felt like a knife through my heart as I crumpled with pain. It was the truth and the truth hurt. I could hear my father's voice inside my head.

You're a liar. Consent form? I never signed any consent form. That's why I know you're a liar.

I felt completely defeated. My back slid down the wall and I slumped onto the mattress. I wanted to collapse in a heap and die, because she was right – Dad didn't want me. All he wanted was his son. My mind and body were already broken, and now Milner would take away my innocence. I laid down on the bed and let the nurse do her worst. I inhaled a sharp intake of breath as the needle pierced my skin and pumped a chemical into my body. In many ways, it was a relief when I felt myself turn to stone. I was unable to move. I'd been numbed and rendered useless – unable to help myself.

Let them do their worst, the voice whispered. *Let them. You've nothing left to live for, not now. Not anymore.*

I blinked and watched silently as the nurse packed away her things and got to her feet. She was just about to leave the room when she turned to me one last time.

"Now you know the truth, you'd do better to behave in the future." Her shoes clacked as she turned on her heels and left.

My tears continued to puddle against the mattress. I heard the sound of footsteps approaching, but they sounded different to the last, they were less pronounced. They were flatter shoes – men's shoes. Milner was here. I spotted him out of the corner of my eye as he came into the room. He was carrying three cushions under one arm, which he laid on the floor. I watched as he leaned over and pressed one of the buttons on the tape recorder. Milner was talking, but I wasn't listening. I'd heard something else – I'd heard a squeak.

There was a mouse – there was a mouse in the room.

Milner's voice droned on in the background, but I'd already tuned out. Instead, I was listening out for the squeak of the mouse. I tried to lift my head up so that I could hear a little better.

There it was again – the mouse. He was squeaking, talking to me to let me know I wasn't alone.

I thought of the little rodent, scuttling around between the walls, carrying the news. The mouse was my friend and my witness. He was there to protect me because he hated Milner as much as I did. He knew what happened to little girls inside this room.

Squeak.

I felt comforted by his sound. His voice was letting me know that everything was going to be alright because he was there with me and I wasn't alone with Milner. I had a friend, I had the mouse.

Squeak.

The sound was so regular, about a minute apart, that I almost knew when it would happen.

Squeak.

He was letting me know. He was trying to tell me he was here to help.

My mind began to wander as I thought of the little mouse living inside the skirting board. How much he dreaded the toothbrush treatment because he didn't like someone scrubbing at his front door. I grinned.

Yes, that was it! He lived in the skirting board.

I was still thinking of the mouse when Milner placed the wire mask over my face.

Drip, drip, drip.

The smell of the fluid made my nostrils flare as the room disappeared and I fell backwards into a long, dark tunnel.

Please help me, little mouse, I prayed.

When I came around I was facing the wall. I'd been moved. Milner was speaking, but then I heard it again.

Squeak.

He was still there with me. I pictured him with his brown body, pink nose and slim tail.

Drip, drip, drip.

More wetness, more blackness. Nothing. And then Milner's voice speaking to me through a fog of medication.

"Tell me about your brother?"

I mumbled, trying to form a sentence, but my mind wouldn't let me.

"Do you like your brother?" he probed.

Little mouse, where are you? I panicked.

Drip, drip, drip.

When I came around I was on my back with Milner's face looming above me. I could feel his hot breath against my skin, and I wanted to claw it away. Claw away every trace of it. I felt a dead weight pinning me down against the bed – something hard against my body.

Drip, drip, drip.

Blackness enveloped me. I awoke, but this time I was on my stomach, my face pressed against the sticky rubber mattress.

Little mouse, speak to me, I begged.

Milner was asking something about spelling, but I couldn't work out what he was trying to say. Then he asked something else.

"Is your little brother naughty? Does he annoy you?"

I want to shout and scream that I loved my brother. I tried to speak, but Milner was there.

Drip, drip, drip.

I came to once more and heard a squeak.

Thank goodness, he's here. The mouse is still here. Everything will be okay as long as I'm not alone with the doctor. He'll help me. The little mouse will help me. He'll go and fetch help. Run, little mouse. Go and find someone...

"You like that, don't you?" Milner's voice said.

Drip, drip, drip.

The room was so dark that I guessed he'd closed the door, but I knew the mouse could see. He'd seen it all. My father hadn't believed me, but the mouse did, because he knew the truth.

Drip, drip, drip.

Blackness overwhelmed me and I disappeared. It was a relief. I wanted to be as far away from Milner as I could get.

"Oh, you poor, poor child," he said. "Tell me about your friends."

Drip, drip, drip.

I came to, but now I was facing the doctor. I'd been moved again. I was just beginning to wonder what had happened to the mouse when I heard him squeak again, but no one had come to help me.

Maybe I was the only one who could hear him?

But he was all I had, so I had to trust him. I had to believe he'd help. There was no one else.

Drip, drip, drip.

Blackness took me once more. I woke up, this time facing the wall. I saw Milner's hand as he leaned over me, holding the mask against my face. I felt a pressure against my back. It was Milner; he was holding himself against me. I drifted in and out of consciousness. Finally, he removed the mask and I came up gasping for air. The pressure against my back had stopped, but I felt a sharp sensation as a needle was pressed into the skin of my buttocks. I started to fade away far from the room.

"Good girl," Milner whispered in my ear.

Meanwhile, the reels on the tape recorder continued to record everything, squeaking along with every other turn...

Chapter 17

The Silent Rage

When I came round, I was back in my bed in the hospital ward. I could still smell the liquid chemical lingering on strands of my hair. As soon as I smelled its familiar scent I felt physically ill. My wrists were sprained and sore from where they'd been tied above my head. The dormitory was empty apart from the identical beds all made and neatly turned under. I wondered how they'd transported me from the treatment room back to the ward because I'd never seen a hospital patient's trolley.

Maybe someone had lifted me up and along the corridor and had placed me back in my bed in a drugged-up stupor?

I didn't have a clue because I had no recollection. I'd once asked Christine how they moved patients around and she told me that they dragged them by the arms. At first, I hadn't believed her, and then I remembered Emma being dragged from the communal room like a dead animal. If they could do it to her, they could do it to anyone. I winced and closed my eyes. I didn't want to get out of bed because I was sore down below again – swollen and wet, as though I'd pissed the bed. But I hadn't. I was still only 12, but I knew I'd been messed with. Someone had put something inside me to leave me so sore down below. Christine had explained what she'd done with boys, and I now knew what sex was and what happened. Still, I didn't want to ask any of others because I didn't want them to know I was a virgin – I didn't want to become a target. Fluid continued to trickle out along the top of my legs. It was a reminder of Milner and the treatment. I remembered Edna and what she'd done to me with the spoon in her bedroom.

Was this the same? I wondered. *Had Milner examined me or worse?*

I thought of Liam and how he'd made Edna stop.

He'd put a stop to this right now, if he knew, I thought bitterly.

But no one knew, not even Dad. I'd told him some of what happened in here, but he didn't know the full story.

Why didn't I have a mum like everyone else? Why wasn't I normal?

Both Dad and Edna had told me my mother wasn't a nice person, but nothing could be worse than this. Nothing. I knew Mum wouldn't let them do this to me.

A pain shot up from my groin and through my body like a bolt of electricity. I closed my eyes and groaned with pain.

I had to ask someone, ask a nurse what had happened to me.

Despite the pain, I must have drifted off to sleep because I dreamed of my mother. We held hands as I skipped along the path, wearing a clean, fresh, ironed uniform. I didn't want for much, just what other little girls had – a mum and a normal life.

"Barbara, Barbara…" a voice called. It cut like a razor through the middle of my dream.

"Mum," I gasped.

I opened my eyes, hoping I'd finally see her – my lovely mum – but it was a nurse. She was leaning over my hospital bed, holding two small paper cups in her hand.

"Come on, medicine time."

The brown syrup stuck to the roof of my mouth because it was so dry. I tried to swallow the tablets but gagged as I did so.

"Don't worry," she was saying. "I'm going to bring you some lovely marmalade sandwiches."

Why are they always marmalade?

The nurse returned with my sandwiches and a glass of water on a tray, which she laid across my lap. I grabbed the glass and gulped the water down greedily.

"Nurse," I called as she turned to walk away.

She was younger and friendlier than the others, so I decided to take a chance.

"May I please talk to you for a moment?"

She perched herself on the edge of Christine's bed and looked at me.

"Yes. What's the matter?" she asked.

"Well," I said, averting my eyes from her. My face flushed red as I considered what to say and how to word it. "I don't understand something. Whenever I come back from treatment I feel really uncomfortable… uncomfortable down in my, erm, privates. It's just that it, er, feels as though I've wet myself. Not a lot, but a little bit."

I looked down at the tray of food balanced across my lap, grabbed a marmalade sandwich, and crammed it inside my mouth to try and hide my embarrassment.

"Don't worry," she said getting to her feet. "It's okay. It happens to lots of girls who have had treatment. It's all part of it. You'll be as right as rain in a day or two."

She stood over me and adjusted the pillows behind my back, as though she'd wanted to look anywhere but at me.

"Now just eat your sandwiches and then you can get up and go downstairs for your tea."

I was only young, but I sensed that even the nice nurse didn't want to talk about the treatment. She'd just cut the conversation short. I watched glumly as she took the tray from my lap and disappeared. With my sandwiches eaten and my legs unburdened by the weight of the tray, I decided to try and get out of bed. Placing both feet flat against the floor, I doubled up as a pain shot across my abdomen. I gripped my stomach. I looked up for the nurse, but she was nowhere to be seen. I grabbed both beds to try and steady myself. As I did, the top blanket pulled away revealing a patch of fresh blood on the sheet. I was in pain and now, upon seeing the blood, I was frightened.

What was wrong with me?

Suddenly, the nurse reappeared.

"Oh, you're out of bed," she said, coming over to help.

I felt sick and dizzy as the room continued to spin around me. A fear rose inside me and I began to sob. Big, angry tears cascaded down both cheeks.

"Oh, come on, Barbara," the nurse cooed.

I was upset but I looked at her and pointed across at the bloodied sheet.

"It's okay," she soothed. "You just got your period, that's all. It happens to all girls your age. Didn't your mother explain these things to you?"

The word "mother" had felt like a dagger to my heart.

"No," I whispered.

My mother never told me. As a matter of fact, she's never spoken to me, I thought as I continued to cry.

She went off to fetch me a sanitary towel.

"Listen," she said handing to it me. "Go and have a wash and you'll soon feel better."

I made my way along the corridor to the bathroom and used a flannel to clean myself. Then I got dressed. Although I was back in my clothes, I didn't want to go downstairs and face the others. I didn't want to see anyone, not even Christine. I just wanted to stay in bed and hide from the world. But the nurse was determined I'd make it in time for dinner.

"Come on," she said, leading me towards the stairs.

As soon as the door to the communal room swung open, I heard the counting.

22, 23, 24…

I was back in the middle of hell.

I spotted Christine's chair. I staggered over and fell down into it heavily.

"Are you alright?"

It was Christine.

"Yes." I smiled, trying to put on a brave face. "Everything's fine."

But everything was far from fine. I was sore, bleeding and my body was doubled up in pain.

There was an unexpected rush as girls scattered away from the window like a flock of starlings. He was here.

I focused on the ground.

"Why, why, why?" I mumbled, rocking backwards and forwards. I turned sideward and stared at Christine through tear-rimmed eyes.

"Why does Milner have to do this to us?"

But she didn't reply, she just shook her head sadly.

Everyone froze as we began another twisted game of musical statues, with Milner picking out his prey through the net curtain. I stared hard at the floor. I didn't want to see him. I didn't want to be part of his sick game. The door opened and a nurse stepped inside the room.

"Andrea Brown," she called out.

I clamped both hands flat against my ears because I didn't want to hear it. I didn't want to hear the name. Inside, I was screaming.

I can't stand any more of this...

Once the girl had been led outside and the door had closed, the room breathed a sigh of relief. It returned to normal, whatever that was. Jane tapped her way across the floor, performing a heel-to-toe routine. She held out both arms and began to sing and smile.

"By the light... of the silvery moon."

Christine looked over. By now, I was trembling with rage. She realised, stood up and walked over to the back of the room, where she sat at one of the dining tables. She knew I was about to erupt and didn't want to be caught up in the explosion. Meanwhile, I remained sitting in the chair, like a ticking time bomb ready to go off at any moment. A silent rage continued to simmer within me. It was as though my desire to find my mother had returned with a vengeance. I had to, no I *needed* to find her, if not just to prove to the bastard of a treatment nurse that I *did* have a mum, and she *did* care about me. If only someone – anyone – would tell me something about her. Even her name would be a start. Dad was always introducing me to his girlfriends, saying "meet your new mum". But I didn't want to meet a 'new' mum – I'd met enough 'new mums" over the years to last me a lifetime. I just wanted to meet my real mother.

Was that too much to ask?

Sometimes, I'd dream she was a beautiful princess, who lived far away in a big mansion. Other times, I'd imagine she was dead. I'd picture myself wandering around a graveyard trying to find her gravestone. I'd drape flowers around it – a daisy chain that I'd made for her – and I'd pray to God to keep her safe.

"Barbara, Barbara…"

I jumped with a start. It was the nurse, she was standing behind me.

"Barbara, your medication."

I opened my eyes and realised I was facing the wall. My face just centimetres away from the cold, painted plaster. I shuddered. I was slowly becoming a zombie like the other girls. I turned around, swallowed my medication and returned to face the wall. It had become my comfort zone – a place I could go to when I needed to feel safe. Unlike people, the wall couldn't hurt me. It couldn't ask questions or say anything to upset me. It was just a wall – cold and unfeeling, like everyone in here.

They're trying to break you, a voice whispered inside my head.

Fear had ruled everyone inside the hospital, and I was sick of feeling frightened. I even wondered if I'd been put inside Aston Hall to stop my mother from finding me.

Yes, I convinced myself. *That's why she hadn't been to see me – she couldn't find me.*

I had Christine, but I didn't trust anyone else, so I continued to stare at the wall. At least that way I wouldn't have to protect myself. I wouldn't have to lie or cover up the fact that I was still a virgin. I wouldn't have to do any of these things because the wall couldn't hurt me.

If your dad cared, then you wouldn't be in here. The treatment nurse's voice hissed inside my head.

What are you? You're nothing but a dirty tinker. Dad's voice boomed. Soon, it'd begun to chime in time with the nurse's voice, until I couldn't escape. I clamped both hands against my ears to try and stop the voices, but they were there – trapped inside my head. Tears pricked at the back of my eyes, but I shook my head, willing them to go away. My throat closed as though it was trying to choke me. I heard Jane's voice as she brushed past, dancing and twirling away to herself. A shiver ran down my spine as I pictured myself trapped inside the hospital forever.

One day, I'll be old, like Jane, I thought. *Maybe I'll grow old in here like her? Maybe I'll never see the outside world again. Had Jane only been a child when she'd first come here? Maybe that's why she dressed and acted as though she's still a little girl because in her head she was one.*

I wondered why she never got picked out for treatment.

Maybe she's too old?

The thoughts continued to swirl around inside my mind as the count continued.

32, 33, 34…

"Sit down, Barbara. Are you alright?" Christine asked, resting a hand against the top of my arm.

But I didn't move. I didn't want to. I continued to stare at the wall. I pictured being held down on a table, my hair shaved at the sides and two wet sponges planted against both temples. I pictured the evil treatment nurse flicking a switch with her finger, and my body convulsing as electricity pulsed through me.

"Come on, Barbara," Christine coaxed, trying to move me away.

I was just about to shift when I spotted something. A shadow had appeared as Jane passed behind me. The shadow of her outstretched arm had merged with my own.

She was in my space. I couldn't even have my own space!

A rage boiled up inside me. I felt it shooting through every vein in my body, from the tips of my toes to the hair follicles nestling on top of my scalp. I wanted to scream, punch and shout, but I didn't have an ounce of energy. I was ready to explode. But someone had thrown a thick heavy bomb-proof blanket across my anger – a numbness. I shifted away from Christine, dipped forward and rested my forehead against the cool wall. I needed space to think – to think of Mum. At least in my dreams no one could take her away from me. In some ways, I craved more medication just so I could shut off and live alone – alone in my dreams. I opened my eyes but the wall had gone. Instead, I was sitting at the dining table with everyone else. Christine held my hand and I felt her give it a reassuring squeeze. I knew she was trying to make me feel better, but nothing or no one could. I glanced down and saw that I had a fork in my hand. I was shovelling food into my mouth, but I couldn't taste it and I didn't want to eat because I had no appetite, only a burning desire to escape. Christine's mouth was moving. She was saying something, but I couldn't make out the words. Her voice sounded warped and distorted by distance and time as though she was calling to me through a very long tunnel.

"Are you alright?" a voice asked, slicing through my fog of medication.

It was the cutlery nurse. I didn't answer because I knew it'd take too much effort. Instead, I remained silent. Time continued to shift, blur and melt into one long moment without natural pauses. I opened my eyes and found myself outside in the corridor. The nurse was holding me – propping me up – her hand under my arm, helping me upstairs to the dormitory. She guided me to bed number one – my bed. I sat down on it but had no energy or interest in wanting to move. The nurse noticed and helped me undress. As she did, she spotted the sanitary towel sticking out of the top of my knickers.

"I'll go and get you a clean one," she said as she whipped my nightdress over my head and covered my body.

Moments later, she'd reappeared with a fresh sanitary towel before pulling the other one out of my knickers, but she seemed confused.

"Why are you wearing this, Barbara?" she asked waving it about in front of me accusingly. "You don't need it."

I stared at her blankly, numbed and unable to speak. Inside my head, the voice answers for me.

I haven't started my periods, yet. It screams. *I was bleeding earlier because someone did something to me, but no one will tell me what.*

But I don't say any of these words. I don't say anything, but sit and watch as she pulls back my bed covers.

"Hop in," she says breezily.

Her face clouds over, and I know she has seen it – the blood on my bedsheets. She seems baffled. I'm bleeding, but I'm not. Unsure what to do, she pulls the top bedsheet over the soiled one to try and cover it up.

"I've got a headache…" I mumble as I climb into bed.

"Alright, I'll go and fetch you some painkillers."

Time shortens again, and she's back by my bedside almost immediately, only now she has a second nurse with her. The first one hands me two tablets and a tumbler of water.

"Sit up," she says.

I do as she says, but then she asks me to get out and stand up. I turn to see both nurses inspecting the blood on my sheet. They look at it and then at one another. But no one speaks. The second nurse looks at me.

"Have you cut yourself?"

I don't say a word, but the first nurse answers for me.

"No, I checked her when I undressed her."

They order me to climb back in bed, so I do. I turn onto my side and look out of the window at the big chimneys protruding from the distant landscape. Within minutes, I'm asleep. I dream of my mother. She's holding my hand as we fly through the air like Peter Pan and Wendy. We fly high up into the sky, clearing the tall chimneys, but suddenly the chimney pots snag against our nightdresses. I panic because we can't clear them. We're trapped. I'm trapped. Suddenly my mother vanishes and I'm all alone. I'm alone and terrified that I'll be trapped inside the hospital forever.

Chapter 18

Fighting Back

I'd been at Aston Hall for five months and had slowly begun to adapt to the daily routine. Girls came and went, but I didn't bother getting to know them because as soon as I did, they upped and left. The only constants in my life were Christine, the cutlery count and my daily medication. I found school easy, but all I'd learned was how to look after disabled children and take them to the toilet. We did simple maths, a bit of English and art, but that was it. Every day, I returned to Laburnum Ward for my medication and lunch.

I underwent another treatment at the end of April, but this time, I'd given up, so I didn't fight the nurse when she'd started to inject me. As Milner had walked into the room, I waited for the chemical to take me and send me to sleep – away from him and that oppressive little room. The mouse had seemed to have vanished, because I no longer heard him squeak. I'd hoped and prayed that he'd gone on a journey to get help, not just for me, but for all the children.

Dad hadn't been to see me in ages, and I wondered if I'd ever see him again. The only way I managed to cope was to convince myself that the treatment nurse was right – he didn't care. In turn, this fuelled my desire to seek out my mother. But I'd learned to have patience – the drugs had taught me that. I'd learned how to tolerate Jane and her incessant dancing and even allowed her to teach me some basic routines.

"That's right." She smiled, tapping across the room. "Just follow me."

I did it because I needed to break up the monotony of the daily grind. Soon, it was May Day Bank Holiday, and the nurses told us that maypole dancers would be performing in the village. Jane was beyond excitement.

"I hope they'll let me dance with them," she sighed wistfully, clutching her hands against her chest. "I was a famous dancer, you know. I danced all over the world…"

Her voice continued to drone on in the background as everyone listened to the nurse.

"So you'll all be going into the village to watch the dancers, and, as long as you're good, we'll take you to the shop so that you can buy something for yourselves."

Someone squealed as excitement gripped the room. The girls organised themselves in three different groups.

"You'll come with me, won't you?" Christine asked, linking her arm through mine.

"Of course." I grinned. I couldn't believe it. This would be my first time back out in the real world since Dad had come to visit.

I remembered the money he'd given me that was hidden in my bedside cabinet.

"Don't worry," I whispered to Christine. "I've got enough money for both of us to spend."

It was a lovely, bright and sunny day when we left the hospital. We walked in groups of twos, as I linked arms with my best friend. It only took about ten minutes to walk there. We laughed when we saw the maypole dancers because the men were dressed in skirts, holding ribbons as the music played. We covered our mouths and began to snigger until soon we couldn't stop the tears from streaming down our faces.

"Don't Barbara," Christine laughed, clutching her sides.

"What?"

"Stop it! You keep making me laugh."

I wasn't sure what I could buy with the money because everything had changed. Decimalisation had been introduced, and I didn't understand any of it. I held out the old brown pennies in my hand. None of it seemed to relate to the prices on the sweets.

"It's okay, Duck," the shop assistant said in a broad Derbyshire accent. "We still take old money here."

I wasn't sure what I should buy, so I picked out lots of chewy sweets because I figured they'd last longer. As we walked, I considered whether or not to make a bolt for it. The nurses had seemed preoccupied because there were so many girls to watch. I thought better of it. I'd not had treatment for over a week, and I didn't want to be punished. I knew that if I ran then I'd end up having electric shock treatment. I just couldn't risk it. We left the hospital after lunch, around one o'clock, and stayed in the village for an hour. All too soon it was time to return. My heart sank as we approached Aston Hall, but I'd had a brilliant day – the best day since I'd arrived at the hospital. Although we were soon inside, the atmosphere was joyful and everyone was buoyant from a good day out. It was also a Bank Holiday Monday, so we knew that Dr Milner wouldn't be coming. We filed back inside the communal room, and, as the nurse locked the door, Jane began to dance across the room. The day had lifted everyone's spirits, but particularly Jane's. For once, no one minded if she sang and danced. No one cared, because we were happy. One of the nurses walked over to the fire escape, at the back of the room. It was usually kept closed, but today it was open.

"You can sit outside if you want, girls," the nurse said.

Christine and I looked at one another in astonishment and scrambled excitedly to our feet.

This was the best day ever!

It felt lovely to sit outside and feel the sun on our faces. We found a patch of grass, lay down and spread out. It was wonderful to smell and feel fresh grass beneath my skin instead of the cold rubber mattress. My heart had felt light, like a bird set free from its cage.

"I wonder why we've been allowed outside," I remarked, as I scoured the grass for daisies to make a chain with.

"Dunno," Christine said, shrugging her shoulders. "But it's a bit odd, don't you think?"

"What?"

"Well, first they let us go into the village to watch the maypole dancers, and now this."

I ran my nail across the stem of a daisy and split it apart so I could thread another one through.

"Suppose," I replied concentrating on my flower. "But I'm not complaining."

Christine smiled.

"Me neither," she said covering her eyes against the sunlight.

It'd been such a lovely and unexpected day, but Christine was right. There was something odd about it.

We were given our medication, and the cutlery count began as usual. Soon, it'd been laid out and our dinner served. I was halfway through eating mine when I spotted something strange.

"Look at that." I nudged Christine with my elbow.

"What?"

"Flowers, over there," I said, gesturing with my eyes towards the window.

She followed my gaze and her mouth fell open.

"I've never seen flowers here before," she whispered.

Something definitely wasn't right.

We'd finished our dinner and all the plates had been cleared away when we heard the sound of car engines outside. Everyone shifted in their seats to try and look out of the window. Someone gasped as Dr Milner's car parked outside. I knew he couldn't have come to do a treatment because we'd just eaten, and he'd never let us eat beforehand.

"Why's he here on a Bank Holiday Monday?" a girl whispered across the table.

But no one knew.

Everyone started to get a little jittery, until five minutes later, when two large, posh-looking black vehicles pulled up alongside Dr Milner's car. Everyone craned their necks to see who it was. I lifted up from my seat to see four or five men and two women climbing out of both cars.

"Who do you think they are?" someone asked, but I didn't answer because I could see the nurses out of the corner of my eye. They were all busy, straightening their hats and smoothing out their uniforms to try and look smarter.

I watched as the group walked towards the main door. They looked very grand indeed. Moments later, a nurse opened the door, smiled warmly and welcomed them inside.

But who were they, and what had they come for?

Dr Milner came in first, followed by the rest of the group. We looked over at him in startled horror because he never came into our room; he only ever looked inside it to choose his next victim.

"Carry on, girls," he smiled with a wave of his hand as though he did it every day. "Don't let us disturb you."

He remained there, standing in the doorway, smiling and chatting to the visitors, who seemed very important. I glanced over at the two women. They were dressed in fancy clothes, with matching bags and shoes and beautiful diamante brooches on their lapels. It was obvious these weren't ordinary visitors – these were dignitaries. Whoever they were, Dr Milner seemed desperate to impress them. I couldn't hear what he was saying, but every so often, he'd throw back his head and laugh as though someone had said something hilarious. But through his sheer presence alone, he'd brought fear into the room. I didn't care that it was a sunny day outside or that the fire escape door was open, none of that mattered because Milner was here in *our* room, in *our* space, and he was laughing and joking away. He was making small talk as though we were all part of one happy family. No one moved because he was here. Instead, we all froze, watching and waiting for him to leave. As he did, he bade us a fond farewell with a cheery wave of his hand.

"Carry on, girls." He smiled like a friendly, trusted headmaster.

But no one smiled or waved back. We just watched as the group filtered out into the corridor and Milner signalled over at one of the nurses to lock the door after him. In less than a second, the smile had slipped from his face and he was back to normal. The door closed and he was gone. It was only then that the room let out a collective sigh of relief.

The following days returned to normal, passing by in a blur of routine, cutlery counting, and Jane singing and dancing. Although it had started out as any ordinary day, 10 May 1971 had left me uneasy. I couldn't explain or put my finger on it, I just sensed something in the air.

I left for school with Frank in the morning as normal, but as soon as we returned later that afternoon and I spotted the window of the treatment room I knew it would be me who'd be chosen. Sure enough, straight after medication, my name was called. In fact, I was called before Milner had even arrived in his car. It was almost as though he'd asked for me especially. With my heart beating ten to the dozen, a nurse led me to the bathroom to be washed, weighed and placed in the horrible grey gown. Then I was taken to the side room.

"We're waiting for Dr Milner," she said as she closed the door and left me sitting in the darkened room. I felt the cold rubber mattress as it stuck against the bare cheeks of my bum. I tried to shift. As I did, I thought I heard a noise. I thought of my friend, the little mouse who lived in the skirting board. I'd already given him a name – Marmaduke.

"Hello, is that you?" I called out into the darkness.

I listened so hard that my ears hurt.

"Marmaduke, are you here?"

But the room was silent.

"Please be here. Please be here for me, Marmaduke," I whispered. I was afraid to be alone.

I decided to lie down on the mattress. I discovered that if I folded my legs up inside the gown then my skin wouldn't touch the cold rubber. It made me feel a little better, but I cursed the nurse for leaving the shutters closed. Even if she'd opened them a bit then perhaps I wouldn't feel so afraid. My senses remained on high alert as I listened out for Milner, the squeak of the trolley or the squeak of Marmaduke.

"Are you here, Marmaduke?" I whispered again, willing him to give me a sign.

I was so busy listening out for noises that I was unable to sleep. The room was freezing, so I pulled both arms inside the gown and held them against my chest to try and keep them warm. I didn't have a blanket, just a cold rubber mattress. A short time later, I was still listening when I heard the squeak of the hospital trolley. I pictured the treatment nurse with her severe face and cold heart, pushing it closer to the room. I hated that nurse and prayed it wouldn't be her that gave me my injection. There was the scraping of a key in the lock as the door opened and she stood there, her shadow lit from behind by the light in the corridor. It was the horrible treatment nurse. Although I despised her, I had a plan. Her comments about Mum had upset me so much that I'd worked out how to get my own back. As she wheeled in the trolley, I sat up on the bed. I spotted the kidney-shaped dish with the needle in it. I longed to stick the needle in her to see if she liked it. I'd even considered it, but the fear of electric shock treatment stopped me. I watched as she went through the motions and unravelled the grey-white bandage in her hand.

"Oh, it's you," she said as though we were in a completely normal situation. "I've done you a few times before, haven't I? What's the name now?" She said as she looked down at a piece of paper on the trolley. "Yes, that's right, you're Barbara. Now, you know what's going to happen."

She held the bandage, ready to tie my hands together.

"That's it, right arm over left."

I did as she said and took a deep breath for courage as she approached and began to bind my wrists together. I looked at her close up. She looked older than I'd remembered. It was the bitterness – it was etched across her face. I hated her with a passion and I wanted her to know. I was ready. I cleared my throat before I lost my nerve. The sound made her look up.

"Do you have a daughter?" I asked.

"That's none of your business," she snapped, trying to focus on the bandage.

"Well, I have a mother, and everyone says she's bad, but I don't know her."

The nurse glanced up, wondering what was coming next.

"Yes, I don't know her, but I know for sure that she would never be as bad as you, and do to children what you do."

The bandage tightened against my skin as she pulled it hard and glared back. I wanted to cry out but didn't want to give her the satisfaction.

"Do it as tight as you like," I said defiantly. "You're not going to make me cry."

The nurse smirked back.

"Your ankles are next."

I gulped, but I didn't want to show weakness.

"That's fine. Do what you want, I don't care anymore."

"Is that right?" she said, raising her eyebrows in mock surprise.

"Yes."

She told me to lie down and pump my fist to bring up a vein, but I wondered why she'd not tied my ankles together.

Maybe she'd changed her mind?

I watched as she prepared the injection. She mixed a small sachet of powder with some saline solution. Then she drew the newly mixed solution up into the needle and gave it a couple of taps with her finger to rid it of air bubbles. She put the needle in the dish and rubbed a finger against a vein in my arm. As the needle pierced my skin, the nurse applied more pressure than necessary to cause more pain. Within minutes I was a statue, unable to move. My eyes followed her and the trolley as she left the room. Seconds later, another figure appeared. It was Milner. He placed his three cushions on the floor next to the mattress. I felt something sharp against my face – the wire mask. There was a trickle of liquid, coldness and the familiar smell.

Drip, drip, drip.

The room went black and my mind blank as I drifted away and under. I don't remember how long I was out for, because I had no recollection of waking up to Milner's questions. I didn't believe it was possible to dream in such a state, but I was aware what was happening, if only from snatches of different sensations and a numbed sense of my surroundings. My mind felt as if it'd been removed from my body. When I finally came to I felt the sensation of being carried in someone's arms. I was lifted from the mattress and taken from the room.

At last, it's over. I can go back to my bed, I thought.

But it wasn't. Instead of the usual smells and sounds of the dormitory, I was carried outside. I felt something over my face, and I blinked as I felt my eyelashes brush against the surface of something – a white sheet. I'd been draped in a sheet and now I was being taken somewhere.

Oh God, the black van! I panicked even though I couldn't do a thing about it.

I'm not dead, I reasoned, *because I can feel the hotness of my breath, billowing back and warming my skin, underneath the sheet in the cold night air.*

I decided it was safer to play dead. There's the sound of a car door opening.

It is the black van!

I was lying across the padded leather seat of a car as I tried to peer through the sheet, but it was impossible. Instead, I listened out for voices and heard Milner's voice. The leather of the car seat stuck against my naked skin.

Where am I going? What's Milner going to do with me?

Suddenly, a hand lifted the blanket but too quickly for me to see who it belonged to. The wire mask pressed hard against my face.

Drip, drip, drip.

I slipped under once more, and drifted in and out of consciousness. As my body shifted around, I realised that I was on the back seat of a car, and the car had started moving.

Where's Milner? Is he driving? Is it his car?

The motion of the car continued to rock me as the sheet lifted again.

Drip, drip, drip.

The rest of the journey passed by in a blur. I'm drugged again and again. I have a vague memory of a mansion – the one I'd passed on my first day here.

Someone had taken me to that mansion, but why? More importantly, what had they done to me there that they couldn't do in a hospital?

The room was dark as I lifted myself up and gasped for air. Fresh air, air without the stench of the chemical. I sense that I'm not in the treatment room because it doesn't smell. I've been taken somewhere different.

You're in the mansion, a voice inside my head whispered.

I tried to focus, but I was confronted with the mask.

Drip, drip, drip.

Milner's voice flooded the room as the questions began once more.

"Have you got your period?"

Normally, I found it impossible to lie, but somehow I did.

"Yes," I whispered.

But I hadn't. It was a fib, and it was also the last conversation I had with Dr Milner.

When I came around I was back in my bed inside the hospital dormitory. As always, I was alone. I looked down and sighed. There was a pool of blood on my bedsheet and I was lying in it. Milner had made me bleed again. I hadn't started my period, but whatever it was that he'd done to me, it was enough to make me bleed.

Many years later, I discovered that a social worker had been to visit me on 12th May, and, although I'd been given treatment on both 10th and 11th May, there's no mention of it in her report. Instead, she later noted I'd been 'sick in bed' when she'd called, and that she'd seen me on the ward. Although she hadn't questioned what was wrong with me, she concluded that I 'seemed calmer and more controlled'. I was neither. I'd spent 48 hours drugged up by Milner. If only that social worker had probed a little deeper, then maybe I and hundreds of others – both boys and girls – wouldn't have had to suffer.

Chapter 19

Telling Someone

The next couple of months passed by in a dreary routine, until soon it was August. I was told my father would be coming to take me home for the weekend. I could barely believe it – a whole weekend away from Aston Hall. I waited by the window and watched as Dad pulled up in his van. This time, he wasn't late.

"Bye then," I said, hugging Christine. "And I'll go to the paper shop and bring you back a copy of *Bunty*."

"Promise?"

"Promise."

I felt it was the very least I could do after the friendship she'd shown me.

I was excited as I climbed into the back of the van and waved goodbye to my friend. She lifted a hand, crossed two fingers and waved back.

Dad's van reversed, turned and began to pull away. As we drove slowly along the tarmac drive, I spotted the treatment nurse walking towards us.

"Dad, please stop," I begged.

"Why?"

"I want to say goodbye to the treatment nurse."

Dad smiled and, thinking she was a friend, pulled up alongside her. The nurse stopped dead in her tracks and looked over at me as I turned the handle and opened the side window.

"Goodbye, nurse!" I said, waving manically. "I'm going home for the weekend with my DAD," I said, emphasising the last bit.

He was shocked, as though he wasn't quite sure what he should do or say.

"Dad, this is the nurse who puts needles in me and ties my hands and feet together."

My father's face looked shocked as he glanced from me to the nurse. But she didn't say a word – she didn't have to – the guilt was written all over her face. Instead, she turned and walked away. I expected him to ask me more, but his mood changed.

"Don't say a word. I don't want to hear it."

I knew I'd embarrassed him, but it seemed a small price to pay for getting my own back on the nurse. The rest of the journey continued in silence, apart from the radio blaring away in the background. I could tell that Dad was annoyed. He thought I'd shown him up, but all I'd done was tell the truth. I was determined I'd use the weekend to convince him that I wasn't lying and that those terrible things really did go on at the hospital. He flicked the van indicator and pulled in at a transport cafe.

"I need a cup of tea," he said by way of explanation.

He returned to the table with a mug of tea and a knicker-bocker glory for me. I grinned as I plunged the long, silver spoon in so I could scoop up a last bit of every flavour. It tasted heavenly. I was so busy lapping up my ice cream that I didn't notice Dad fidgeting in his seat, clasping the hot mug of tea in both hands.

"Listen, Barbara," he began.

I swallowed my mouthful and put down my spoon; he looked serious.

"I don't want you to tell anyone else about the hospital. Don't mention it to anyone else, do you understand?"

I licked the ice cream from my lips, but said nothing.

"If you do, I'll not be bringing you home for weekends. Understand?"

I nodded glumly.

"But why?" I asked. "Christine's my friend; won't I be allowed to talk about her?"

He shook his head.

"Listen, you tell anyone who asks that you're in boarding school. That's it, boarding school. Do you understand, Barbara?"

I looked down at the table and blinked hard. I realised that he was ashamed of me and the fact I was in Aston Hall.

"I can take you back there at any second if you start to play up."

The words had put the fear of God into me.

"I won't mention it. I won't tell anyone…" I promised. But I couldn't help myself, and soon the truth had come spilling out. "…but they have been injecting me… in a room. It's like a cell, Dad."

He sighed and shook his head in despair.

"But I don't have any reason to run away now, please believe me, Dad."

He glared as though he was beginning to lose all patience with me.

"Come on," he said abruptly. "Let's get going."

I hurriedly scooped up as much dessert as I could fit in my mouth. It had been so long since I'd had a treat and I didn't want to leave any of it.

As soon as we climbed back in the van, I could sense an atmosphere. Dad sat staring at the steering wheel. He was gripping it so tightly that his knuckles flashed white. For a moment he was silent and then he turned to me.

"You're a liar. And do you know how I know you're lying? I never signed no consent forms, so your lies will have to stop. You hear?"

I nodded, but I was only 12, and I didn't know what a consent form was.

"Dad, what's a consent form?" I asked. I didn't want to make him angry, but I really wanted to know.

"It's a green form, but I never signed one, so less of the lies."

"I'm not lying," I whispered, but it was too late – I knew he didn't believe me.

"Just don't mention that place to anyone."

"Alright."

"It's bad enough you being a tinker, but in a mental hospital as well?" He sighed, as he twisted the key and started up the engine. "You'll make a holy show of me."

The van spluttered and soon we were back on the road. I wanted to keep on his good side because I didn't want to be taken back to the hospital.

"Janice is at home," Dad said, changing the subject. "She's cooking us a nice supper, but don't you go saying anything to her."

"Yes, Dad."

"She's going to be your new mum from now on, so you better be showing her some respect."

"Yes, Dad."

I stared out of the window. I didn't want him to see my face because I didn't want a new mum, I wanted my real one.

My father had moved into a high-rise tower block, but I couldn't get over how tidy his flat was. *Janice was a good influence*, I thought as he took my coat and hung it up.

"Come on," he said, hurrying me along the hallway. "Janice is cooking in the kitchen."

She was busy straining potatoes as we walked in.

"Hi, Barbara." She smiled.

"Hello, Janice."

I liked Janice, because deep down I knew she was a kind person, but her life was worlds apart from mine. She had a son, called Martin, who went to boarding school. I think that's where Dad had got the idea from.

"How's school?" she asked, carrying two full plates of food into the front room for us.

I glanced over warily at my father.

"Yes, it's good, thank you," I said, taking the plate from her.

As I tucked into my food, I could've sworn that I could hear the distant counting of the cutlery nurse.

The room was almost too quiet to eat.

After dinner, Janice disappeared off into the kitchen to do her hair. She was getting ready for an evening out with Dad, so I sat and passed her the rollers. Every so often, she'd tut as a loose strand became uncurled and had to be wrestled back into place. She did a full head of hair with only a small, frameless mirror balanced precariously on her lap. The television was on in the front room, blaring away to itself. To the outside world, we looked every bit the normal family, when in truth we were three strangers sitting in one room. I watched Janice as she pulled out a cigarette from a silver case, perched it in her heavily lip-sticked mouth, and lit it. Dad had always hated people smoking and I wondered what he thought of Janice's habit.

"You can put some records on, if you like?" Janice suggested.

I looked over at Dad. He was busy combing his hair in the mirror, but he nodded to let me know it was alright. I wandered over towards the back of his chair where he kept the record player and turned it on. I half-expected a nurse to drag me away and when nothing happened, I breathed a sigh of relief. I'd felt honoured to be allowed to complete such a mundane task. The sound of Elvis Presley's voice filled the room so I began to tap dance and twirl my hands around in the air, just as Jane had taught me.

"What are you doing?" Dad asked a little bewildered.

"I'm dancing, like Jane does," I said without thinking.

"Who's Jane?" Janice butted in.

"Oh she's a dancer. She's danced all over the country, even the Royal Albert Hall."

The words tumbled out of my mouth before I'd even realised what I'd said. Dad didn't look happy.

"Right, that's it. I'm getting my shirt on and we're going to a party." He leaned over to give Janice a peck on the cheek. "Barbara, you clear up those plates, wash and dry them."

I stopped dancing and did as he asked. I knew he'd only said it to get me out of the room.

I didn't mention Aston Hall, I thought as I scrubbed the dishes. *Only the people there.*

Janice changed the record to an Elvis LP and soon 'Are you Lonesome Tonight', filtered through to the kitchen. I was lost in my thoughts when my father appeared at my shoulder.

"You never mention anything about that place," he whispered. "You never mention those mental defectives again, understand?"

"Yes, Dad."

He leaned in closer.

"You're going back on Sunday, but I can take you back any time."

It was the last thing I wanted. Not long afterwards, they left and I was all alone. I felt exhausted from the journey, and the come-down from the medication. Yawning, I lay down on the sofa and fell asleep. When I awoke, it was the following morning. Someone had covered me with a blanket, and Dad and Janice were asleep upstairs in bed. I got up and turned on the television. Not long afterwards, Dad came into the room, scratching his head.

"We're going to town to do some shopping," he told me.

I only had one change of clothes in my carrier bag, but I rushed off to the bathroom to get dressed. As I came out of the bathroom, I bumped into Janice. She was wearing a flimsy baby doll nightie.

"Morning, Barbara. Are you looking forward to going into town?"

"Yes." I grinned.

The truth was, I could barely believe it. I was actually getting to do normal things like other little girls did. I went back downstairs and waited with Dad.

"Do you like Janice?" he asked.

I nodded.

"Good. You better show her some respect."

Once she was ready, the three of us piled into the van and headed into town. Dad was flashing his money in front of his new girlfriend, which suited me because it meant I could take advantage and get him to buy me lots of new things. I ended up with nearly a whole new wardrobe, and Janice played the part of my mum with aplomb. That afternoon, they disappeared to get ready to go out again. Although I'd be all alone again, I didn't mind because I had the television and record player to keep me company. Once they'd left I tried on all my new clothes and even helped myself to Janice's rollers and make-up. For once, I felt good about myself. Being back at Dad's felt like being on holiday – I had the freedom to do silly little things that other children took for granted such as watching whatever I wanted on TV and turning the record player on. There was a fire in the front room. It had two electric bars that heated up at the flick of a switch, which got me thinking. I'd be returning to the hospital the following day, so I decided that I needed to prepare myself. Dad had asked me to tidy up before he went out, so I'd started to pick up dirty cups and empty out Janice's ashtrays. I spotted the silver foils from packets of cigarettes she'd smoked and hit on a brilliant plan. I walked over to the fire and turned it on. I watched until the bars started to glow red, then I switched it off again. I took a sliver of silver paper from the fag box, twisted it between my fingers and stuck it between the grill so it made contact with the electric bar. I was determined to find out what electric shock treatment would feel like.

I needed to be prepared.

The metallic paper sparked as soon as it hit the bar and then it began to singe, leaving brown burn marks along the edge. I was disappointed because I'd not felt a thing. I needed more electricity and more paper.

I need to leave the fire on for longer next time.

I switched it back on, but this time I counted to 20, and turned it off just as the orange glow had begun to fade. Pushing the paper through, I felt a small spark of electricity but nothing else.

I need to make the paper thicker to get more power.

I searched for more empty cigarette boxes and pulled out all the silver paper I could find. Twisting it, I made the probe longer and thicker and rested it against the electric bar. A series of electric shocks soared through the paper and up along my arm. I held it for as long as I could stand before dropping it onto the floor.

Ouch! I winced; that had hurt.

Elvis had stopped singing, so I went to turn the LP over, and returned to the fire. I was holding the paper against the fire when I heard Dad's voice from the doorway.

"What the fuck are you doing?"

I turned to see him with Janice at his side. She was holding a shocked hand against her mouth.

"Answer me," Dad demanded.

I was mute with fear.

"Are you trying to set the whole place on fire, you mental defective?"

His words cut me through to the bone.

"Get up!" he roared.

I leaped up from the floor, dropping the silver paper as I did. Dad was raging and started to lecture me on how many people I could've killed if the fire had taken hold. I started to sob because I was worried he'd tell the hospital. If he did, I'd surely get electric shock treatment. I was crying so much, that his voice softened and he slumped down in his chair.

"God knows what they teach her in that place."

Janice stayed calm and tried to reason with me.

"Come on, Barbara. Tell us what you were doing and why?"

I looked at Dad and then at her. I was too frightened to tell them why I'd done it because it would mean I'd have to mention Aston Hall, and he wouldn't like that.

"Answer her!" Dad insisted. "Tell her what you were playing at."

I took a deep breath. My stomach turned over, making me feel sick with nerves.

It was now or never. This was it.

I looked up. They were both staring at me, waiting.

This was my chance to tell them once and for all.

But I was so scared that I thought I'd choke on my own tears.

"Come on," Janice coaxed, wrapping a gentle arm around my shoulder. "It's alright. Just tell us."

I looked at Dad as I blurted the words out.

"I did it because they're going to give us electric shock treatment."

"What the fuck…" he said, leaping to his feet. He flushed bright red. He was embarrassed – ashamed of me – even though I'd kept my word and hadn't mentioned the hospital once. Dad dipped forward to try and grab me, but I was fast.

"Stop it! Leave her alone," Janice said trying to calm the situation down.

My father stood back and composed himself as Janice took control.

"Now, let's see what else she has to say. That's not a normal thing for a child to say," she reasoned. "Tell me again, Barbara, what is it you're frightened of?"

Dad glared at me over her shoulder and grabbed his car keys off the sideboard.

"Get your bags. You're going back right now. And you're not coming out for weekends again. Do you know how many people you could've killed doing that?"

The car keys were jangling in his hand, but Janice grabbed them from him.

"You're driving nowhere with all that drink in you," she scolded.

He looked at her and then at me and realised he'd been defeated. In a huff, he slumped down heavily into his chair. I sidled up to Janice because I knew she was on my side.

"Right," she said, "let's get to the bottom of this. Now tell me again, Barbara, and tell me the truth. Why did you stick paper in the fire?"

"Because of the electric shock treatment," I whispered.

Janice sat down on the sofa in shock. She shook her head in disbelief as Dad stared hard at the floor.

"Barbara, where's your boarding school?"

This was it. I had to tell her. I had to tell them both what Milner had been doing to me and the other children.

I took a deep breath for courage and soon, the words had tumbled out into one long sentence without pause or breath.

"It's not a big, posh, boarding school. It's a hospital… and they're injecting me and giving me treatment… and putting a mask over my face and pouring a funny smelling liquid on it that knocks me out... but no one believes me... and I have to take medication all the time... and they strip me naked and put me in a room with a stupid gown on... and then Dr Milner lies down next to me... and I always bleed after treatment... but they do it to everyone, but not Jane..." I gasped, my voice finally trailing off.

I crouched on the sofa next to Janice, pulled my knees up against my chest, and began to sob uncontrollably. Although I was distraught, I also felt an utter sense of relief as though a big, heavy weight had been lifted from my shoulders. The silence in the room seemed to last for ages, and I was terrified what would happen next, especially when Milner had found out I'd told my father. It was a warm summer's night and the front door was open. A cool breeze drifted into the room, and for a moment I considered running out onto the balcony and jumping to my death. Anything had to be better than going back to the hospital.

I felt a hand against my shoulder. It was Janice.

"Everything's going to be alright," she promised, giving me a hug.

My tears had stuck my face against the plastic sofa. I tried to look at Dad because I thought he'd be angry with me, but he looked utterly broken.

"Right," Janice said, lighting up a cigarette. "What's this all about, Barbara? Tell us everything about this electric shock treatment."

Suddenly, I'd lost my nerve. I didn't want to make things any worse for myself or go back to the hospital, so I said nothing.

"Don't be scared," she said. "Your dad's not angry, are you?"

I looked over at him and I was shocked – shocked, because for the first time in his life Dad was crying.

Chapter 20

Escaping the Terror

"They gave me treatment," I said, my voice barely a whisper as I looked over at Janice.

Her brow furrowed.

"Repeat that, Barbara."

I repeated everything I'd said earlier about the treatment, the mask with the dripping liquid, the injections and Dr Milner. I even repeated the bit about me bleeding after treatment.

"She's a liar," Dad said, interrupting me. "She's always lying."

But Janice wasn't convinced. She rested her back against the sofa, took another long drag of her cigarette and considered me.

"Well, if my kid was coming out with stories like that I think I'd be checking it out."

"But I never signed any consent forms," my father tried to reason. "So she must be lying."

For some reason, Janice believed me and stuck to her guns.

"How would a kid this age know anything about ether and injections?"

My father sat up and thought for a moment.

"You're right, but she could have read about it in a book."

Janice blew out a huge lungful of smoke and tutted.

"Come off it! I wouldn't send her back until I'd checked it all out," she said, her face deadly serious. She picked up her handbag, pulled out her purse and took some money from it. "Barbara, be a good girl and nip over to the shop to get me some fags. Here's some money for going," she said, slipping a little extra into my hand.

I didn't need asking twice. I also knew what the extra money meant – it meant take your time. I felt cold, chilled by the shock of it all, so I pulled on my cardigan and headed out of the flat. I hoped by the time I returned that Janice would have persuaded Dad I was telling the truth and I wouldn't have to return to that hellhole of a hospital ever again. I pressed the button and waited for the lift to come, but I didn't feel well. My hands began to shake and cold beads of sweat collected along my forehead. The lift pinged, so I stepped in and pressed the button for the ground floor. My head was racing along with my heart.

Was fear doing this to me?

I stepped out of the lift and walked out of the block of flats. There was a wall in front of me, so I sat on it. I felt strange, as though I wouldn't be able to make the few yards walk to the shop. I was desperately trying to breathe in fresh air because I felt as though I was going to pass out at any moment, but I was too frightened to stand in case my legs gave way. An old lady passed with a shopping trolley stuffed full of newspapers. I recognised her immediately, it was Mrs Watson.

"Hello, Barbara." She smiled.

But I didn't feel well enough to even answer. Mrs Watson stopped in her tracks and came over.

"Are you alright, Barbara? It's just that you don't look very well."

"I… I… I… just feel a bit…" but as I jumped off the wall I lost my balance, so Mrs Watson had to catch me.

"Come on," she insisted. "I'm getting you home."

She knocked hard on the half-open door of Dad's flat.

"Hello, is anyone in? I've got Barbara with me… and she's not very well."

I put out my hand and pushed the door before almost falling in through it. Janice had heard the commotion and came running.

"She's not well," Mrs Watson told her.

Janice took me and laid me down on the sofa.

"Oh my God," she gasped, "she's burning a temperature."

"That child needs a doctor," Mrs Watson said, butting in.

I physically flinched at the word 'doctor'.

Dad had also seemed concerned.

"Are you alright?" he asked, staring down at me.

By now, my arms were shaking and I had terrible pains in my stomach.

Janice nipped through to the kitchen and returned with a glass of orange cordial.

"Here," she said, placing it on the coffee table, right next to me.

By now my temperature was so high that I felt chilled and couldn't stop shaking.

"She must have the flu or something. She's as white as a ghost," Janice fretted.

I don't know if I passed out or fell asleep, but when I awoke hours later I felt dreadful. I tried to lift the glass from the table but my vision was fuzzy and my hands were shaking so much that I couldn't match it to my mouth. In the end, I gave up.

"Are you alright, Barbara?" I could hear Dad, but I couldn't see him because everything was blurred.

My head was pounding as though I'd just had treatment, and then I realised – I'd not had my medication for a couple of days. I heard Janice and Dad's voices in the distance, but they sounded distorted and removed as though they were calling to me from the top of a mountain. I tried to open my eyes again, but the light was blinding, so I shut them again. I didn't realise it, but I was having my first cluster migraine attack – something I'd suffer with for the rest of my life.

Sunday was a complete blur, and by the time I fully came around I discovered it was Monday. I still felt groggy, but better than I had been. My father was sitting in his usual chair, but he'd washed and changed his clothes. He'd given up the oil rigs in favour of truck driving, and he was sitting there ready for work.

"How are you feeling? Are you alright?" he asked me.

I nodded but I didn't want to get up because I felt so weak.

Dad sat with me. A few hours later, I heard the whistle of the milkman and the chink of bottles as he delivered milk outside the door. It was eight o'clock. I looked over at Dad, my throat too dry to speak, and wondered what time he'd be taking me back to the hospital. I tried to reach the juice again but my arms felt too shaky. My father had noticed and got up and gently tipped the glass towards my lips. Then he helped me sit up. I retched as though I was going to be sick, so he ran out to fetch a mop and bucket, opening up the front door to let some fresh air circulate into the room.

I was violently sick but he cleaned it up, before taking the mop and bucket away.

"Come on," he said gently. "You lie back down."

I did as he said. The cool air wafting over me made me feel a little better as I drifted off to sleep once more. When I woke hours later, my father had gone but Janice was sitting there holding the phone in her hand. As I came to, she put the telephone receiver back in its cradle.

"Are you feeling any better?"

I nodded. "Where's Dad?"

"He'll be back soon. He's just gone to the Social Services office. Now, come on, get up, love. You've been on that sofa for three days. Let's get you washed and dressed. Do you feel up to that?"

I didn't, but I didn't want to upset her because she'd been so kind to me. I went into the bathroom and used a flannel to wash, and then I dressed myself.

"Better?" she asked as I walked out into the hallway.

I nodded, because I didn't feel much like talking. I sat down on the sofa as Janice brought me a plate of toast and cup of tea. But she didn't leave; instead she sat down and held my hand.

"Barbara, I worked in a hospital for a very long time. Did they give you tablets or anything in that place?"

"Yes, they did. They gave me a lot," I replied, my voice a hoarse whisper.

I grabbed the tea and tried to steady the cup by wrapping both hands around it. I was still a bit shaky and I was worried I'd spill tea everywhere and make her angry. But she wasn't, she was far from it. A short while later, the front door closed and Dad came into the room.

"Oh, you look better." He smiled.

I immediately felt better for seeing him. He pulled a piece of paper from the inside pocket of his jacket, sat down and began to dial a number.

"I'm going to fix your hair up so it's pretty, would you like that?" Janice asked me, but I wasn't listening. I was too busy trying to eavesdrop on Dad's telephone conversation.

She continued to talk, drowning out my father's voice, until he finally put the phone down.

"Right, have you got your bags packed?" he asked.

I had. My bags were always packed. I didn't have much with me and everything I did have was inside a plastic bag.

"Yes, Dad," I replied in a small voice.

I could picture Aston Hall and the slow drive up the long tarmac drive. I felt numb with fear. I wanted to die.

"Good," he said, getting to his feet. "Because you're not going back to that hospital."

My heart skipped a beat.

Had he just said that? Had I heard correctly?

I knew I had. I immediately started to sob, until soon I couldn't stop myself.

"Why are you crying?" he asked a little puzzled. "Why, you don't want to go back there, do you?"

"No! No! No!" I gasped. "Thank you, Dad!" I said running over to hug him. "Thank you for getting me out of that place."

My heart suddenly felt light because I didn't have to go back there. I wouldn't be locked up in that horrible place or the treatment room by the wicked nurse. But best of all, I'd never have to see Dr Milner again.

Chapter 21

The Approved School

"Right," my father said, grabbing his van keys off the side. "I've got to go to work, so you stay with Janice and be good until we sort out where you're going next."

He came over and rubbed my head fondly. "You'll be alright." He smiled as he leaned forward and kissed Janice on the cheek.

"Be good now. See you later, Janice."

"I love you, Dad," I called.

I stayed in the flat for a week, but I continued to suffer the effects of drug withdrawal. Janice was lovely, and she bought me magazines, and chatted to me about fashion and make-up. But I felt sad for Christine, because I'd never got to say goodbye or give her the magazine I'd promised.

A few days later, a lady from Social Services rang.

"She wants to tell you something," Janice said handing me the phone.

"Hello."

"Is that Barbara?" the lady on the other end of the line asked.

"Yes."

"My name is Susan, and I'm calling to let you know that you're being transferred to Blackbrook House in St Helens. That'll be your new home from now on."

"New home?"

"Yes," Susan said. "It's an approved school for Roman Catholic girls. Anyway, someone will be along to pick you up in the morning."

My heart sank. I was on the move again.

"Do I have to go?" I asked Janice after I'd put the phone down.

"Yes, your dad has gone to an awful lot of trouble to get you transferred, so I don't think he'd be happy if you didn't go."

I understood that I couldn't stay here forever, and this Blackbrook House had to be better than the hospital.

Anything had to be better.

The following morning, I was collected as arranged. I didn't have the chance to say goodbye to Dad because he'd left for work, but I knew he'd come to see me at my new home. I was driven to St Helens in Lancashire by the social worker. The journey seemed to take forever and I must've fallen asleep because she had to wake me up.

"Barbara, we're here."

We turned into a long driveway, and I pressed my face against the window as we approached the largest house I'd ever seen. It was a grand red-brick building with huge cream pillars that held up the front entrance porch.

"Hello, I'm Sister Jenny," a nun said, stepping forward to greet us from the car.

She ushered us in through the big wooden door into a beautiful hallway. There were doors on both my left and right that led into different rooms. She beckoned us through the first door on the right, and sat down behind a huge mahogany desk in a grand office. She gestured with her hand for the social worker to also sit down, but there was only one chair so I remained standing.

"Alright, Barbara," Sister Jenny began. "I've heard a lot about you. Now are you going to promise me you are not going to run away from here?"

I looked over at her. She was a nun, and as a Catholic, I didn't dare lie to a nun. I thought about her question and tried to work out an answer. Deep down, I knew the moment I got my first chance, I'd be off down the road, looking for my real mother. I cleared my throat.

"Sister, all I can say is I promise to do my best not to run, but I can't promise I won't. I do promise my very best though."

A twitch appeared at the corner of her mouth as she tried her best not to laugh. I didn't understand what was funny.

"Well, Barbara, I like your honesty," she said, still smirking. "Do you think we can learn to trust one another? If I trust you, will you trust me?"

"I'll try, Sister."

"Now tell me. Why did you give me that answer – that you promise not to try and run away?"

I looked over at her.

"Because you're a nun, and I cannot lie to you. If I do, I'll get a black mark on my chest forever and then I'll never go to heaven."

Just then, another nun entered the room. She was there to show me around.

"Well, just you try your best," Sister Jenny smiled, "and I'm sure we'll get on famously."

My bedroom was on the right-hand side, off a long corridor. I was delighted to discover that I had a bedroom all to myself. The room just had a single bed, wardrobe, cabinet and sink in it, but it was all mine. I realised that Blackbrook House had so much more to offer than Aston Hall. As well as our usual lessons, we had cooking, sewing and typing classes. But best of all, there was no medication, no cutlery counting and no Milner. I soon settled in and made friends easily. At Blackbrook, I had so much more freedom, even though I was still technically locked in. But instead of drugs, we were 'treated' with prayers three times a day, mass, confession and Holy Communion. I hated the religious side with a passion, but it was better than the hospital. Sewing classes were my favourite, and soon I'd learned how to sew and cut my own patterns. I decided that I liked it there so much that I would try not to upset the nuns. In the back of my mind there was always the very real fear that I'd be sent back to Aston Hall, and I didn't want to risk it. At dinner time, the tables were laid out in a proper manner and we were trusted with our cutlery.

I was so happy that I soon became known as the joker of the school. Dad would telephone me every Wednesday, and we'd chat about what I'd been doing, so, unlike the hospital, there was always that to look forward to. At weekends, we were allowed home to see our parents, but I stayed at Blackbrook because Dad was often working. But I didn't mind because there was a kind priest there called Father Jones. He'd take us to the beach at Southport or to the park in St Helens, where we'd hire out small rowing boats for the day. Once, we were at the beach when Father Jones pulled out a camera and started taking photographs of me in my swimming costume. Although it was entirely innocent, it caused a lot of trouble. Not long afterwards, Father was in the convent talking to a lady, who it later turned out had been a social worker.

"Hello, Barbara," he called cheerily as I rushed past on my way to a lesson.

"Hello, Father," I said waving back and smiling. Without thinking, I blurted out something that had been on my mind. "Father, did you get the pictures you took of me at the beach back yet?"

The woman's face dropped as she turned from me to Father Jones. I knew instantly that I'd said something wrong, even if I didn't know what it was. The woman beckoned me over and took me to one side.

"Did Father Jones take your picture?" she asked.

I didn't answer, because if there'd been one thing I'd learned at the hospital it was the less you said, the better. Still, twenty minutes later, Sister Jenny summoned me to her office. I was terrified that I was being sent back to the hospital. Big frightened tears welled in my eyes as I waited to be called in. I finally walked into the room with both my arms poker straight down my sides and my heart pumping. Sister Jenny was sitting behind her desk wearing a black habit that'd been starched within an inch of its life.

"Hello, Barbara," she said.

My eyes darted over to the chair where the lady who'd asked me about Father Jones was sitting.

"Is this the girl?" she asked the lady.

She nodded.

I'm in real trouble now, I thought as I began to panic.

Thoughts of the treatment room, the mattress and the long needle flashed through my mind. I heard counting, the squeak of the treatment trolley and Jane tap dancing, as the treatment nurse's determined face loomed into view. My head felt light and my legs weak until they buckled underneath me and I fell to the floor. When I came around, I was being carried along on a canvas stretcher. My head began to throb and I blacked out again. When I finally opened my eyes, I was inside my room, but it was spinning. I felt weak, but somehow I climbed out of bed and tried to open the door. I tried the handle but it was locked. It sent me into a panic as I rushed to try and open the window, but it would only budge a fraction. By now, my anxiety was at fever point because I was certain I was about to receive treatment.

It was fight or flight.

I started to kick the door to try and open it, but it wouldn't move. Gripped with fear, I grabbed the bedside cabinet and began to hammer the door with it.

*I'm trapped. I'm all alone and he's coming. Milner's coming…
I have to get out of this room.*

The nuns heard the noise and came running, but they couldn't get inside because the smashed-up furniture was blocking the door. There was a side window panel, but it had a wire mesh running through it so it was impossible to break. I peered through, trying to work out which nun had the injection in her hand.

"Calm down, Barbara. Calm down," a voice called from the corridor. "We can talk about this."

But I didn't want to talk, I wanted to escape. I continued to smash everything up.

"You're only making things worse for yourself. Behave and calm down otherwise we won't put your Dad's call through to you on Wednesday."

It was enough of a threat to make me stop, and I fell onto the bed with exhaustion. The nuns asked me to move the furniture so they could get into the room.

"If you don't, then we'll have to call the police and take you back to Aston Hall."

I gasped and picked up a sharp piece of broken wood. My hands trembled as I held it aloft.

"If Milner comes near me I am going to kill him. I will put this stick of wood right through his throat, and I will kill him. I'll not stop until he's dead. And if any of you have an injection for me, you won't get it in me because I will kill you all," I screamed.

Suddenly, the voices went quiet. There was a pause, and then one nun spoke.

"Barbara, who is Milner and why do you think we'd inject you?"

I was silent.

Was it a trick?

"We wouldn't do that," she insisted. "We're not allowed to. Why, what other stories have the girls been telling you?"

"They're not stories," I cried. Angry tears streamed down my face. "It happens. Why, don't you give an injection before electric shock treatment?"

The nuns looked at me through the glass in bewilderment.

"No, we'd never do something like that."

"Yeah," I said, wiping my nose with the back of my sleeve. "I bet your mate the other nun, or Milner is out there ready with the mask for me. I'm not stupid."

The nun seemed baffled.

"Why don't you have a rest and we can talk and find out what's wrong."

She sounded so calm that I knew she was telling the truth. After all, nuns didn't lie. They asked me to unblock the door, but I desperately needed to lie down, which I did. A short while later when I'd woken up, I unblocked the entrance, but outside it was quiet. I waited until a young nun, called Sister Mary, came in to see me. She asked me why I'd destroyed my room and explained how privileged I was to have one all to myself. Within minutes, four other nuns entered the room. They grabbed my arms and legs, and I was carried along the corridor and put into a room with padded walls.

It was like the treatment room.

My heart pounded as I spotted a single mattress on the floor. I was stripped to my underwear, and then they checked my hair for slides or clips or anything I could use to hurt myself. The nuns left and closed the door, leaving me with just a single light in the middle of the ceiling.

This is it, I thought. *This is where Milner comes in. Please God, no more treatment*, I prayed.

I shivered because there was no blanket and I was freezing cold. Then the door opened and Sister Mary walked in holding a blanket.

"In an hour I'll bring you some food," she said.

I was starving hungry, but her words had made me feel better.

They wouldn't be giving me a blanket and food if Milner was on his way.

A little while later, I was allowed to go to the bathroom. I'd wanted to look down near the pipes to see if my friend the mouse was there, but Sister had insisted on keeping the door open so I wasn't able to look for him. Then I was led back to the padded room.

"How long will I be in here?" I asked Sister Mary as she handed me a jumper.

Sister Bridget answered for her.

"As long as it takes for you to behave yourself."

Even though they were nuns, I felt I couldn't trust a soul as I sat trapped in the padded room. I missed Christine so much and wondered how she was getting on. A short while later, Sister Mary appeared with tea and a plate of toast.

"Who's waiting outside?" I asked, eyeing both her and the food warily.

"No one," she said. "Well, Sister Margaret was there but she's gone to check on the others."

Anxiety twisted inside my stomach.

"Sister Mary, can I ask you something please?"

"It depends what it is."

My head throbbed so much that I just wanted to escape and leave the room, even if only for a short time.

"Can you get me a mask and drip liquid onto it? I just want to black out today so I can stop the pain in my head."

Sister Mary looked horrified.

"What would a young girl like you know about ether?"

Ether? Was that what the strange smelling liquid was called?

But I didn't reply because I was worried I'd make things worse for myself. And she never asked.

Sister Mary got up to leave but promised to bring me a book to read. She returned with a copy of *The Railway Children* – one of my favourites; I read it cover to cover.

The following morning, I was taken to get washed and dressed, and then I was allowed to go for breakfast. I was allowed back into my bedroom, only minus the bedroom cabinet that I'd smashed up. It took almost two months of living at Blackbrook before I realised that Dr Milner had no power over me anymore. I never forgot Christine. I even wrote to her, but I never heard back so I'm not sure if she ever received my letter. I continued to excel at school and everything was going well, until one afternoon during a history lesson Sister Jenny called me out of class. I immediately went into a blind panic.

What had I done wrong? Was Milner here?

As I stood up to follow her from the class, the other girls jeered.

"Ooo, someone's done something wrong."

It made me feel worse. Girls were never called out of class unless they were getting moved. My nerves were in tatters. Sister Jenny realised I was nervous.

"Don't look so worried. You have a visitor. It's your dad; he's come to see you."

I couldn't believe it. A huge grin spread across my face, as my spirits soared up to heaven. I was simply ecstatic. It was Dad's first visit, and on a school day too!

I followed Sister down the long polished corridor into a small room with a huge window and a line of chairs. I'd never been inside it before. The room was empty, but the sister told me to take a seat while she went to collect my father. I couldn't stop grinning as I sat with my back to the window, facing the door. I pulled up my socks and smoothed down my skirt and hair. I wanted to look my very best for him. I smiled as the door began to open, and I pictured myself rushing into my father's arms. But there was someone with him – a young girl. She was short, slim and very pretty, with blonde hair. I studied her – she looked about the same age as me. She stared back intensely, as Dad looked between us and spoke.

"Barbara, meet your sister, Karen."

"Sister?" I gasped, looking at her. "I have a sister?"

Dad nodded as they sat down in front of me. My emotions were all over the place. I was in a state of shock. I had a sister, but no one had thought to tell me until now. I eyed her up and down, but she looked much shorter than me.

"How old are you?" I asked.

"Fourteen."

My heart sank. She was two years older than me, and she was sat next to *my* dad.

"Which one's your mother?" I said, firing another question.

Dad interrupted.

"Listen, Barbara, she came to find me, but she's been looking for you for a very long time so I drove her here. She really is your full-blooded sister. I've taken the day off work so you could meet each other."

But I was both angry and upset. It'd been a shock, and now a crippling jealousy had begun to creep in.

"Who's your mother?" I demanded.

"She has the same mother as you," Dad interrupted.

No, no, no! The voice inside my head screamed. *I'm an only child!*

But it seemed I wasn't and never had been. My head was thumping so hard that I thought it'd explode. I was furious with Dad. He'd only come here because my sister wanted to see me, not because he did.

"Where's Janice?" I asked.

He hung his head.

"She's left you, hasn't she?"

I knew it; Janice had left him like all the others. It was just so predictable.

"Where's my mother? Tell me now, where is she?" I said, turning my attentions back to the girl.

"She's in Ireland," she replied. "And she doesn't want you, she never did."

I wanted to punch her in the face. I wanted to hurt her because she'd stolen my father's affections from me. Slowly, I began to piece things together in my mind.

If Mum had left when I was a baby then she must've taken Karen with her, leaving me behind.

My perfect vision of her had vanished in an instant.

"So you're my so-called sister are you?" I said with my voice raised. "Is she a dirty, rotten, lying tinker like me then, Dad?"

At that moment, the door opened and Sister Jenny walked in.

"I thought I heard raised voices," she said her eyes darting around the room. "But this is a convent, so I must be mistaken. I think visiting time is over," she said, directing the last bit at Dad. "Barbara has an education to deal with. Please say your goodbyes."

My heart felt as though it'd been ripped in two as I watched the strange girl walk out of the room with my dad.

It should be me, I thought bitterly.

Every dream and hope I'd had about my mother disappeared along with them. This girl had our dad, but I had no one.

Sister Jenny ushered them along the corridor, while Sister Mary came to usher me back to my room.

"Keep her off class for the rest of the day," Sister Jenny whispered.

As I watched him disappear, I knew it'd be my last chance.

"Dad, Dad wait," I called as I broke into a run.

They stopped and turned as I ran up towards him.

"Never come to see me again," I told him.

Sister Jenny gasped.

I turned to my so-called sister. "And as for you... you never come again. You're not my sister. I only have a brother."

The girl looked me square in the eye.

"Yes, you do have a sister, whether you like it or not."

"Get out of my face," I snarled.

Sister Jenny was horrified.

"Barbara, whatever's come over you, talking like that? Where are your manners? Now, say sorry to your dad. He's driven a long way to visit you, and we've bent the rules so you could see him and your sister."

But I couldn't keep it in any longer.

"Dirty, lying tinkers don't say sorry, do they, Dad?"

By now Sister Jenny had heard enough. She turned to my father.

"If I thought you'd come here to upset this child then I never would've allowed it. Please don't come again without proper arrangements and advance notice, especially if you have some upsetting news for the child. Now, Sister Mary, could you show the visitors out and I will take Barbara."

She grabbed my hand as though I was a five-year-old and led me into the dining room.

"Sit down. Let's have a cup of tea and see if cook has a nice cake for us."

I knew she was being kind, but her goodness made me want to weep. Soon, tears were flowing thick and fast down my cheeks.

"There, there," Sister said, rubbing my shoulders with her hand. "Let those tears out now."

I rested my arms on the table and lowered my head down onto them and sobbed my heart out. I cried for so long that my head was throbbing.

"Come on," Sister said eventually. "We have to leave because they need the room for tea time."

Chapter 22

Baths and Broken Glass

I went up to my bedroom and sat on the end of the bed.

"Barbara, you are a lovely girl. You have a good heart, and you always want to help. I don't like to see you like this. If you ever need to talk, just tell any of the staff, and we can have a chat to see if I can help you."

I dried my tears as I listened to her. Sister Jenny was such a kind person.

"You're different to the other girls because you have no mother. They all have mothers in this unit, yet they do not respect them. You're not the kind of girl we normally get in here. Everyone likes you, including the staff. You work hard in class, the only problem was when you barricaded yourself in your room that time, but we can forget that."

She continued to chat, but my mind had begun to wander. I thought of Dad and the strange girl sitting next to him in his van.

She'd taken my place.

A fury boiled up inside me.

Why had he taken her and left me here? If she was my sister, then why hadn't they taken me with them? Aren't sisters supposed to stick together?

281

"…so you carry on as you are, Barbara," Sister was saying. "Most girls who come in here end up in borstal, but you're not borstal material."

The word borstal caught my attention.

"Is that prison?"

Sister sighed, "Well, sort of, but you are better than that. You stay good, work hard at school and you'll do well in life."

"I have a bad headache," I mumbled.

"Alright," she said getting to her feet. "You've had a long day, so I'll get Sister Mary to bring some tea up to your room."

Once alone, I sobbed myself to sleep. I awoke hours later but it was pitch black. I checked my watch – it was quarter to six and I was still dressed in my clothes from the day before. I replayed everything that had happened. Burying my head against my pillow I wanted to scream because I'd lost everything, including my perfect illusion of my mother. The dream of her had kept me going for so long but now it'd vanished. The girl had said Mum didn't want me, and then she'd left with my dad.

I have no one.

I looked through my bedroom window and watched the sky slowly turn lighter as morning began to filter through. I wondered what I should do now.

Maybe I should kill myself?

I knew about suicide because a few girls had spoken about it back at the hospital. Looking up, I spotted a brass catch on the tall window. The nuns used it to put a pole in to open it. But now I saw it as the perfect place from which to hang a noose. Grabbing my bed sheet, I tied a large loop in and tried to thread it through the hole, but it was impossible – the catch was too small. In the end, after trying for the best part of an hour, I gave up. I calmly laid the sheet on my bed and tidied my room. But I had no interest in anything or anyone. Up until that point, I'd always been the joker, but in the days and weeks that followed, I found I preferred my own company.

One day, Sister Mary stopped me in the corridor to tell me a new girl was moving into the room next to mine.

"So you'll soon have someone to chat to."

A short while later, the school bell rang so I picked up my books and headed to class. I bumped into Sister Mary and the new girl, who was called Susan.

"You're going to be neighbours," Sister said by way of introduction, "so Barbara will show you the ropes."

After class, we had dinner and then I headed back to my room. I'd only just sat down when there was a knock at my door. Before I'd had the chance to answer, Susan had let herself in and was looking around my room, picking things up.

"How long you been here?" she asked.

"Oh, about five months."

She wasn't listening; instead, she was rifling through my books. Then she picked up my hairbrush and started brushing her hair with it. I was gobsmacked. I watched as she picked up some hair slides and started putting them in her hair, leaving them there. I was just about to say something when she picked up a bottle of talcum powder and tipped it all over the floor. Then she rubbed her shoes in it to make more mess.

"All the girls were telling me how they don't like you. They tell me you're a grass. You're up the nun's arses, they say."

I shook my head because it wasn't true, but Susan hadn't finished.

"I know how to deal with twats like you," she said. "I haven't been to borstal for nothing, and I hate grasses."

I gulped. Susan was tougher than anyone I knew.

"When you've finished cleaning up this mess, you can get in my room and clean that. If you do, I might spare you today's beating."

I was already feeling vulnerable, so I took her seriously. Susan was tall, with long dark hair, and I was simply terrified. She looked at me and left the room. I got down on my hands and knees and started to clean. Moments later, she reappeared in the doorway.

"Come on. My room now. Get it done."

I did as she said, hoping I wouldn't get a punch or a slap. But when I entered her bedroom I couldn't believe my eyes. The bed had been stripped and all the drawers had been pulled out of the cabinet. There were clothes everywhere, and she'd even emptied a tube of toothpaste and smeared it across her window.

"Get on with it," she snapped before leaving the room.

I worked quickly because it was almost time for school, and I knew the nuns checked your room when you were in class. If you didn't keep it clean then you were given black marks. Three black marks would ground you, meaning no outdoor trips, while six marks lost you all privileges, including home visits. I panicked to get it done. But as I wandered back into my own room, I discovered that Susan had gone back and destroyed it again. I panicked as I glanced down at my watch – I had less than five minutes. I'd just finished when the bell rang. Breathing out a sigh of relief, I grabbed my books and made my way down the corridor to find Susan waiting for me. She dug her fist hard into my back as we walked along. But the day went from bad to worse as she continued to torment me, throwing pencils and bits of paper. At dinner time, Sister Mary came over to speak to us.

"How are you settling in Susan?"

She looked up and smiled as though butter wouldn't melt in her mouth.

"Fine. Me and Barbara are great friends, aren't we?" she said, giving me a nudge.

I tried to look at Sister Mary, pleading with my eyes for her to get me away from this monster, but she just smiled and turned away. During dinner time, Susan stole my dessert.

"You won't be wanting this, will you?"

After lunch, we were having exercise outside when Sister Mary called me over.

"You are going right back up to your room. What's going on with you? I've just been up there and it's a pigsty. That's two black marks for you!"

I shot Susan a hateful stare because I knew she'd done it, but she just laughed.

Back in class, it became clear that she'd managed to win everyone over. All the girls were giggling and sharing jokes, and every time I glanced over they burst out laughing. Susan passed me a note:

We all know you're the grass, it read.

I'd reached breaking point. Standing up, I turned to her and began to shout.

"You're the fucking grass, and you better back off me right now. I don't care how many borstals you've been in, I ain't no grass."

"Barbara O'Hare. Get over here now!"

It was Mr Jones, the teacher. He was a large man in his late forties, with a beard and untamed brown hair that curled up at the edges like an old piece of bread.

"Over here," he shouted.

He pulled his chair away from his desk as I approached and told me to bend over his knee. I refused, so he grabbed me, put me over his lap, and slapped my backside with his bare hand. It'd stung, but not as much as the humiliation.

The bullying continued for another two months, until one day in assembly. Susan was surrounded by her troops, sniggering and making snide remarks. I snapped and lunged forward, grabbing her hair. But she was quicker, and she punched me so hard that she knocked me out. When I came around I was being carried away on a stretcher. I was checked over by a nun, who gave me another three black marks for fighting. Now I had five to my name. Although I had a big red lump on my forehead, I was sent back into the exercise yard. I immediately spied Susan out of the corner of my eye and marched over to her.

"Oh yeah," she smirked. "What are you going to do about it?"

I grabbed her head and kneed her hard in the face, not once, but four times, until blood came spurting out of her nostrils. Then I began to punch her. By the time I'd finished, Susan was in a bloodied heap on the floor. The nuns came running and dragged me off to the padded room, where I was left for three days. It was when I was in there that I met a new nun. Her name was Kathleen, she was Irish, and she had dark-brown eyes like the pit of hell.

"I want to see Sister Jenny," I said.

But she told me it wasn't possible.

"This sort of thing wouldn't happen in Ireland. If it did, I'd know how to deal with it. You're nothing but a wicked girl to hurt that other poor girl as you did. Now I suggest you use your time in here to pray for forgiveness."

I was just thinking what a bitch she was when Sister Mary appeared.

"Can I see Sister Jenny?" I asked, knowing that she'd fight my corner.

But Sister shook her head sadly.

"No, Sister Jenny has left. She's gone into retirement."

I was heartbroken. Jenny had been my only friend in there besides Sister Mary.

The following day, horrid Sister Kathleen returned.

"Pray, girl. Pray for being so wicked and evil. Pray forgiveness," she hissed before slamming the door.

Then Sister Mary returned to check on me.

"How's Susan?" I asked, desperate for news.

"Not good," she replied. "In fact, you might be arrested for grievous bodily harm."

Sister handed me my clothes and I was allowed to wash in the bathroom. As I passed Susan's room I looked inside – it was empty.

I was fed and given water over those few days, but by the third, I was told I was free to leave. Sister Mary had brought another new nun along with her called Sister Elizabeth. The two nuns left together, but moments later, Sister Elizabeth popped her head back around the door.

"Shush!" She whispered with a finger against her lips. "Listen; tell your social worker that they put you in this room. They are not allowed to treat you like this. Don't tell anyone that I spoke to you, because I won't be here long. Just make sure you tell her or your parents about this."

I nodded.

"But you must promise me that you won't tell them what I said."

"Promise."

She left the room. To this day, I wondered who she was because within the week she'd left for good.

I never found out what happened to Susan, but I was never charged and she'd left by the time I'd come out of solitary confinement. With Susan gone, life returned to normal. One day, I swapped beds with a girl in the dormitory. There were two other dorms with ten beds in each. Although I'd been grateful for my own room, I missed the camaraderie of a dorm, so when a girl called Sarah offered to swop for the night I jumped at the chance. The evening was hilarious, and it ended in an almighty pillow fight. There were feathers everywhere, and Sister Kathleen went crackers, but it was worth the telling-off because it'd been so much fun.

"I wonder why Sister Kathleen came and not Sister Jenny?" I remarked to one of the others.

She pulled her sheet away from her face.

"Haven't you heard? Sister Jenny died of a heart attack – that's why she disappeared."

I was heartbroken. I'd loved Sister Jenny because she'd not only shown me compassion, she'd been one of the few people on my side. I cried that night and for weeks after. I also knew that with Jenny gone, Sister Kathleen would have more power.

There were four baths inside the bathroom. They each had half doors so the staff could see over the top of them. The rule was you stripped off in your room, went to the bathroom with a towel wrapped around you and waited in line for your bath. Each girl was allowed five minutes in the bath, which included time to wash her hair. One day, Sister Kathleen was in charge. I lined up until it was my turn. Sister asked me to raise both arms, and although I wasn't sure why, I knew better than to try and argue. She pulled out a tube and rubbed some white cream into my arm pits. Within moments, my skin was on fire. I didn't realise, but it was hair removal cream and it stung like hell.

"Oh, do shut up crying," she scolded as I whimpered in the corner.

I ran my hand towel under the cold tap and put it under both arms to try and ease the pain, but my skin was blistered and red raw. I took my bath hoping the water would cool it but it made it worse. The following Sunday, I lined up again, grateful that I'd already undergone hair removal. A girl called Jean was standing in front of me as Sister Kathleen led the proceedings. Jean was a small, shy girl, who wasn't any trouble to anyone. We watched as Sister ran a fresh bath for her. As she did, I noticed her put a tumbler glass on the side, next to the taps. I thought it was odd. Once the bath was full, Sister beckoned Jean forward and closed the half-door. A minute later there was a dreadful scream as Sister Kathleen pushed open the door. I looked into the bathroom to see poor Jean kneeling in the bath. She was howling in pain, with blood gushing from her backside. The blood was streaming down both legs turning the water blood red.

"Come on. Stand up, let's get you out," Sister Kathleen said, without a hint of sympathy in her voice.

Sister Mary came running in to help. An ambulance was called to take Jean to hospital, but I knew what I'd seen. It'd been no accident. Sister Kathleen had taken perverse pleasure in hurting others, especially little girls. As for poor Jean, we never saw her again.

Chapter 23

Marmaduke

Lots of officials suddenly started to visit Blackbrook. I couldn't be sure if it was because of what had happened to Jean or it was just a coincidence. But after that, every girl's social worker came to speak to her, including mine. I remembered what kind Sister Elizabeth had said, so I told her about the padded room.

"Can you show me?" she asked.

I led her down the corridor, but the nuns had placed a huge, metal wardrobe over the front of the doorway to conceal the entrance.

"It's behind there, I swear."

I was certain she didn't believe me, but she stopped and asked one of the nuns what was behind the wardrobe.

"Oh, that old thing," she replied with a wave of her hand. "I don't know. It's far too heavy to move. In fact, we never have. She's just telling stories."

I was stunned. I knew the nun was lying, but the social worker chose to believe her rather than me. Strangely, that weekend, whether by chance or to keep me quiet, a nun took me into Liverpool's C&A to buy some clothes. I felt ashamed as shoppers saw the nun and turned to look at me in pity.

"Aww, poor little mite. She must be an orphan."

The words cut me to the quick because I wasn't an orphan, I had two parents, but it seemed they didn't want me.

The following Friday, I was allowed another treat. I was allowed to travel back to Dad's on my own. It would be my first journey in ages – I could barely wait. A nun dropped me off at the train station with a list of trains that I needed to catch, the times and where I needed to change.

"Here's your father's telephone number. Ring him when you get to the station," she said, thrusting a piece of paper in my hand.

Dad told me which bus to catch, but by the time I'd arrived he was getting ready to go out. I didn't mind because I had the TV for company and the place to myself.

"Here," he said putting four pound notes on top of the mantelpiece, "just in case you need anything."

I didn't spend it; instead, I curled up on the sofa and watched TV. The following morning, Dad was still fast asleep in bed, so I nipped out with the money in my pocket to see what I could find. I was walking along the high street when I passed a pet shop. I did a double-take, there he was as bold as brass, playing in the window. I watched as he ran around on a red plastic wheel. It was Marmaduke, the mouse who had saved me in the treatment room. He was just as I'd imagined him to be, with a small brown body, huge dark eyes and a long, slinky pink tail. I dashed inside the shop and asked the shopkeeper if I could buy him.

"Which one? There are dozens."

I looked for Marmaduke and saw him scuttling across the cage.

"That one. The little brown one!" I said pointing him out.

I was so excited that I thought I'd burst! The shopkeeper put him in a box, and I bought him some food and hurried home. As I neared Dad's flat I realised that I had no keys, so I pressed the intercom. It took him a while, and when he answered he sounded tired and grumpy.

"It's me, Dad."

"Go and play."

"But I need the loo," I lied.

I heard him groan and he pressed the buzzer and let me in. I didn't use the lifts; instead, I climbed the stairs, placing Marmaduke and a handful of wood shavings in my duffle coat pocket.

"Thank you," I said, stroking the soft fur on top of his head. "You saved me in hospital, now it's my turn to save you."

As soon as I walked into the flat I could smell perfume, and I knew there was another 'new mum' waiting.

"Alright?" Dad asked, popping his head around the living room door.

I nodded and smiled, my secret safely tucked up inside my pocket.

Dad closed the door and I heard the tell-tale clack of stiletto heels as they left the flat. But I didn't care because I had Marmaduke, and I'd never be alone again. With the coast clear, I started searching for something that I could put my new pet in. I found an old sweet tin and used Dad's hammer and a nail to knock some air holes in the top of the lid. Then I ripped up some old loo roll for him to nest in. For once, I couldn't wait for the weekend to end so I could take my mouse back to Blackbrook. I didn't see my father until the following morning, but I had to leave because my train left at ten o'clock. Stuffing my clothes into a plastic bag, I said goodbye to my father and headed for the bus. Once on the train, I grabbed a seat next to a table and gently lifted Marmaduke out of my pocket to play with him. As soon as the train pulled into St Helen's station, I popped him back inside the tin to keep him safe. I couldn't wait to be in my room with the door shut – just me and Marmaduke. I briefly said hello to the other girls and then disappeared off to my bedroom, saying I had homework to do. I emptied out the drawer from my bedside cabinet and made him a new home inside.

"You were there, weren't you?" I whispered as he stopped to clean his face with his tiny paws. "I know you were there and you saw everything that doctor did to me. You're the only one who believed me, do you know that? Everyone else thinks I'm a liar, but I'm not. You know the truth, Marmaduke."

He looked up at me with his big eyes and I knew he'd understood. He'd listened to me when others had failed to and he'd given me a reason to carry on when I had none.

My new school skirt had two zipped pockets on either side. The pockets were deep, so I put Marmaduke in one, his food in the other, and I took him to school. In class, I put my hand up and asked if I could go to the loo. But I didn't need to; I just wanted to spend precious time with my new friend. Whenever

I woke up in the dead of night from a bad dream, Marmaduke would be there to comfort me. Although I'd left the hospital, the hospital hadn't left me. I was still haunted by it, even in my sleep.

The regime at Blackbrook changed again with a new influx of Irish nuns. I always found the Irish nuns to be the strictest. One day, I decided I'd had enough. I made a run for the front wall and tried to jump it, but the caretaker grabbed my foot and managed to drag me down. He took me to Sister Bernadette, a formidable nun, who possessed the same cruel streak as Sister Kathleen.

"Trying to run away, were we?" she scolded; as she marched me out to the driveway, by the wall. "Right," she said, letting me go. "I'll teach you to run, and run you will. Now take off your shoes and socks."

I looked at her dumbstruck.

"I said take them off, otherwise it's three days in the padded room for you."

She marched up and down in front of me, cracking her walking stick hard against the ground.

"Right, I'm going to count to ten, and if you don't run it will be the rap of my stick until you do."

She started to count, so I pulled off my shoes and socks.

"Eight," she shouted, banging the stick against the ground. I flinched and took to my feet. This time I cleared the wall easily. I began to run but the field was full of long nettles.

"Oww," I cried, as my feet and legs were stung thousands of times. I carried on running because I was frightened what she'd do to me if I stopped.

The Hospital

With my feet cut to ribbons by broken twigs and my legs on fire with nettle stings, I came to a halt. I climbed back over the wall, desperate to feel the cool short grass underneath my feet. By the time I'd reached the main entrance, Sister was waiting.

"Do you still want to run?" she smirked.

I limped back into the school, where I was given a bottle of calamine lotion and some gauze to try and take away the sting. I was kept inside my room as punishment, but at least I had Marmaduke with me. Later that evening, I heard footsteps outside in the corridor, so I quickly hid Marmaduke in his drawer. There was a knock at my door.

"Barbara," a voice called. It was Sister Mary.

"What happened to you today?" She asked as she perched on the end of my bed.

I told her all about Sister Bernadette, the walking stick and the stinging nettles.

"It's not Blackbrook I'm running from. It's the horrible new nuns that have come over from Ireland," I complained.

Her face fell and I knew she had something to tell me.

"What is it?" I asked.

"I'm sorry, Barbara," she said, taking my hand in hers, "but I'm leaving for London."

"But what will I do? What will I do without you?"

She explained that most of the nuns left after a year, and now it was her time to move on.

"Listen, I can tell you're upset, so when your dad rings I'll put him through to you. How about that?" she suggested.

Although I had even more black marks against my name, I knew Sister Mary was as good as her word. Sure enough, at seven o'clock that evening, Dad was on the phone waiting to speak to me.

"Hello," I answered – my voice urgent and panicked.

"How are you doing?"

"Dad, please, please ask the social worker to come and see me."

I had to get out of Blackbrook.

"And Dad?"

"Yes?"

"I miss you, but I can't remember what you look like. Could you send me a photograph so that I can see you before I forget?"

My father went silent on the other end of the phone as I heard him choke back his emotions.

"Dad? Are you still there?" I asked.

"Yes."

"Something happened. I have to tell you."

"Don't tell me over the phone because they listen in," he warned. After my time at Aston Hall it was clear that my father didn't trust anyone. "I'll get your social worker to come and see you."

Then he changed the subject. He told me he'd bought something, and had posted it in a parcel.

"Has Elvis done another LP?"

Dad laughed.

"No, it's the new single by Michael Jackson."

I loved Michael Jackson, everyone did, and I couldn't wait to play my record to everyone in Blackbrook house. After the phone call, Sister Mary took me back to my room and I told her all about the record.

"Oh, you do know that's from a film. It's about a boy and his pet rat. I read about it in a magazine. I'll have a look for it and bring it to you."

I could barely believe it. It was as though my father was a mind reader.

Did he know about Marmaduke? No, don't be silly, no one knew about him.

True to her word, Sister Mary brought me the magazine, which contained the lyrics to the song 'Ben'.

"Wouldn't it be wonderful if we could all have a friend like Ben," Sister said, winking at me as she got up to leave the room.

Did she know?

I checked on Marmaduke, but he was there, curled up and fast asleep in his tin. I spent the rest of the night memorising the lyrics so I could sing along when the record arrived. As soon as it did, I played it to death. It was 1972, I was 14, and I'd been in Blackbrook over a year. The following Monday, my social worker arrived just as Dad had promised. My legs had healed over so I couldn't show her my nettle stings, but she wasn't interested because she'd come to tell me something.

"You're leaving Blackbrook for a hostel for girls. It's closer to where your Dad lives."

"Is that like a borstal?" I asked.

"No, not at all. Now, go and pack your things because we're leaving today."

I was so happy that as soon as I'd left the office I found Sister Mary to share my good news.

"Are you excited?" she asked.

I nodded, gave her a hug and skipped down the corridor to go and pack. Within minutes I was ready to leave. I'd tucked Marmaduke in my coat pocket and put his tin inside the carrier bag so no one would see. As I left, Sister Mary called after me.

"Have you forgotten something?" she asked, holding a clear plastic bag aloft in her hand. It was full of Marmaduke's food.

I gulped.

"I thought I could smell a mouse in your room," she smirked. "Then every time you emptied your pocket wood shavings would fall to the floor."

I knew then that I'd been rumbled. I wondered if she'd tell, but then she walked over, took me in her arms, and hugged me for all she was worth.

"You're a special little lady," she whispered, with tears in her eyes.

"Bye, Sister Mary, and thank you."

"What for?"

"For being so nice and kind to me."

Suddenly, the social worker loomed into view.

"Are you ready? We'd better hurry up."

"Bye," I said as I waved to Sister Mary.

"Bye, Barbara."

As I left the other girls were lining up for dinner, but they all came over to hug me and say goodbye. I left Blackbrook with happiness in my heart and Marmaduke inside my pocket.

Chapter 24

The Letter

The social worker was lovely to me as we drove to the hostel.

"What's it like?" I asked as the car travelled along a small country road.

"The hostel? Well, it's different to Blackbrook. From the outside it looks like a normal house, and there are only three other girls living there, so it's all very relaxed."

"So it's not like Aston Hall? It's not like the hospital?"

The social worked stared at me.

"I wouldn't mention Aston Hall to anyone, if I were you."

"Why?"

"Because it won't look good on you," she replied.

I didn't know what she meant, but I presumed she thought people might judge me because I'd been inside a mental hospital.

We eventually pulled up. With Marmaduke tucked safely inside my coat pocket, I grabbed my bag and we headed over towards the door. We were greeted by a young woman, who showed us in with a smile.

"Kitchen's through there," she said, pointing towards a room at the back of the house.

I was struck by the atmosphere. The social worker had been spot on; it was very relaxed. A washing machine swished away inside the kitchen and there was a big pile of clothes on the floor, waiting to go in. There was a radio blaring away in the background, playing the latest chart hits, as the phone began to ring loudly in the hallway.

"Can someone get the phone?" a voice called from upstairs.

I instantly decided that I was going to like it here. To the outside world, it was just like a normal, busy house.

"This way," the woman told me as she led me to a bedroom that contained a couple beds. There were posters on the wall, shoes scattered around the floor, and the beds were messy and unmade. To my utter relief, this place was nothing like Aston Hall or Blackbrook. It was exactly how I'd imagined a normal teenager's bedroom would be. I was introduced to the other girls and members of staff, and everyone was friendly and welcoming.

You've landed on your feet here, Barbara, I thought to myself.

But there was one thing worrying me – Marmaduke.

How would I keep him a secret when I had to share a bedroom with other girls? In many ways I was free, and maybe now it was time for Marmaduke to be free.

I unpacked my clothes and went downstairs into the office, where there was a woman in her early twenties waiting for me.

"Let's talk about rules," she began.

Here we go… I thought, as I steeled myself for a long list of dos and don'ts. But there weren't any; it was all pretty straightforward.

"So I can just walk out of the door at any time?" I repeated, barely able to believe it.

"Yes, as long as it's after 7am, and you're back in by 11pm. Now, are there any more questions or is there anything that's worrying you?"

I thought about Marmaduke.

I had to tell her.

"Yes, I have a little secret that I need some help with."

She leaned in towards me.

"What is it?" she asked, genuinely concerned.

"I have a mouse. He lives in my pocket. Look, I'll show you," I said lifting the flap so I could lift Marmaduke out.

The woman smiled and started to laugh.

"Well, she said, looking relieved. "We don't normally allow pets here; however, I think in this instance we can break the rules just this once. But we'll have to get him a cage so he has a home."

She made a few phone calls and before long, Marmaduke had a home of his own. With him settled, I walked into town to the shops with one of the other girls. I still couldn't get used to my new-found freedom, after spending the best part of two and a half years behind locked doors. A whole new world had opened up to me and I intended to grab it with both hands. Soon, Monday arrived, and the other girls left to go to college because they were all 16 and over. I stayed at the hostel and busied myself, washing my clothes and playing with Marmaduke. The following day, I was sitting in the kitchen, chatting to the others when a member of staff walked in. He was holding

303

a pile of letters and he started to hand them out. I was new, so I didn't expect anything but the man turned to me.

"Oh, Barbara, I almost forgot. There's a letter for you." He handed me a pale blue envelope. "And it's an international one."

"But who's it from?" I asked.

"I don't know. Open it and you'll find out."

I'd very rarely received letters in the previous home, apart from the odd parcel Dad had sent, so I was puzzled. I stared at it as though it was treasure in my hands. There was writing on the front where an address had been crossed out. It had come from Blackbrook, but had been forwarded on here. It felt thick, as though there was lots of paper folded up inside.

Maybe it was from Christine? Maybe she'd got my letter after all?

The suspense was killing me, so I tore it open.

My eyes scanned the first page.

Hello, Barbara.

I hope you're well.

I looked at the address at the top of the letter. *West Midlands.*
But I didn't know anyone there.

I read on, trying to decipher the scrawled handwriting. It asked me how I'd been and told me that she'd been trying to get hold of me, but it'd been Karen, my sister, who'd told her where to find me. I fast forwarded to the last page and there it was, written in black and white.

Your ever-loving mother.

I almost dropped the letter in shock.

It was Mum, and she was alive! Not only that, but she was looking for me. I knew Karen had been lying. Mum had wanted me, and now she'd written to me. This letter proved I'd been right all along.

I held the letter against my heart. I could barely believe I was holding something that my mother had once held in her hand. It was the closest I'd ever been to her. I looked around for a member of staff.

"Where's Walsall?" I asked.

"Oh, about 30 miles away."

I couldn't believe it. Mum was only 30 miles away from me, and I had her address – a post office in Walsall. Wow, I thought. Mum owns a post office!

I told the staff that I was going out for the day to meet my mum. They didn't try to stop me, but gave me money on the understanding that I'd stay in contact and call them if I got into trouble.

"I promise."

I pulled on my new brown skirt, baby-blue blouse and pink cardigan, and fixed up my hair so that I'd look my very best. This was the biggest moment of my life – I was finally going to meet her. I asked the bus driver where the post office was and showed him the letter.

"Don't worry, I'll drop you off right outside," he offered.

"Thank you. It's just that I'm going to meet my mum." I smiled. "She owns it."

The bus seemed to take forever, but every mile we travelled I knew was another mile closer to her. Getting off the bus, I walked into the post office but it was busy, so I took my place in the queue. I craned my neck, and then I saw her – a lady behind the counter with bright red hair. My heart was beating as I neared the front. I waited my turn, walked up to her and placed the letter on the counter. I'd expected her to come rushing out and hug me, but instead she looked at me blankly.

"Can I help you?"

"I'm looking for my mum," I said, my eyes searching hers for some recognition.

"Alright, where does she live?"

I pointed at the letter.

"Here, I think."

The woman looked puzzled as her brow furrowed. My heart sank because I knew in that split second it wasn't her.

"Can I read it?" she asked.

I nodded, with tears pricking at the back of my eyes.

What will I do? I'd come all this way. What if I can't find her?

The postmistress read the letter and then looked up at me.

"Ah, I see. No, what you need to do is go straight over the road and walk up the lane. You will find them all up there."

I wanted to ask her what she'd meant by "them" but the next person in the queue had already stepped forward, so it was time to leave. I wasn't sure quite where to go, but I followed her directions and passed half a dozen smart houses on the left. I wondered if my mother lived in one of them, but then I spotted more trees and a field beyond. A long road stretched out in front of me but I continued to walk. Before long, I could smell bonfires and then I heard voices, laughing and joking. There was a small canal bridge, so I crossed it. As I turned a corner and cleared some trees I saw it before me – a huge gypsy camp with around a hundred caravans parked up on either side of the road. I heard the neigh of horses that had been tied up on long pieces of rope, pegged to the side of the road. There were lots of dogs. They started to bark as soon as they saw me, alerting the camp that I was there. I felt extremely nervous, but I was desperate to find my mother.

A scruffy little girl with long red hair rode up alongside me on a horse. She had a dirty face and a trail of snot streaming down from one nostril.

"Where you going?" she asked. She was only about eight, but I was flabbergasted because she was riding the horse bareback.

"I'm going to meet my mother," I replied, walking away, but she continued to follow.

I was holding the pale-blue envelope and she spotted it.

"What's your name?" she asked suddenly.

"Barbara, why, what's yours?"

The girl stopped in her tracks and pulled the horse to a sudden halt, and then she jumped off. She looked me right in the eye.

"You're my sister."

My mouth fell open, but before I could answer I was surrounded by other gypsy children. The dogs were going mental, barking at the sudden rush of excitement, as the girl led me over towards the gypsy camp. One of the children went to fetch an adult and a tall bear of a man dashed over and stared at me.

"Oh, my God!" he exclaimed, putting a hand to his mouth. "Yes, it is. It's Barbara."

Before I could say a word, he threw his arms around me tight. News had spread and soon women and children had come rushing over to say hello. I was handed wads of notes, jewellery and other trinkets as everyone rushed to welcome me into the camp. I felt overwhelmed as I was pulled this way and that, but the man led me towards a caravan and out of the mayhem.

"I'm your uncle John," he said, beaming at me, "and this," he said, gesturing towards an old lady sat in the corner of the caravan, "is your grandmother."

The old lady looked up at me and, grabbing a rosary around her neck, burst into tears. She bowed her head and crossed herself, thanking God for my safe return. Soon, the kettle was boiling and endless cups of tea had been made and drunk as my grandmother told how she'd always prayed for my return.

"I can't believe it," she said, cupping a gentle hand against my face. "You don't know how long I've waited for this moment."

Her caravan was homely with a wood-burning stove in the corner and crocheted cushions scattered everywhere.

"But I can't crochet corners," she confessed. "So I call them my spare wheels."

She kept chickens for eggs, and made fresh soda bread every morning, giving the loaves to other families on the camp. She knew everything about plants and trees, and was the doctor of the camp, making up ancient concoctions to cure illnesses. She was without doubt the most wonderful person I'd ever met in my life, and it was quite clear everyone else felt the same. The kids of the camp adored her, while the adults had the utmost respect for her – the matriarch. I sat with her all day, laughing and joking, and talking about family. As we chatted, I was shocked to discover I had six half-brothers and sisters.

"So where's my mum?" I asked finally.

"Oh, she's out, but she'll be back soon," Uncle John replied.

I could barely wait. Soon it was dusk, and all the adults went to the pub, with the women going off to play bingo. Uncle John took me to my mother's caravan so that I could wait for her. It was a beautiful caravan with mirrors and highly polished chrome both inside and out. There were grand tea sets of Crown Derby on show and the lights worked on gas, even though there was none to light them. My sisters and brothers told me the caravan next door was where they slept, and the 'show' one used by Mum and my stepfather. I also discovered that I was the oldest.

"So, what have you been doing all this time? Where have you been living? Do you live in a house? I bet you've lived the life of a princess," one of my younger sisters said, as they fired one question after another at me.

If only they knew about the hospital, I shuddered.

That's all in the past now, I reasoned. *This is my new life, here with my brothers, sisters and Mum.*

Around nine o'clock, the caravan door opened and a woman walked in. It was pitch black, but I knew in an instant it was her – it was my mother. I was sitting on the edge of the bed as nervous as hell, trying to make her out in the shadows.

I saw a ringlet of long hair nestling against her throat as she lunged forward to grab me.

"Oh, my baby!" she said, throwing her arms around me dramatically.

It was the moment I'd waited for all my life, but suddenly, sat there on the bed, I felt really uncomfortable. Her exaggerated burst of emotion had felt totally false.

"Come on," she said. "We're going to the pub."

I sat there feeling shy and uncomfortable in the middle of the pub, surrounded by strangers. As the hours passed, everyone became drunk. Someone had started to sing, and soon everyone had joined in. There were endless stories of family and of Ireland. I belonged there, but I felt strangely removed from it all. Mum looked just as I'd expected – tall, with curly, long, red hair. In fact, I was the spitting image of her. I also met my step-father in the pub but disliked him instantly. I couldn't put my finger on it; I just got a really bad feeling about him.

"Come on," Mum said, "We're back off to the caravan."

I followed them both, but she directed me towards the old caravan where all the children slept.

"Would you like a nightie or pyjamas?" she asked.

"Pyjamas."

She cackled with laughter.

"Get in that bed. Pyjamas? You'll be lucky around here."

I realised she was not like how I'd imagined her. She was callous and cold – the total opposite of my grandmother. Broken-hearted, I crawled into bed, surrounded by half a dozen strange children, who were now my new family. The following morning, Mum came into the caravan and started to cook breakfast. I realised how hard-faced she looked as she talked of women she didn't like and of bare-knuckle fights.

"Get in the car," she said after breakfast.

"But where are we going?" I asked, climbing in.

"You'll see."

As we drove there, she asked me if I wanted to stay with her. I hesitated. I barely even knew her.

"We'll have a grand time," she promised. "You won't have to go to school; you can help look after the horses. Just think, all that freedom, Barbara," she said as she continued to paint the perfect picture to entice a 15-year-old girl.

We pulled up outside the office of Social Services, and my mother proceeded to inform them that from now on I'd be living with her.

"I'm going to take care of her now. She's my daughter."

The social worker was perturbed and invited me into a side room.

"Are you sure, Barbara?" she asked.

"She's my mum. Everything will be fine," I insisted, even though I wasn't entirely convinced myself. But my longing to be part of a family was so strong that I was willing to take a chance.

Mum grinned as we got back in the car and drove back to the camp.

"That told them," she smirked.

As soon as we'd returned she asked me to look after "the babies", meaning all my younger brothers and sisters. But

I didn't have a clue because I'd never looked after children before; I could barely look after myself.

My step-father took an instant dislike to me, and told me that I was good for nothing.

"You're only good for one thing," he sniffed, although I didn't have a clue what he meant. "Make me a cup of tea."

My younger sister took me under her wing and showed me how to clean the caravan.

"It must be scrubbed and gleaming, and you must have the fire lit before mother comes back, or we'll be in for it," she warned.

I swallowed down my nerves. It seemed my gut-instinct had been right. When she returned later that evening to cook dinner, she looked at the trailer and turned up her nose.

"It's filthy," she scolded, looking around for my younger sister. "Come here, you," she said, trying to grab her. "You know how I like it. This isn't good enough. You should know better. You better learn quick, or it'll be you next," she told me.

The other traveller girls came over to chat to us the next day, as we scrubbed and polished the caravan to Mum's exacting standards. In truth, the show caravan was so clean that every surface had shone like a mirror. But she'd inspect it with eagle eyes.

It felt as bad as being inside one of the children's homes. Every day I scrubbed, cleaned, and made constant cups of tea for my step-father. He made me feel uncomfortable and I avoided being left alone with him. Instead, I'd find sanctuary inside my grandmother's caravan. He didn't hit me, but he tormented me, and he particularly liked me to rub his head every night when my mother wasn't around. It made me feel uncomfortable because it seemed too intimate – the sort of thing a wife would do for her husband.

The following evening, after my step-father came home from the pub drunk, he sat down and demanded that I rub his head. Only this time I was prepared. Before he'd come in, I'd smeared my hands with hair removal cream and I worked them deeply into his hair and across his scalp. The following morning, he awoke to find half a head of hair nestled on his pillow. I tried not to laugh as he patted a hand over his bald patches.

"I think I'm sick," he gasped. "I need to get myself to the doctors."

He'll never ask me again, I thought to myself.

Shortly afterwards, I packed a bag and ran away. As I stood there, trying to hitch a lift at the side of the road, I thought how ironic it was. I'd spent my life running away to find my mother, and now that I had, I couldn't wait to get away from her. I telephoned my father, but he didn't want to get involved. I think he was angry that despite all his best attempts to secure me in a better place, I'd thrown it all away for my mother. I hitchhiked to London, where I lived on the streets. I spent my first night sleeping on a park bench near Trafalgar Square, covered in bits of old, broken cardboard. One day, I stayed in a hostel in the centre of the city. The following morning, I got chatting to a kind, homeless man in his twenties. He was called Taffy. We'd just said goodbye outside the hostel when a Chinese man approached me.

"You want work, you want money. You want a good job?" he asked.

I nodded. It was all I'd ever wanted. He told me to follow him into a nearby phone box, where he made a phone call in Chinese. Afterwards, he put down the receiver and turned to me.

"Okay you've got the job, you come with me."

I grinned, absolutely thrilled it'd been that easy. I was just about to walk off with him when Taffy came over and tapped me on my shoulder.

"Whatever you do, don't go with him, because every girl who does is never seen again."

"But I'm going to get a job," I protested.

"Please, don't go. I'll look after you. I'll help you get a job, I promise. Listen, this is no life for a young girl. Why don't you smarten yourself up and try and get a job in a hotel? They're crying out for girls like you."

I thought for a moment.

"What, you really think someone would give me a job?"

"I don't think so, I know so."

Sure enough, I landed a job working in a hotel, which suited me fine because I needed a roof over my head. I also needed somewhere to hide from my mother. I worked hard and had saved up a bit of money. With some experience under my belt, I knew I'd easily get another job, so I left and went to stay with my grandmother. Days later, my mother arrived at the camp, looking for me. I ran again, back to London, where I begged from tourists. I shoplifted nice clothes to sell and to wear until I found another job. I'd saved up enough money to pay my fare back to Liverpool, where a friend from Blackbrook lived. I secured a job in a chip shop, which I loved, but then I found better paid work in a Greek restaurant. It'd been three long years, but with a job and a good place to live, I'd finally started to make my own way in the world. Nobody could tell me what to do anymore; I was my own boss and only responsible for myself. I was 18-years-old, with my whole life in front of me, and I felt great.

Chapter 25

Going Back

It is 1995, Oasis is blaring out of my car speakers, I am driving along when I pass a red-brick fire station in Allerton, Liverpool. I hadn't even been thinking about the hospital, but the sight of those bricks and building with its large windows triggers something inside my brain. In a split second I am back there. Dr Milner is lying on top of me, raping me. I can feel his hot breath on his face. I'm stopped at traffic lights, but now I cannot move. Car horns beep behind me, but I'm frozen. Thankfully, my friend, who is sitting in the passenger seat, helps me park the car up. Even then, it still took me another half an hour to stop shaking. By the time I'd returned home, my children thought I'd been in a car accident because I was still such a state.

* * *

Over the intervening years, the hospital had never left me. Shortly after I had started working at the Greek restaurant as an 18-year-old, I had fallen in love with a wonderful Greek man who I met there and with whom I sailed around the world as a stowaway on the boat he worked on. I'd fallen pregnant but, sadly, our relationship didn't meet with his Greek Orthodox parents' approval and I had found myself back in Liverpool preparing to be an unmarried mother in a world where that still carried a stigma. I gave birth to a beautiful daughter and married a man who was looking for a green card, so I could purchase some respectability. We had two more girls and a boy together and I fostered many others – determined to save children from the fate I had suffered. But my marriage of convenience was beginning to fall apart. I was still haunted and I hadn't realised how powerful those demons were until that day when I'd brought the traffic to a halt.

I visited my GP and told him what had happened. I'd expected sympathy or understanding, but he seemed totally unconvinced.

"There is no history of you being at that hospital," he insisted, looking at my medical notes.

Instead, he prescribed me anti-depressants and sleeping tablets. I realised then that I couldn't let this go. I had to do something. I had to fight back and expose Milner and that hospital for what it was. I went to see my uncle, my dad's brother, and I told him I'd been drugged as a child inside Aston Hall hospital. I wasn't sure what I could do or who else I could go to, but my Uncle Paul was well educated so I was certain he'd know what to do. He telephoned the hospital, and we were both invited to go in for a meeting. We found out that Dr Milner had died back in 1976, so I knew I wouldn't be able to get the justice I so badly craved. But I was determined to find out the truth and get the answers to questions that had burned inside of me for 30 years. I had to be strong, if not for me, for the other victims that were suffering in silence. As we drove up the long tarmac drive, I felt my stomach turn over.

"Are you alright?" my uncle asked, placing a concerned hand on my arm.

I took a deep breath to try and calm my pounding heart.

"I'm alright. Let's do this."

We rang the doorbell and waited for someone to let us in. As we stood in the entrance hall, I was right back there as a terrified 12-year-old girl. A girl frightened of her own shadow, a girl who had been petrified of every doctor and every nurse she'd come into contact with since.

We were led into an office. One of the managers asked what was it that we wanted to know.

"I want to know why I was a patient here when my father never signed any consent forms," I began.

But she couldn't answer me, so I fired my next question.

"Okay, tell me why I was injected at just 12 years old?"

Again, the room was silent. She had no answers to give me, but she brought out a file – my medical file from Aston Hall. I looked inside but was disappointed because it only contained a few sheets of paper. I couldn't prove it, but I sensed there was more paperwork only it was being kept from us.

"And I can take these?" I asked, presuming that I could.

She shook her head.

"No, I can only show them to you."

I felt as though new people were trying to cover up for what had gone before. Disgusted, we got up to leave. As I did, I spotted a nurse walking towards me. Although she was greyer and older, I recognised her immediately; she'd worked at the hospital back in the day of Dr Milner.

I made a snide remark, but she refused to listen and astonishingly started to defend him.

"Dr Milner was a pioneer in his field…" she began.

I'd had enough. I was no longer a scared little child. I was an adult now, and I wasn't frightened of her or anyone else. That child had gone; she'd gone and found her voice. A fury boiled up inside me as I turned and pointed my finger right in her face.

"A pioneer, you say? And tell me. He was a pioneer in what exactly, because he knew what he was doing."

I knew I had to leave before I said or did something I might regret. But the nurse was determined to have the last word. As I walked across what had once been a ward but was now an office, she called after me.

"Shall we destroy your files?"

Was that a threat? I thought as I turned to look her in the eye.

"Do you think I would give you that pleasure?" I said, spitting the words out. "No, keep them because I'm coming back."

As I turned and headed for the door I pictured myself standing there as a terrified 12-year-old girl staring at the wall – staring because it was the only thing that couldn't hurt me. I stopped in my tracks and turned to the nurse.

"Always remember this. Children have memories. I remember you and I will never forget what you did to us all."

In a fury, I lifted up my hand and grabbed a handful of my hair in my fist. "Go on, try and pull my hair now…"

My uncle realised I was about to explode, so he led me from the room and tried to calm me down.

"Not like this, Barbara."

I knew he was right. I had to do it properly. On 20th March 1995, he wrote a formal letter to the hospital, asking for answers and what drugs had been given to me as a child. But we didn't receive any real answers. It spurred me on because I knew I had to expose the hospital for what it had put me and hundreds of other innocent children through. My fight had just begun.

Chapter 26

The Fight of My Life

I tried to fight, telling GPs and anyone who would listen about what had happened at Aston Hall. But I continued to hit a series of brick walls. There was no mention of the hospital in my medical records; not a trace. It didn't make any sense, I even started to doubt myself.

Why wouldn't it be in there? Maybe everyone was right, maybe I was crackers?

But I knew what I'd been through, how they'd locked me up and what Milner had done. Even though I insisted I was telling the truth, it seemed that no one believed a woman who'd once been locked inside a mental hospital. It was as though people had already made their minds up before I'd had the chance to state my case. Around late 1997, the internet was just coming into general use, although back then it was a dial-up connection so it was temperamental, to say the least. Spelling had never been my strong point, so I'd typed in the words Ashton hospital, instead of Aston, and found nothing. The flashbacks and nightmares continued, but I didn't have computer training, so I wasn't sure how and where I'd find information.

Meanwhile, my relationship with my husband continued to worsen to the point where we lived as strangers. I desperately wanted him to leave but he refused. In the end, I started drinking heavily. I'd buy vodka, and soon I'd got into a daily routine of drinking and sleeping – anything to block out the anxiety and the flashbacks of my time at the hospital. After four months, I decided that I needed to sort myself out, so I booked a holiday to stay with relatives. I stayed for almost two months. The sunshine, fresh air and space gave me the chance to breathe and clear my head. It also gave me the strength to do what I should've done years before – tell my husband to leave. I flew back into Manchester airport, and returned home a different woman. My husband got up and walked into the kitchen to make me a coffee, but when he handed it over, he did what he always did and took a mouthful first. It was his way of controlling me, but not anymore.

"I don't want it," I replied coldly.

I'd had enough and he knew it. He got up, picked up his cup and walked out. As he slammed the front door behind him, I ran over to it.

"Goodbye, and don't come back."

It was 1998, and he'd left for good. Our son was just 13, but I knew our lives would be better from that moment on. I felt he'd tried to poison people against me, including my own children, by labelling me 'mad Barbara'. In the meantime, I continued to foster children. Over the years that followed, I fostered around ten children, officially and unofficially, and I was proud to do so. If anyone was in need, I'd try to help out.

If I could prevent just one child from going into care then it'd be worth it.

In early 2000, I started to suffer with gynaecological problems. I was seen by a doctor who advised me I had polyps.

"You need to get these seen to, otherwise they could turn cancerous."

But the thought of going into a hospital had filled me with terror, so I put up with it, hoping that it'd all go away once I'd reached menopause.

I continued to try and fight for justice from my time spent in Aston Hall, but I was met with a wall of silence. It felt as though the medical profession had closed ranks. I felt helpless.

How could I – a middle-aged woman – take on a fight like that?

I had the will, but no money or legal representation, and solicitors cost money I didn't have. Despite this, my desire to expose the truth never left me. But then I was faced with a new challenge, and one that would become the fight of my life. By 2011, my children had grown and fled the nest. With the ghost of Aston Hall always there in the background of my life, I began to suffer from depression. Then I began to feel physically unwell, with heavy bleeding and a crippling pain in my lower back. Something was wrong, but I was too terrified to go and seek help, because it'd mean going to see a doctor in hospital, and Milner had left me with an acute fear of both. My head was a mess, but with my symptoms growing worse I knew I had to tell someone. I drove to see my Uncle John at his house in the West Midlands. Over the years that had followed, I'd kept in touch with Uncle John because he'd always shown me such kindness. Uncle John is a bear of a man – loving and tough, but with a heart of gold, and I knew from the time I'd spent on Mum's gypsy camp that he was always the person to go to in a crisis.

"Hello, Barbara." He smiled as he opened the door.

His partner, Mandy, was in the house, so I sat them both down and told them I had something to tell them.

"I'm very, very ill," I began.

John's face crumpled as I delivered the news.

"I'm bad, and I think it might be cancer," I continued. "But I'm not going to fight it. I'm tired, and I'm sick of fighting. I've been fighting all my life."

"You will fight this," John insisted, holding the top of my arms. "You're strong; I know you can fight this."

Then he threw his arms around me and started to cry.

"Don't cry," I begged, because I couldn't bear it. I loved him so much.

"Look," he said, finally composing himself. "You can go to the hospital and get help, or we'll drag you there."

Somehow the tears and words of this wonderful man had pierced through my depression. As his tears soaked into my shoulder, I realised that I did matter and that my life was worth living. There were still people out there who loved and cared about me, even if I didn't care about myself.

My uncle had always been a successful bare-knuckle fighter, and he never backed down – not even to cancer. He was right, but I needed him with me if I had any chance of beating it.

"I need you to fight with me," I told him.

324

"I'm with you every step of the way," he insisted.

For the first time in my life I had a moment of pure clarity.

I had to fight. I had to fight it so that I could live and expose the truth about what had happened to me all those years before. I had to get the truth out there, if not for me, for the hundreds of other children who had suffered. It would be the fight of my life, but I needed to live so that the truth could be heard.

I swallowed my tears and drove home. I lay down on the sofa, but was woken shortly afterwards by crippling stomach pains. I looked down to see the cream sofa had been covered in blood clots the size of chopped liver. The extreme blood loss terrified me. Even though the thought of going to a hospital had frightened me more, I knew I had to do something. It was either that or bleed to death.

You've left it so long that they probably won't be able to help you anyway, a voice inside my head taunted as I travelled to the hospital.

As I walked inside Liverpool's women's hospital, I felt my breath become shallow as I tried to calm my pounding heart. I looked over and spotted a doctor walking towards me. He was middle-aged, with grey hair and glasses. I stopped dead in my tracks, unable to move, because I thought it was him. It was Milner.

Keep calm, Barbara. He won't be here. Milner is dead. He died a long time ago. He can't hurt you now.

The doctor didn't even register me as he passed by and turned left down another corridor.

I felt the panic subside and my heart slow.

You have to do this. You have to tell someone. There's something wrong, and if you don't get help you will die.

I steeled myself and forced one foot in front of the other as I made my way to the front desk. I told the lady all about my symptoms – 11 long years of blood clots and crippling abdominal pain. I was called into a treatment room by a nurse. A female doctor came in moments later. She examined me, and I was admitted that afternoon. Two days later, I was in theatre having a biopsy. I knew it was cancer before they'd even told me. But three weeks after the biopsy it was confirmed. I had stage 2B cervical cancer. A male doctor broke the news to me. I'd asked to see a female doctor, but he was the consultant and I was his patient. Instead, I insisted that two nurses be present at all times.

"We don't know how this is going to go," he said honestly. "The tumour is inoperable. Basically, it's wrapped around the whole of your cervix."

"Am I going to die?" I asked numbly.

"I certainly hope not, but I suggest we give you chemotherapy to try and stop it from spreading and internal radiotherapy to try and shrink the tumour."

It was a sobering experience, being diagnosed with cancer. All the small worries in life suddenly disappear because they're not relevant. Nothing matters anymore, only living. In a daze, I headed back to my car. I blinked back my tears, turned off my phone, put my favourite CD in the car player, fastened my belt and drove. I didn't have a plan, I just drove. One road melted into another as I drove around for hours. I'd hit rock bottom and there was nowhere else left to go. Then I thought of Uncle John and how upset he'd been. I thought of Milner and what he'd done to me, and then I thought of all the other children who'd suffered inside that hospital. As I thought of them, I dug deep and found an inner strength – one I didn't even know I had. I knew then that I had to fight the cancer and stay alive so that I could fight and get justice for all those silent victims.

Chapter 27

True Survivor

It took me four long years of gruelling hospital visits, treatments and check-ups, but I was finally told I was in remission for cancer. Somehow, I'd survived. My fight to stay alive gave me a new impetus to fight for the truth for all the children who'd been experimented on at Aston Hall, in Derbyshire. I went back to my doctor's practice and told them I'd been abused as a child at the hospital. I also wanted to know why the hospital admission had been left out of my medical records and waited for answers.

In June 2015, I googled images of the hospital. Somehow, I'd hoped that by seeing them and revisiting my hospital prison as I was now – a strong cancer survivor – I'd be able to put them into context. Although there was no mention of Aston Hall in my medical notes, I knew, I just knew, that I'd not imagined it. This had happened to me and it had happened to countless others – I just had to prove it. After looking on a few pages, I stumbled across an internet site called Urban Mayhem. My fingers froze against the keyboard as my eyes scanned derelict images of Aston Hall hospital – my prison for eight long months. A shiver ran through me as I brought up one photograph after the other – it was exactly as I'd remembered it. This wasn't in my head as everyone had led me to believe – this was where I'd been held against my will, pinned down, drugged and abused. As my eyes scanned to the bottom of the page, I found a comment. It had been left by a lady who also said she'd received treatment at the hospital. For the first time in over 46 years of not being believed, I realised I wasn't alone. Someone else had suffered what I had. I left a message saying that I, too, had been a victim. The lady searched for me on social media and then messaged me over Facebook. We became friends, but what she told me next almost blew my mind – she was in contact with a third woman, another victim of Milner's who'd also been abused and experimented on. Now there were three of us.

"There must be more," I insisted. "There must be so many people out there, like us, that are searching for answers."

I knew there was only one thing for it.

"I'm going to set up a survivors of Aston Hall group on Facebook. It's the only way to get more victims to come forward."

Together, we decided where we should go from there and what we should do next in our bid to get someone – anyone – to listen. I realised if we were going to be believed then we'd have to try and prove it, and the only way to do that would be to get hold of our files. I had to make the call. I steeled myself, and dialled the number and a woman answered.

"Hello," I began, "I used to be a patient at Aston Hall hospital. Could you tell me, how I go about getting hold of my medical files, because my GP has no trace of them in my medical records."

There was a silence and then the woman spoke.

"We have some here, but many of them were lost years ago in a flood."

I felt the blood drain from me.

"A flood?"

"Yes, that's right."

"But how do I know if you still have mine?"

The woman took my name and contact details and promised to look into it for me. I urged the other women to do the same. Miraculously, all three files had escaped the flood, and now we had them. At last, we had concrete evidence that we'd been held in a mental hospital as children. But I was worried.

How would we be able to prove what Dr Milner had done to us?

Ripping open the brown paper envelope I pulled out the photocopies of my medical notes. The writing was awful and faint in places, and the notes had been taken from microfilm, but sure enough, written there in black and white was concrete proof that I'd been injected with a drug called sodium amytal, as well as other medication. Grabbing my laptop, I typed in the words 'sodium amytal' to see if anything came up. I was desperate to learn more about what I'd been given. To my horror, I found out it was also known as a truth serum and it had once been administered to shell-shocked soldiers after the Second World War. It was also a powerful sedative and was once used to treat insomnia. I soon discovered that the recommended maximum dose for an adult is one gram, as it is highly addictive and it can be lethal if too much is taken. I'd been injected on different occasions with 120mg.

But, if it was a truth serum, then why had Milner knocked us out with ether, especially if we'd already been injected with a sedative?

It didn't make any sense. And that's when it hit me and I started to tremble. Of course, the drug was to make us comply, whilst the ether had rendered us unconscious. It was unbelievable. No wonder Dad and everyone else hadn't believed me. Nobody knew what was going on behind those doors. We were human toys. Just a piece of meat for someone to play with.

By now, word had begun to spread and soon we had 30 members. I contacted NHS Derby and Derbyshire police, who asked me to provide a video statement. For the first time, I felt fired up – things were finally moving. Then we hit another brick wall. I tried to get the press to take the story in the hope that other survivors would come forward, but they didn't. Then the police decided not to investigate further. I was heartbroken, because after all these years, I felt everything come to a grinding halt. But I found help in the most unlikely place. I'd heard of another group on Facebook called CSA Nottingham. It was also fighting for justice for the appalling abuse their members had suffered in children's homes. The group was due to have a meeting with the head of Nottingham police, who they told about our ongoing fight as survivors of Aston Hall. Amazingly, the powers intervened and decided to take another look at our case. We each handed over copies of our files as evidence – we'd all been given the same truth serum as children. The group continued to grow in strength as more members came forward. We helped them obtain their hospital files and were there as a support network to emotionally pick them up when they felt down. I discovered that like me, a lot of the other survivors had suffered with depression. We also had one thing in common – cluster headaches, which I believe are a direct result of the drugs Milner pumped us full of when we were kids.

As the police investigation gathered pace, I started to carry out my own investigations. I discovered that Milner had used his patients for medical experiments – something I can prove from official medical research documents. I also believe that he allowed others to experiment on children at Aston Hall. Whether this was for reward or status in the medical profession, we shall never know because he took it to his grave. I also believe that although the hospital was owned by the NHS, both Cherry Ward and Laburnum Ward, which was mine, were owned by the Home Office – make of that what you will. I'm not sure who paid Milner's wages as a doctor. I also understand his research papers were burned following his death, and that the hearse carrying his coffin had driven right past the grounds of Aston Hall, where he'd presided daily as doctor and master over the poor terrified children inside.

What kind of man would do that? It was as though, even in death, he was still trying to have the final word.

I plugged away, trying to get a journalist to take on the story, but with Milner now dead, and therefore unable to be held to account, it was difficult. One day, my telephone rang.

It was a journalist from the *Derby Evening Telegraph*, called Isaac Crowson. Unlike other reporters, Isaac not only listened to me and believed what I had to say, he also printed the story the same day. Afterwards, I was contacted by a BBC reporter called Simon Hare. By complete coincidence, it transpired that Simon knew my uncle – the one who'd written a letter to the hospital all those years before. Like Isaac, Simon ran a piece on TV later that day. Meanwhile, the *Derby Evening Telegraph* began to receive a huge response to their story and soon I had 48 survivors join the group, with more contacting the police or NHS Trust direct. The whole campaign had begun to gather fresh momentum. I still needed to get a solicitor on board, but every time I called one, I could almost hear the disbelief in their voice as soon as I uttered the words 'mental hospital'. In sheer desperation, I rang a barrister's chambers. By chance, the telephone was answered by a barrister, who asked me to come in the following day because he knew a solicitor he thought would be able to help. As I relayed my shocking story to the two men, they listened. They not only listened, but Stephen Edwards, my brilliant solicitor, agreed to take on my case and those of the other survivors. He soon became a tower of strength to us all.

One day, my phone rang. It was Isaac, who had some news. Our plight had been taken to Prime Minister's Question Time in the Houses of Parliament. The MP for Derby had spoken directly about the ongoing investigation to David Cameron, who was then Prime Minister. Mr Cameron agreed that our case needed to be thoroughly investigated. He responded by saying:

"I'm very happy to give my honourable friend that assurance (of an inquiry). She is absolutely right to raise this. They are very serious allegations and it is vital the full facts are considered. My understanding is the police, the local authority, and the NHS are working together and there is an inquiry process under the Derbyshire Safeguarding Children Board in line with its procedures. I would encourage anybody who knows anything about this to come forward and give their evidence to that board."

Today, the inquiry – Operation Hydrant – into wide-scale abuse at Aston Hall Hospital in Derbyshire is still ongoing as more and more victims come forward. I believe that there are thousands of victims out there. As I write this, we have since been invited to the Houses of Parliament so that our voices can finally be heard after years of silence.

In July 2015, BBC Radio 4 ran a special investigation piece into Dr Milner's treatments at Aston Hall. They spoke to many victims, including myself. Critics have tried to argue that the drug sodium amytal can leave patients with something called false memory syndrome. But how can so many different people have the same false memory – that they were drugged and abused by the same doctor?

During this process, I've learned lots of things I've found hard to deal with. But it was my dear father who picked me up and rescued me, as he did again and again throughout my troubled life. My dad would be the first to admit he isn't perfect, but I owe him a huge debt as, despite everything, he was the one who saved me from Milner and from Aston Hall.

I cannot blame him for not believing me initially, after all I've had trouble getting others to do the same many years later. But I have, and I will continue to fight for the truth.

As the inquiry progressed, I read a book by a lady called Teresa Cooper, who'd also been abused in care. Teresa's story triggered me to write this book. The saddest part of my story is there are no photographs of me as a child. Disturbingly, the only photographs are those that the stranger in that room took of me as I lay there for Milner, drugged up and naked. It makes me shudder to think who has looked at them since or where they are now.

People tell me that I'm strong because I blew the whistle, not only on Milner, but on Aston Hall hospital. I've found it both distressing and ultimately healing to talk about the abuse I suffered there. By forming the group and writing this book, I feel I've finally given a voice to all those children who suffered in silence. All those frightened children no one believed are being listened to now, and we won't stop until we get justice.

Afterword

In 1993, Aston Hall hospital closed its doors to the last patients of my ward, Laburnum, as well as all others. Locals had petitioned to keep the hospital open as many of them worked there, with many denying knowledge of what had happened inside, or that there were children there at all. When I returned to Aston Hall in 1995 to see my files, I drove away feeling so angry and yet so strong. I told the nurse there that I would be back, and I have kept my bitter promise.

I had a fight in me that I had to follow through. I had to understand what drugs had been given to me, and what effect they could have on my children. Were they to blame for my little girl having a hole in her heart, plus a heart murmur? Or my little boy being born a grunting baby? A million questions flashed through my mind as I drove the roads I had been taken along as a 12-year-old child. The tall, fat chimneys still terrified me – I never thought I would ever see the other side of them. That is when I realised how strong I had become. There is not a prison in this country that is as tough as Aston Hall was, and also there is no crime in the modern world that would justify the torture we all suffered.

Reading through my files from both Social Services and Aston Hall, I find so many flaws or cover-ups. Dates, places and times are contradicted, and in my notes I was referred to as patient number 4. That is how they saw us – like numbered sheep. Our survivor's group have found out Milner was a registered NHS doctor, but it was the Home Office that paid him, and the Home Office who owned the two wards used at Aston Hall by Milner. The Home Office sold them in 1995, while NHS Derby sold the other nine wards. The Secretary of State for Health is the defendant in the lawsuit for what so many people at Aston Hall suffered.

Milner may be dead and gone but his path of heartbreak and trauma lives on. In a strange way, I wish I could forgive Milner and Aston Hall for what I suffered. They made me the strong woman I am today. The only thing that has changed since my visit in 1995 is that it is no longer just me fighting – WE are ALL fighting back. We now know we had the right to walk out of Aston Hall any time we wanted as children. We were classed as informal patients, so no one had the right to hold us against our will under lock and key, and certainly not to drug, assault and abuse us. I specifically did not have a court order on me to demand I be detained. Instead of breaking me, Milner and Aston Hall have made me stronger than I was ever meant to be. I used my strength in my fight for justice and answers. I know it may be years before any of us survivors will see justice and, although we may never get the full facts or truth, at least we will be able to make some kind of sense out of it.

I found writing my story the best therapy – trying to talk about it was not working for me. But a screen did not get upset at my tears. Since writing my story, my hair and nails have suddenly started to grow and I can think a bit clearer. It feels like a big, black, horrible balloon has deflated inside me and I can breathe at last. I would advise anyone who is dealing with this kind of PTSD to write down their experiences and feelings, no matter how long it takes. Then, do what you want with it. I burnt my first go and I let the wind take away all the burnt paper. I still have nightmares, panic attacks and flashbacks that have been part of my life since I was young. But I understand them better now. Sometimes they fit together like parts of a jigsaw. Others are so horrific it can take a long time to get over them. But I wish you to find strength from my book. Do not be downtrodden – open up, speak out and get everyone talking about abuse. The abused child in me, silent for nearly 60 years, has been set free by sharing. Us survivors know we cannot change the past, but we can expose the truth and share our story. We just might make a difference for tomorrow's children. To any survivors or family members reading – please find strength from it, and the positive in it.

Remember, you are only alone until you speak out. Then you will find there are thousands of survivors who understand. Many more survivors are coming forward with their own horror stories of Aston Hall, spanning over the decades Milner was medical superintendent. The sad thing is many of his victims don't feel able to come forward and speak out, because their family do not know they were ever admitted to a mental hospital, and must live with their secrets hidden inside them, unable to get support. I have spoken to many other survivors and, after hearing their stories, I now know I was one of the lucky ones – many suffered far worse 'treatment' than me. Each day, more evidence of Milner's abuse is being revealed. My own story has been told, but the full and horrific truth of treatment at Aston Hall hospital is yet to come out.

Barbara O'Hare, February 2017

<u>Barbara O'Hare</u> d/b ███████ .

Religion: Roman Catholic

There appears to be little information on Barbara's early history.

Barbara

                    officially received into care in ████████████

On the ████████████   asked for Barbara to be removed from
the foster home, due to Barbara's constant wanderings, and staying out all night,
and also due to a build up of difficult behaviour, i.e. petty pilfering and
deceitfulness. Barbara has always been difficult at school and last term
Barbara was transferred from Cardinal Newman School to Wainbody Wood School for
the maladjusted. She appears to have settled down at Wainbody Wood School.
(I enclose a report from Cardinal Newman School).

Barbara was placed at The Grange children's home on the ████████████ , and
              the superintendent has constantly complained about her difficult
behaviour.   has stated that Barbara is openly aggressive and abusive
towards anyone in authority.   has also said he has reason to believe
that Barbara was shop-lifting on her way home from school. However. it is felt that
Barbara is not maladjusted, but just anti-authoritarian. However. it is felt that
Barbara may be extremely maladjusted.

However, on the ████████████   Barbara absconded from The Grange, and
it was felt that in Barbara's interests she should be placed in a remand home,
and be seen by Dr. Milner, to ascertain what help could be given to her.

                    ████████████

                    <u>Child Care Officer</u>

REPORT FORM

C.R. No.

Name of Child

Sheet No.

PAS 2949. 6/13

Date	A full report is asked for as to health, welfare, conduct of the child, the condition of the home (including the sleeping and the living accomodation) and clothing, any complaint made by or concerning the child, religious attendance and use of leisure
	about.

During the visit I was unable to see Dr. Milner as he was away on holiday. However I felt that Barbara was improving and the staff nurse told me she felt that Barbara would be in Aston Hall for a few more months and then would be able to move out to another situation. However I am still a bit concerned about this because the only possibility for Barbara at the moment is for her to go to Stoke House

Barbara   now developing a much more positive relationship with father who appears to be much more interested in them.

From ....

To .... Director of Education

OUR REF. : ███████

YOUR REF : ███████

19 71

Re. Barbara O'Hare ███████

With reference to your memorandum concerning the above girl, Barbara was admitted to Breadsall Remand Home, Derby, on the ███████ 70. She was then admitted in January 1971 to the Adolescent Unit of Aston Hall Hospital, Derby, for treatment. She has responded to treatment. However, she will remain at Aston Hall for a further two or three months. I am sorry that we could not let you know when Barbara would definitely return to Coventry, as it depended on her response to treatment.

However, I feel that in the present circumstances, that her place at Wainbody Wood School should be no longer retained.

C.R. No. 65328

REPORT FORM

Sheet No. ....

Name of Child ... Barbara O'Hare ...

P & S 3349. s.11

A full report is asked for as to health, welfare, conduct of the child, the condition of the home (including the sleeping and the living accomodation) and clothing, any complaint made by c concerning the child religious attendance and use of leisure.

Date		Init of C

███████ Contacted Breadsall Remand Home but they could not tell me a definite date when Barbara would be going to Aston Hall.

███████ Visited Barbara at Aston Hall on the ███████ 71.
During this visit I saw Barbara's headmistress at school and also Dr. Milner. Apparently Barbara is improving in her school work and has now seemed to settle down a little bit. I had a discussion with Barbara just before she was going to see the psychiatrist. First of all she was rather aggressive towards me and told me that she did not like being in Aston Hall, but I pointed out to her that it was to help her in her school work and also because Dr. Milner felt that she would benefit from staying at Aston Hall. However when Barbara calmed down she seemed to be more reasonable and she asked me if she could possibly go home to her father. I again told Barbara that if her father would have her out of care this was what I felt would be the best thing for her.

Name Barbara O'Hare aet 12½   Status

Psychologist's Report.

Date ▓▓▓

(1) Test: Porteus ?
Result: M.A. 10.0   N. 87

(2) Test: Block Designs Test ?
Result: M.A. 10.0   N 87

(3) Test:
Result:

Remarks about behaviour:

Impulsive approach - impulsive, explosive, but in the end cooperative, even if slightly obstinate and argumentative

Miss R. O'Hare,
Aston Hall Hospital,
Laburnum Ward,
Aston-on-Trent,
Near Derby.

Dear Barbara,

I hope that you are now feeling better, and are out of bed. It was nice to see you the other day and you appear to be more settled after a few months in Aston Hall.

How is your project at school getting on? I will have to see it when I come up to see you again. I hope that you enjoy your holiday and I hope to come up and see you again in the near future.

Yours sincerely,

Senior Social Worker.

Tests Assessment:
Tests seem normal (college?)

Aston Hall Hospital

Name   O'HARE, Barbara

Ward Laburnum

M.A   Date of Admission ▓▓▓   Sheet No.

Date   I.Q.   Case No.

Date of Birth ▓▓▓

Epileptic
CLINICAL NOTES   Religion Roman Catholic

'3 5 71 ... T ° 102, P 104 R 22
...
... 250 mg ...

Acknowledgements

There are so many people I'd like to thank that it's difficult to know where to start, so I'll start with the staff of Liverpool Women's Hospital – thank you for saving my life. In particular, Dr Robert MacDonald – may your hands always remain blessed. Thank you also for understanding my fear of doctors.

To the staff at Clatterbridge Hospital – a thank you is not nearly enough.

To my father: you rescued me and were there when I needed you; you never turned your back on me and for that I'll always be grateful. I love you, Dad.

To my children for all their love and support and kindness – I love you.

To Rachel Nally, my foster daughter (and bookworm): thank you for inspiring me to do this.

To Veronica Clark, my ghostwriter and godsend: thank you for your support and understanding nature. God must have blessed your hands for you have been my 'voice'.

To Kitty Walker and Eve White, my literary agents: thank you, Kitty for listening, and Eve for working so hard for me.

To Kelly Ellis at Blink Publishing – you are amazing: thanks to you and the rest of the team for believing in me and my story.

My friend Mary – a Magdalena survivor herself: I love you, girl. Thanks for your support over the past 40 years.

To Teresa Cooper: your book inspired me to write this, so thank you for giving me the strength.

To Mickey Summers and Mandy Coupland who created the Nottingham CSA Inquiry Action Group, and Chairman David Hollas MBE, who brought light to our plight: a big extra thank you, for without you fighting our corner, we would have never been heard.

To the Irish Community Care in Liverpool: thank you for everything, all of you.

To Ruth Evans at BBC Radio 4 for putting our story out there, and Simon Hare, BBC North East. Also, Isaac Crowson, who got the ball rolling.

To my uncle in Derby (you know who you are) and big John, who is not only my uncle but my best friend. Also to 'Mandy' for her support.

To Gertrude Fitzgerald over in Limerick, Ireland: we are family, but we are also friends forever.

To Taffy, a homeless Welsh guy in London: thank you for also saving my life.

Stephen Edwards @beenletdown in Liverpool: I know I've done your head in, but you are a great guy, so thank you to you and all of the staff for your hard work.

Marie McCourt – a truly remarkable lady, who is still fighting to get justice for her daughter Helen: God bless you, Marie. We will win.

Thank you to you all for reading my story. I hope it will either help you or help you to help other survivors out there.

To Philip Lafferty, CSA Group:

"Ask not what the future can do for your past, but what your past can do for the future."

Last but not least, to everyone in the group 'Survivors of Aston Hall', you all say I give you strength – but it is you who keep me strong. God bless you all.

If you were in Aston Hall, we are there for you – feel free to join us on Facebook. If you need help, please contact the Derbyshire NHS safeguarding team on 01332 623700. You can also contact Derbyshire police, asking for Operation Hydrant, on 101.